Successfully Skipper a Sailboat

Successfully Skipper a Sailboat

Modern Lessons From the Fastest-Growing Global Sailing Education and Certification Program

Beginner to Intermediate Skills for 26-to 60-foot Sailboats

GRANT HEADIFEN

Seahorse Publishing

Dedication

To my daughter Alexandra:

"Sail away from the safe harbor. Catch the trade
winds in your sails. Explore. Dream. Discover!"
Mark Twain

Acknowledgments

Many of the photos in this book are courtesy of Beneteau, with photographer
Nicolas Claris.

A big thanks again to Lauren Zykorie for the endless help in editing and telling
me when I was tacking away from the basics.

Thanks to Tom McCarthy of Skyhorse Publishing for his further edits and
patience. The QR codes certainly had us losing sleep. Thanks also to Michael
Landry for the use of his beautiful Beneteau 373 *Siyagruva*.

Seahorse Publishing books may be purchased in bulk at special discounts for
sales promotion, corporate gifts, fund-raising, or educational purposes. Special
editions can also be created to specifications. For details, contact the Special Sales
Department, Skyhorse Publishing, 307 West 36th Street, 11th Floor, New York,
NY 10018 or info@skyhorsepublishing.com.

Seahorse® and Seahorse Publishing® are registered trademarks of Skyhorse
Publishing, Inc.®, a Delaware corporation.

Visit our website at www.skyhorsepublishing.com.

10 9 8 7 6 5 4 3 2

Library of Congress Cataloging-in-Publication Data is available on file.

Cover design by Tom Lau
Cover photo credit: Beneteau and Nicolas Claris

Print ISBN: 978-1-944824-05-1
Printed in China

Contents

Introduction   vii

Chapter 1: Weather and Sea Conditions   1
Chapter 2: Electrical Systems   28
Chapter 3: Auxiliary Power—Diesel Engines   43
Chapter 4: Hulls, Rigging, and Sails   54
Chapter 5: Rules of the Nautical Road   70
Chapter 6: Leaving the Slip, Maneuvering in the
Marina, and Returning Safely   74
Chapter 7: Sailing   89
Chapter 8: Communications   138
Chapter 9: Navigation   156
Chapter 10: Anchoring and Mooring   190
Chapter 11: Safety and Emergencies   211

Afterword   244

Introduction

Grant Headifen

How this book works

This book is unlike any other book you've read. We call it a hybrid eBook. While the book can stand alone on its own as one of the best learn-to-sail books written, it also employs some really cool technology should you decide to take advantage.

Throughout the book, you will see QR codes. When you scan these codes with your mobile device, the book comes alive with interactive animations, videos, and useful websites. This will vastly enhance your learning experience.

To get a QR code reader, simply search on any App store. QR code readers are free. Alternatively, NauticEd also provides a free iOS App that can read QR codes. You can go to www.NauticEd.org/sailing-apps and download the free app there. Once you have it downloaded, click on the hybrid eBook link in the App menu.

Try out your QR code reader now and go to the webpage (http://www.nauticed. org/book-skipper) for this book where we show an introductory video, a promo code to take the test, and any post-publication updates.

NauticEd is one of the world's leading sailing training companies and the only company to employ super high technology systems into its training programs. NauticEd also helps students gain the ICC, the International Certificate of Competence. The ICC was created by the United Nations and is required as a sailing license in many countries. Yacht charter companies worldwide accept the NauticEd sailing résumé and certification system.

Skipper Book
Home Page

This book, then, is not only going to be part of your world-class sailing training but will lead you to a highly regarded sailing certification; one that is accepted globally.

As part of your purchase of this book, you will also have free access to a lot of tools that are introduced here. You'll simply scan the QR codes and a new world of modern sailing training, sailing résumés, sailing logbooks, and sailing badges will be opened to you; ALL FOR FREE.

About This Book

This is a fun course for beginner to intermediate sailors on sailboats in the 26-foot (8 m) to 52-foot (16 m) range, though experienced sailors will pick up some gems as well. We've also taken a unique approach to sailing education: We've made it fun. We tell little stories, we crack jokes and use an informal style of language you'll appreciate. It's in my nature; everyone goes sailing to have fun (that is, since the invention of the engine). So why not have fun while learning how to sail? With that said, however, we are serious about burning into your brain the necessary knowledge you need to have to be a great sailor.

This course presents the theory of learning to sail only (*haa haa* obviously). But, as you will soon recognize, theoretical knowledge is equally as important as practical expertise. Case in point: who gives way in the following crossing situation?

You simply cannot go to sea as a skipper without knowing the fundamentals like this. Operating on the assumption that just keeping out of the way is best, is not good enough. It is irresponsible!

Who Gives-Way

Equally, a true understanding of weather, rigging, engines, communications, anchoring, and safety will keep you out of serious trouble. Having the skills to navigate away from and around rocks and dangerous objects is in the best interests of your life and those of your family and friends. This is all theory. The practical is seeing it in action and experiencing it—holding a steady course, adjusting to the wind, and so much more. Thus, both theory and practical are important.

Upon completion of this book, you will be ready and fully prepared to experience practical training at any sailing training school worldwide or simply get out on your own and try out what you have learned here. We also recommend that you gain lots of experience through friends with boats and at your local yacht club. We wrote an excellent blog on the topic of how to gain practical experience. See it here:

Sailing Bucket List

http://www.nauticed.org/sailing-blog/sailing-bucket-list/

As part of your purchase, we give to you a free electronic sailor's logbook. We recommend that you begin to fill this out. You'll soon learn that you must report your experience in a résumé form to Yacht Charter Companies. Our free résumé-building system works by drawing from your logbook entries. We explain all this with the QR code here:

Skipper Book Home Page

Finally, you're probably already starting to realize the value of this book. This is not just a grab off the shelf and go read book; this book ties you into the world's best sailing training program should you decide to pursue any further knowledge and certification. You're starting in exactly the right place. If you would like the understanding you have gained from reading this book added to your sailing résumé, you simply take the test online at NauticEd.org. You will need to register for the Skipper course. To do this, scan the QR code below. You'll then be taken to a website where you will get $24 off the price of the online course and test.

As an additional bonus for buying this book, we are giving you two free online sailing courses:

1. **Navigation Rules:** A comprehensive course on the International Rules of Prevention of Collision at Sea.
2. **Basic Sail Trim:** An interactive look into wind and how it works with the sails.

Please enjoy these courses with our compliments. Scan the code above and learn how to get these courses for free.

Now, let's get on with learning how to be a great sailor, shall we? To start, let us get you "in the mood" for a fun interactive sailing course. The boat featured in this short video is a Beneteau 38.

Beneteau 38 Video

Chapter 1
Weather and Sea Conditions

The Joys of Sailing

A Beneteau 41.1 Under Sail

Sailing is ridiculously enjoyable! But a serious accident, injury, or loss of life is just not worth it. For the most part, these are all totally avoidable with knowledge, responsibility, and experience. So you are to be commended for taking this course AND for taking it seriously. This is not something to power through and knock out for the sake of it or for the piece of paper certificate. There is information throughout this course that will save lives—yours or a family member's.

Since both weather and sea conditions are major influences in sailing it is important that we begin the book with these essentials.

The biggest killer in boating is weather, so you are well advised to take this chapter seriously, to continuously learn about weather and to be able to identify when it is safe to "enjoy boating" and when it is not safe.

In adverse weather conditions, safe boating is proportional to the size of your vessel. A smaller vessel will get tossed around more and is less able to handle wind and waves. There is also less protection from exposure to the weather.

As you gain experience, you'll begin to be more confident with a rough day out, and a good thrashing around can even become quite enjoyable. But always keep in mind your crew. The best way to scare off a spouse, family member, kid, or friend from sailing forever is to have them screaming on the side rail "TAKE ME HOME." It's much more prudent to introduce people to sailing on a nice day—sunny with 10 knots of breeze is perfect.

If you're an old-timer, remember the TV series *Hill Street Blues*? The sergeant always said to his team, "And hey! Be careful out there."

Same here. Hey, you with the boat, the weather can be a killer. Let's be careful out there. Check the weather and sail to your own confident ability!

Waves, Swell and Depth

Waves, Photo Taken in Martinique

Since it is a good idea to keep your boat on top of the water, it's good to understand the dynamics of water.

Waves

Waves are the product of wind blowing across water.

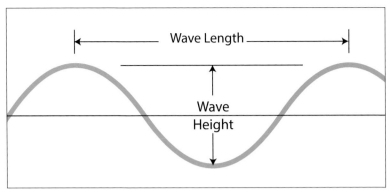

Wave Metrics

Wave height and wave length metrics are shown below. Another important metric is the period. The period of a wave is the time it takes for two consecutive crests to pass a stationary point. The frequency of the wave, although not used much in ocean wave metrics, is the number of waves to pass a stationary point in a certain amount of time, for example, 10 waves per minute is a measure of the frequency; the period then would be stated as 1 wave per 6 seconds.

Since waves are primarily the result of surface wind action, they can be accurately predicted. Waves have troughs and crests. Sailing in moderate seas is safe and easy, but as waves grow, their capacity for doing harm is greatly increased and requires expert sailing skills.

As waves get steeper and steeper their tops become tenably unstable. When propelled farther by wind, the tops fall off, creating breaking waves. Take away the wind and the tops return to being stable but the waves themselves continue because there is nothing to stop them. This resultant wave is known as swell.

Swells

Swells are the result of waves from distant storms sometimes thousands of miles away. Their wave length is long and generally they are not a problem; with one exception: many sailors are subject to seasickness because of swells.

Depth

Sailors need to be a little more cautious than recreational powerboaters. To prevent being pushed sideways through the water by the wind, sailboats have a big long thingy sticking down from the bottom of the boat. It's called a keel. For a medium size keelboat 26 feet to 52 feet (8m to 16m) or so, the depth of the keel

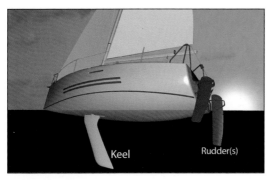

Keel and Rudder Depth

will be around 4 to 7 feet (1.3—2.5 m). The "rudder," which is the steering board thingy at the back, will be slightly shorter than the keel.

Modern reliable **depth sounders** are electronic instruments that determine the distance from the keel to the sea floor by using ultrasound pulses. These devices can be set to alert sailors when sailing close to shore, near atolls, or over other objects where you are uncertain about the water's depth. Fishfinders can be incorporated with depth sounders, allowing sailors to also check for fish activity, should you wish to catch the "big one."

Keep in mind that when sailing over areas that may have highly irregular bottom surfaces, such as coral, large rocks, and sunken objects, you may not have ample time to react to your depth sounder's warnings.

Harbors are notorious for having fluctuating depths due to currents and poorly scheduled dredging. Be wary of water depth any time you sail into a new harbor.

Depth Animation

In the olden days, they used marked lines attached to lead weights to determine depth. Nowadays, we use sonar signals traveling at the speed of sound to measure the depth (and to determine if there are fish around for dinner). Still, a prudent sailor will have on board a backup lead-weighted line. Recreationally speaking, it's not practical to have a bowman calling out the depth of water every minute. Thus, almost every vessel these days has a modern day sonar depth finder. Every experienced sailor will tell you that the cost of a depth finder is worth the investment. If your vessel does not have one, get one.

Offset

Depth sounders have a feature that allows the depth reading to account for the depth of the keel. For example, if your keel is 5 feet deep and the real water depth is 20 feet, you will have only 15 feet of clearance. Thus, you want the depth reading to show 15 feet. Caution however, when you set up your device—the offset number you need to put in is a negative number.

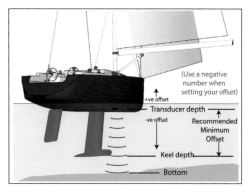

Depth Offset

Tides

Tides are the regular rise and fall of the ocean due to gravitational forces from the moon and the sun. Tides vary in height all over the planet from zero to 50 feet (15 m), but for each specific location they rise and fall a similar amount each cycle.

Be especially wary of tides when anchoring. Anchor at high tide, and you may find your boat resting on the bottom in a few hours. Anchor at low tide and you might find your boat drifting away in a few hours because the amount of anchor rode (anchor line) you put out did not account for the extra depth.

Boat at Anchor

Fortunately, charts are marked with the low tide depth. But this is not all you need to know about tides. Sailing is endlessly technical in its own nature. And further studies are always required.

A Rough Ride

Sailing becomes less than idyllic as sea state conditions worsen. While waves and swell are due to wind there are some effects that can make them worse:

- Current: when current meets waves in differing directions they create a confused heightened state of waves. Often, the waves become choppy and the wave length is decreased.
- When swells meet waves: superposition of these two can vastly increase the height and confusion of the sea.
- Distance from shore: when you have an offshore breeze the waves get larger in height the further from shore
- Depth of water: as water gets shallower wave height increases while also becoming steeper.

Understanding Weather Systems

Weather is a highly complex natural phenomenon. Globally, it is all connected and operates on a multitude of physical laws. Consider these few that constantly bewilder and wonder us:

- Heat travels through space from our very own star at the speed of light.
- Warm air rises while cold air sinks.
- Air wants to flow from high pressure to low pressure.
- Pressure decreases with altitude.
- Warm water releases vapor faster than cold water.
- Warm air holds more moisture than cold air.
- The Coriolis effect turns wind right in front of our eyes.
- The tilt of the Earth creates the seasons.

Predicting weather is one of humankind's most challenging tasks because of the many variables. It is indeed fickle stuff; it can be almost motionless one moment and moving rapidly with tremendous speed and force the next. While there is not an app yet to control the weather, the good news is that there are now many good sources to predict the weather including apps on your smartphone and mobile devices.

Meteorology is the science of weather, and while forecasting weather is not yet an exact science, it is getting mighty good. Before going sailing, be sure to obtain the very latest weather conditions for your local area and prediction for the period you will be sailing.

A Hurricane off the Southeastern US.

Weather Sources

Global weather in general comes from unequal heating of masses of air at the Earth's surface in places called "source regions." The main source regions are the snow-covered arctic and Antarctic plains and tropical and subtropical oceans. Thus, an air mass might be cold and dry, cold and moist, warm and dry, or warm and moist. As the air moves, the planet rotates underneath it. This causes the rotation that we see on weather maps every day.

Air masses at different latitudes move around the planet in different directions. This is because at the equator, air is generally ascending. As surface air moves in to replace the ascending air, it turns west. At the polar regions the air is generally descending. As air at the surface is pushed away from the polar region, it turns east. Due to other more complicated effects, that is, rotation and tilt, air from the equator descends back to the surface at about 30 degrees north and south latitudes. At 60 degrees north and south latitudes, air rises to descend again at the polar regions. This is called the Three Cell Model of General Circulation.

It's not necessary to remember all this detail but only to say that all these forces and movements create general trade winds,

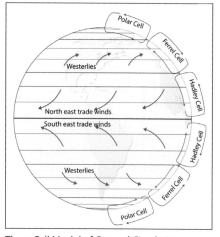

Three Cell Model of General Circulation

which sailors have been using for thousands of years. It's why cruisers go around the world in a counterclockwise direction, sticking to more equatorial latitudes with easterly winds and racers go around the world in a clockwise direction going as far south as possible with westerly winds. These forces and movements also create clashes of spinning air masses. It is these clashes that affect local conditions creating cold and warm fronts and pressure gradients.

When a cold low-pressure mass of air clashes with a warmer mass of moist air things are going to happen like frontal systems, which will be discussed soon.

Pressure

Air pressure is essentially the weight of all the air above pressing down. It is dependent on the density of the air and the temperature of the air in the exact column above. On a weather map, you see lots of circular and curved lines. These are isobars—lines of similar pressure. They are akin to gradient lines of height you see on a contour map showing mountains.

High-pressure areas are normally caused by a phenomenon called subsidence, meaning that as the air in the high cools it becomes denser and moves toward the ground. Pressure increases here because more air fills the space left from the low. Subsidence also evaporates most of the atmosphere's water vapor so high-pressure systems are usually associated with clear skies and calm weather.

A high-pressure system, or "high," is an area where the atmospheric pressure is greater than that of the surrounding area. In some places, highs are referred to as anticyclones. These move clockwise in the northern hemisphere and counterclockwise in the southern due to the Coriolis effect.

A low-pressure system, or "low," is an area where the atmospheric pressure is lower than that of the surrounding area. Lows are usually associated with high winds, warming air, and thus, the atmospheric lifting. Because of this, lows normally produce clouds, precipitation, and other bad weather such as tropical storms and cyclones.

Since low-pressure systems are referred to as cyclones, high-pressure systems are thus referred to as anticyclones.

As one might expect, wind likes to flow from high pressure to low pressure. But notice the words "*like to*." What actually happens is that while wind is moving the Earth also turning, creating an effect on the wind called the Coriolis effect. This changes the wind's flow direction and results in a large circular motion about the pressure center. High-pressure systems spin one way and low-pressure systems spin the other depending on whether they are situated in the northern or southern hemisphere.

As you get closer and closer to the center of a low, the pressure is dropping. This can be measured by a barometer. The lower the pressure the more propensity the wind has to move to the center of the low—which means higher wind speed. If you see the pressure dropping below 1000 mbar (millibars) then a low is approaching. Pressure in hurricanes gets down to about 900 mbar. Anything around 980 mbar will begin to feel uncomfortable for you in terms of higher winds.

Coriolis Effect

The Coriolis effect is a fictional force that appears real in spinning objects like our planet Earth. In the diagram below, the first man rolls a ball to his friend. But by the time the ball makes the distance, the friend has moved. To both, it appears as though the ball was acted on by a constant turning force to make it veer off the original straight path. But there was no such force—it's just an effect that we observe.

Due to the Coriolis effect, in the northern hemisphere, the spin of the Earth makes any air flowing **south** turn west, while in the southern hemisphere, the spin of the Earth makes any air flowing **north** turns west. This is observed by areas of low pressure in the northern hemisphere turning counterclockwise, while areas of low pressure in the southern hemisphere turn clockwise. Essentially then, the winds follow the pressure lines angling in about 15 degrees in low-pressure zones and angling slightly outwards in high-pressure zones. This is depicted by the animation below.

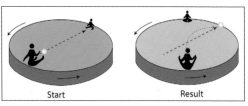
The Coriolis Effect

The easiest way to remember the spin directions is by the saying: "An anticyclone spins anticlockwise in the antipodes." (Australia and New Zealand were referred to the

The Coriolis Effect on Weather Systems

antipodes in the olden days because they were directly opposite of inhabitants of the northern hemisphere.)

Humidity and Moisture

Air holds water vapor in suspension. The amount of water it can hold depends on the temperature of the air and the pressure. For example, when the pressure is lowered by air rising, the air cannot hold as much water vapor and thus the water comes out of suspension, resulting in clouds and rain. In lows, air is rising and thus pressure is decreasing, resulting in clouds. In highs, air is descending and thus increasing in pressure. Moisture is absorbed into the air, resulting in clear sunny days.

Fronts

Fronts are completely different from lows and highs. The term "front" was coined when the phenomenon was understood and documented during the time of World

War I. In a war, when two armies clashed, a front line was established. It was then similarly named when describing the clashing of two opposing air masses. It is important to understand these as they generate significant changes in weather—sometimes fast. By seeing these on a weather map prior to heading out, you will be able to understand what is about to come.

Cold Front

A moving cold mass of air clashing into a stationary warm mass of air creates a "cold front." As the cold air strikes the warm, the warm air is immediately and violently lifted. As the warm air rises, water vapor is released. Thus, at the front line you will see massive clouds and rain and a sudden change in temperature. Isobar lines will also make a directional change due to a sudden change in pressure, thus affecting the wind direction. On the other side of the front, air is descending again and thus you can have good clear visibility after the passing of the front.

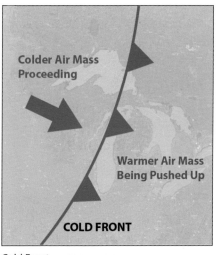

Cold Front

On a weather map, a cold front is represented as such:

Backing and Veering Winds

A wind direction changing to come from a more counterclockwise direction than it is now is called a backing wind. A veering wind is a wind changing to come from a more clockwise direction. For example, say you are in the northern hemisphere and looking north. The wind is coming from the southwest (7:30 o'clock to you). A cold front passes and the winds have changed to the northwest (10:30 o'clock to you). The winds thus changed clockwise—they veered. This is typical in northern hemisphere cold front passages.

In southern hemisphere cold front passages, a typical wind change will be from northwest to southwest—backing.

A cross-sectional view of a cold front in the northern hemisphere is below. Notice drop in temperature and change in wind direction to a more clockwise direction.

Cloud definitions are:

- Ci = Cirrus
- Cs = Cirrostratus
- Cb = Cumulonimbus
- Ac = Altocumulos
- Cu = Cumulus

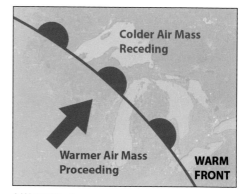

A Cold Front Cross Section

Warm Front

A moving mass of warm air clashing into a colder mass of air will spawn a warm front and is represented on a weather map as such:

A cross-sectional view of a warm front in the northern hemisphere is below. Notice increase in temperature and change in wind direction to a more counterclockwise direction. The wind backed.

As the warm front approaches, clouds will become lower and lower and barometric pressure will decrease because of the rising air. At the frontal boundary, ground fog can be formed due to the temperature change. The worst visibility condition with a warm front will be as it passes and immediately afterward because of the moisture and possible rain in the air.

A Warm Front

A Warm Front Cross Section

Occluded Front

Occluded fronts are linked with areas of low pressure called depressions (more on these soon!). When a depression forms, there is usually a warm front and a faster-moving cold front. The (northern hemisphere) diagram below shows this. To the north of the warm front is the cool air that was in the area before the depression developed. When a cold front catches up to a warm front the result is called an occluded front. A wide variety of weather can be found along an occluded front, with thunderstorms possible, but usually the occluded front passage is associated with a drying of the air mass. Occluded fronts can generate quite stormy weather as they pass over.

In the diagram below, the traveling warm air mass is replacing cooler air. At its leading edge is a warm front.

As the depression intensifies, the cold front catches up with the warm front (remember, a cold front moves faster than a warm front). This is shown below. The line where the two fronts meet is called an occluded front:

A cross section of an occluded front looks like this:

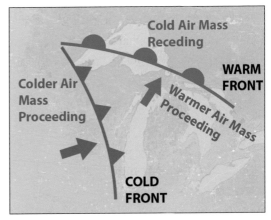

Occluded Front Forming

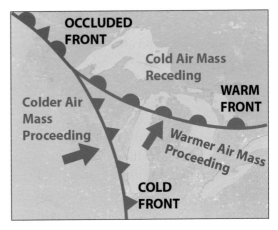

Occluded Front

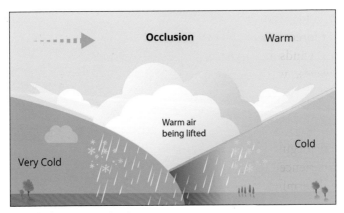

Occluded Front Cross Section

Wind

Winds can be gentle, hardly felt, like zephyrs flitting about in a local area, or they can be vast movements of air moving swiftly across oceans and continents at low and high altitudes.

Sea breezes are a local area scale of the effect of differential heating of air. Experienced sailors know them well.

In the diagram below, a parcel of air over land in summer at noon will be warmed more than a parcel over water. Both are receiving the same amount of solar heat, but it takes more heat to raise water one degree than it does for land. Hence, the parcel over the warmer land will thus rise while the heavier cooler air over the water will flow in under it to take its place.

This phenomenon gives birth to the so-called daytime "sea breeze."

The reverse occurs at night, particularly on clear nights when the Earth can radiate a lot of heat out to space.

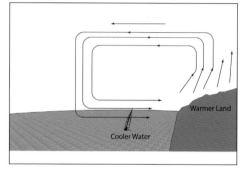

Sea Breeze

Now, air warmed by the water rises and is replaced by the descending cooler air over the land driving the air flow in the reverse direction, creating a "land breeze." This can surprise an unwary sailor, when as the night wears on and he sleeps at anchor, the land breeze alters the wind and his boat swings to a new direction. Did he consider this effect when he anchored?

During daytime hours sea breezes can yield useful sailing conditions just next to a coast, when there might be no wind further offshore and none otherwise shown in weather forecasts.

Light surface winds produce "cat paw" looking waves, whereas stronger winds produce sharper and higher waves. As winds increase, energy is transferred to the water, waves become higher, and spray begins blowing off their crests. Experienced sailors can often accurately determine wind speed by watching the wave.

SYMBOLS EXPLAINED		
Symbol	Wind Direction	Wind Speed
○	Indeterminate Direction	Zero
		1 short barb = 5 knots
		1 long barb = 10 knots
		1 short 2 long = 25 knots
		1 penant = 50 knots

Wind Symbols Explained

When reading a weather map or wind map you need to know the symbols used. Make sure you understand this table, especially the direction. The circles are the head of the arrow; the barbs are the tail.

In compass named directions, the wind directions in the table on page 13 are:

- 5 knots northeasterly
- 10 knots northwesterly
- 25 knots easterly
- 50 knots south-southeasterly

The following table is a rough summary of wind speed and its effect. The column on reefing is of course a matter of choice and boat type. For example, in large catamarans, you'll reef the mainsail first because of its larger size over the genoa. Roller-furling systems allow the crew to reef the sails to any position. However, the sails will typically have marks on them for the recommended first reef and second reef points. Expected boat speed is stated for an average cruising type boat. Race boats can go much faster.

Wind Speed (knots)	Wave Action	Expected Boat Speed (knots)	Effect on Boat and Reefing Recommendation
0–5	calm-ripples	0–2 knots	No heeling
6–10	1–2 ft (0.3–0.6 m)	2–6 knots	Slight heeling
11–15	2–4 ft (0.6–1.3 m) white caps	6–10 knots	Moderate to heavy heeling
16–25	4–8 ft (1.3–2.6 m)	6–12 knots	Reefing required heavy heeling
25–35	6–15 ft (2–4.6 m) spray	6–12 knots	2nd reef required—danger return to base ASAP—seek shelter
35+	8–20 ft (2.6–6.3 m)	6–12 knots	Max reefing–extreme danger seek immediate shelter. Employ storm tactics.

Beaufort Scale

The Beaufort Wind Scale is both historically and visually very interesting. It was designed by British Admiral Francis Beaufort in the 1830s to help large, fully rigged vessels determine their sail requirements. It is a classic and still useful for today's sailors as a guide and component of your dreams to be a frigate captain.

THE BEAUFORT WIND SCALE

Force	Wind (Knots)	WMO Classification	Appearance of Wind Effects On the Water
0	Less than 1	Calm	Sea surface smooth and mirror-like
1	1–3	Light Air	Scaly ripples, no foam crests
2	4–6	Light Breeze	Small wavelets, crests glassy, no breaking
3	7–10	Gentle Breeze	Large wavelets, crests begin to break, scattered whitecaps
4	11–16	Moderate Breeze	Small waves 1–4 ft. becoming longer, numerous whitecaps
5	17–21	Fresh Breeze	Moderate waves 4–8 ft taking longer form, many whitecaps, some spray
6	22–27	Strong Wind Warning	Larger waves 8–13 ft, whitecaps common, more spray
7	28–33	Near Gale	Sea heaps up, waves 13–20 ft, white foam streaks off breakers
8	34–40	Gale	Moderately high (13–20 ft) waves of greater length, edges of crests begin to break into spindrift, foam blown in streaks
9	41–47	Strong Gale	High waves (20 ft), sea begins to roll, dense streaks of foam, spray may reduce visibility
10	48–55	Storm	Very high waves (20–30 ft) with overhanging crests, sea white with densely blown foam, heavy rolling, lowered visibility
11	56–63	Violent Storm	Exceptionally high (30–45 ft) waves, foam patches cover sea, visibility more reduced
12	64+	Hurricane	Air filled with foam, waves over 45 ft, sea completely white with driving spray, visibility greatly reduced

This is pretty hard to remember. Thus, look at the table above and remember the wind conditions force number that you are comfortable sailing in. If force conditions are reported as worse, then you know not to go out or to prepare if you are already out. Generally speaking, force 4 is 11 to 16 knots. This is comfortable for most.

Yacht clubs and some harbormasters may fly flags to indicate any wind warnings. These are not internationally standardized so it is best you check for your country and state (yes, even states differ in the USA). Don't go sailing in anything above Small Craft Advisory and note that a Small Craft Advisory is a warning to those in small craft that conditions are dangerous. If you are inexperienced, you should not go out under small craft advisory conditions.

Here is a table of the most common wind warning flags in the USA, though some other countries also use them.

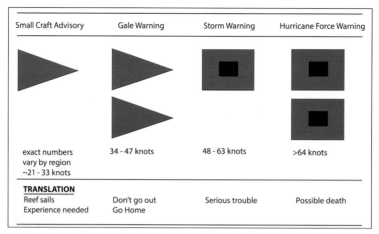

Small Craft Advisory	Gale Warning	Storm Warning	Hurricane Force Warning
exact numbers vary by region ~21 - 33 knots	34 - 47 knots	48 - 63 knots	>64 knots

TRANSLATION			
Reef sails Experience needed	Don't go out Go Home	Serious trouble	Possible death

Wind Warning Flags

Gusts

Gusts can occur at virtually anytime and can be extremely dangerous for several reasons.

- If not properly handled, a gust can overpower the rig and cause the mast to come down (dismasting).
- A gust heels the boat over and throws the crew and gear around.
- A gust heels the boat making the rudder less effective and thus rounds the boat up into wind and into crossing traffic causing a collision.
- A gust can broach the boat when sailing with a spinnaker. A broach is like a round-up into wind, except the boat is held down and on its side because of the spinnaker. It can cause sinking.
- A gust can cause the boom to gybe over unexpectedly, killing crew members with their heads up.

Gusts can be seen coming by a moving discoloration of the water. Good crew members point out approaching gusts to the helmsperson and prepare for action, such as letting out the mainsail traveler or mainsheet. Helmspersons can prepare to adjust course.

Wind Gusts in the BVI

Here is a series of gusts in "The Bight" in Norman Island, British Virgin Islands.

Here is a series of gusts created by katabatic winds in the Marlborough Sounds, New Zealand.

Katabatic Wind Gusts

In General

Always keep in mind that you never want to overpower your vessel since this can lead to catastrophic results. As wind velocities increase, the force on a sailboat's rigging and sails is dramatically increased by the squared power. As examples: if the wind speed doubles from 5 knots to 10 knots, the force on the rigging quadruples; from 5 knots to 20 knots, the force becomes 16 times greater.

Clouds, Fog, Thunderstorms

Clouds

Clouds can give a relatively easy and quick look at what might be coming in the future. Compare these to the two cross sections of warm and cold fronts presented earlier. Notice that both warm and cold fronts are preceded by cirrus clouds. These clouds then are a good indication of possible changing weather in the next few days.

But because there is so much going on in the atmosphere, any serious prediction of weather from cloud observations is difficult unless you are a complete expert. Given that most of us are not expert meteorologists, it is better to heed to the information on your smartphone.

Below are the most common clouds.

Cirrus Clouds: very high and wispy. Possible warm or cold front approaching.

Stratus Clouds: low thick clouds. These are typically rain clouds and are associated with warm fronts and low pressure systems.

Cumulus Clouds: cotton ball shape. Fair weather clouds. Not too much happening.

Cumulonimbus Clouds: tall puffy clouds often associated with severe thunderstorms. Watch out for these.

Altocumulus Clouds: very high small and cotton ball shape.

Fog

Since fog is one of the more menacing
weather conditions because of the risk of collision, it is prudent to know there's a possibility before leaving the slip or anchorage. Fog
banks can often be observed as they move
into an area. Whenever fog occurs, the vessel must have a plan of action. These include:

Fog Enveloping the Golden Gate Bridge

- Knowing and making the proper
  sound signals
- Posting crew to maintain a lookout
- Using radar and AIS if available
- Proceeding slowly
- Using your VHF to contact other vessels and inquire about conditions
  around you

Fog occurs when the air becomes saturated with moisture by a changing temperature and/or air pressure condition. Fog might occur as a relatively local event, often
near shore as it rolls off the land, or it might be much larger, covering a huge area.
Over land, radiation fog occurs when the land cools and subsequently the air next
it cools moisture drops out, forming fog. Remember that colder air holds less
moisture.

Advection fog over the water can be generated by warm, moist air blowing over
a cold sea just like your breath on a cold morning. And unlike land-based morning
fog, advection fog doesn't necessarily mean it will burn off as the day warms up.

The many conditions that could lead to fog formation make it prudent for sailors to know what these are for your local area. However, professional forecasting is
now very good and should be monitored.

Electric Thunderstorms

Electric storms are frightening. On inland waters, they can arrive very quickly,
especially on a hot sultry day. Electric storms are frequently accompanied by high
and very erratic winds. Huge wind bullets, which are sudden wind gusts, can come
seemingly out of nowhere.

While you should always be prepared for a storm, when you observe a heavy
cloud formation rising rapidly with huge white clouds called "thunderheads," it
is time to make further preparations. Get to a safe harbor if time permits. If not,

prepare for a storm: reef the mainsail, lower the jib sail, douse spinnakers, close hatches, keep away from metal objects if possible, put on life jackets, turn off electronic gear. Crew safety is paramount.

If a violent thunderstorm is approaching take all sails down and turn on engines. Reduce the apparent wind velocity on your boat by running downwind.

Weather Microburst

View this awesome microburst video which shows a thunderstorm producing deadly winds.

If you sail in a thunderstorm-prone area, you should consider seeking professional help to install lightning protection gear for your vessel.

Lightning can strike anywhere, on lakes or on the open ocean. Lightning rods on top of masts and connected to metallic pathways to the ocean can help prevent damage to a sailboat.

When encountering an electric storm, it's best to leave the area and get off the water. If this is not possible, get everyone below decks. Do not touch metal objects. While theoretically your mast is insulated from the water in most vessels, at the voltage levels generated in lightning the electrical discharge can jump across the insulating materials. Much of this can be avoided by checking

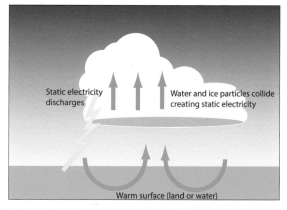

Static Electricity

the weather before you go out to see if there is storming activity.

There is an old myth that says to wrap your anchor chain around the mast and put it into the water to allow lightning to travel overboard and not into the boat. This is certainly a myth and every lightning engineer will tell you that lightning will not travel around the right angle turn from the mast to the chain.

Weather Predictions

Before modern-day digital forecasting and its cool electronic toys like Doppler radar and satellite imaging, sailors feared the weather on every outing, and rightly so. Bad weather and death were potentially always just around the corner. Today the cool toys tell us just about everything. But that means that the modern-day sailor must use and understand how to use the cool toys. There is no room on Earth for the lackadaisical recreational sailor who goes out on the water without checking the forecast.

Philosophers have repeatedly said, tongue firmly in cheek: We all talk about the weather but there are very few things we can do about it. While this is still true today, we have real-time knowledge about approaching weather conditions and can be better prepared. Gone are the days when a hurricane will hit without warning. In September 1900, 8,000 people were killed in Galveston, Texas, during a category 4 hurricane. They simply did not know it was coming nor did they have time to get out of its way.

Galveston Hurricane 1900

Today, information about weather conditions is updated in real-time and made available to every mariner. Even at sea, mariners can get instant information via satellite. And even better, computer weather forecasting models are mature and predictions are accurate. Everybody has their own favorite personal weather anecdote, based on aching joints or running noses, about what the weather will be like. These folk tales should not be taken too seriously, but weather forecasts should.

Weather Forecast Terms

Table of Terms Used in Forecasting	
Gale Warnings	Average wind is expected to be F8 or more or gusts 43-51 kn
Strong Wind Warnings	Average wind is expected to be F6-7. F6 is often called a yachtsman's gale
Imminent	Within 6 hours of the time of issuing the warning
Soon	Within 6-12 hours of the time of issuing the warning
Later	More than 12 hours from the time of issuing the warning
Visibility	GOOD = greater than 5 miles (8 km) MODERATE = between 2 to 5 miles (3.3 km to 8 km) POOR = 0.6 miles to 2 miles (1 km to 3.3 km) FOG = less than 0.6 miles (1000 m)
Fair	No significant precipitation
Backing	Wind changing in an anticlockwise (counterclockwise) direction. e.g. from NW to SW
Veering	Wind changing in a clockwise direction. e.g. from NE to SE
General Synopsis	How and where the weather systems are moving
Sea States	Wave heights: SMOOTH = 8 in to 20 in (0.2–0.5 m) SLIGHT = 8 in to 4 ft (0.5–1.25 m) MODERATE = 4 ft to 8 ft (1.25–2.5 m) ROUGH = 8 ft to 13 ft (2.5–4 m) VERY ROUGH = 13 ft to 20 ft (4–6 m)

Weather Information

Nowadays, sources of weather information are virtually limitless. There is no excuse not to use what's available and it is an amateurish mistake to be caught out unawares by weather because you did not bother to look. Yes, you might be miles out to sea when a weather system develops or a tropical depression turns in your direction, but you will know it is coming and you can form a tactic to outrun it prior to its arrival. Cook, Drake, and Magellan had no such luxury.

Here are the major sources or weather information:

- VHF radio, fixed mounted or handheld
- Online Internet access
- Weather fax
- Television and radio stations
- Streaming audio from a list of USA and Canadian sites
- Smartphone and tablet apps
- Subscription services for serious sailors who need and want accuracy

Streaming Audio
Weather

VHF Radio

Tuning into one of the 1 to 9 VHF weather channels designated for your area will provide a local forecast as well as for close surrounding areas. This information is updated and repeated continually, 24 hours a day. A quick search on the Internet will give the VHF channel for your local area.

The Internet

Weather information is constantly gathered, updated, and disseminated by a vast number of websites. A quick search will render ones to your liking. Here are some common USA and global ones.

NOAA (National Oceanic Atmospheric Administration)		Wind Guru	
NWS (National Weather Service)		The Weather Channel	
Weather Underground		Predict Wind (subscription— highly accurate data)	

Apps

PocketGrib

One of our favorite apps for weather information is called PocketGrib. This clever app downloads on demand an extremely small **GRI**dded **B**inary file and overlays into the software in the app. You can select anywhere in the world for which you want the information and you get a forecast up to five days. The reason it is so cool is that the data packet is extremely small, which saves on cell data rates if you are in a place where you're using roaming data.

Tap the image for an animation. Notice that as the animation plays the conditions change with date and time. It ends with a tabular view of the same. Watch it a few times.

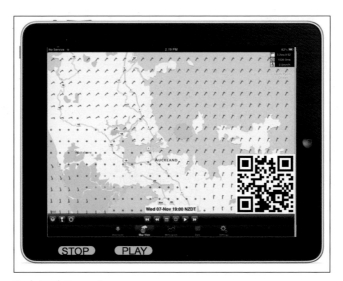

PocketGrib Animation

Here are links to the PocketGrib app:

PocketGrib for iPhone   PocketGrib for Android

PocketGrib for iPad

Weather Underground

Besides being a good website, the Weather Underground app WunderMaps is also pretty good. It uses the Internet directly to present information.

Here are links to the Weather Underground app:

 WunderMap
by Weather
Underground - for
iPhone and iPad

 WunderMap
by Weather
Underground - for
Android

Here is a screen shot of the WunderMaps app showing radar and frontal systems:

WunderMaps App

PredictWind

PredictWind is also a web *and* app source of information. Some of it is free and some is a paid subscription.

 PredictWind - for
iPhone and iPad

 Predict Wind - for
Android

Other Apps

With apps getting added seemingly every day we're supplying this widget to search for apps on the iTunes store.

Other Apps

Subscription Services

Subscription services are by far the best source of information and most have a semi-limited free version for which you can sign up. Or, for $20 bucks a year you can get amazing detail—sometimes down to 1 km resolution. There are packages specially designed for sailors including forecast tables and graphs, wind maps, swell maps, rain maps, cloud maps, isobar maps, sea temperature maps, GBIB files, weather routing, tides, currents, departure planning, GPS tracking, forecast alerts, real-time observations. And all this information is in one place! If you're serious about sailing, you should be subscribing to one of these services. At the very least, have a poke around the companies listed below to see what they offer. Plus, if you're into racing, this is going to give you a huge advantage.

PredictWind

This is a web based subscription service. You get all the information via the web down to 1 km resolution. To the right is an example of winds off the coast of New Zealand for a specific day. Colors represent wind strengths—or you can view by a data table. PredictWind also has apps for iPhone, iPad, and Android.

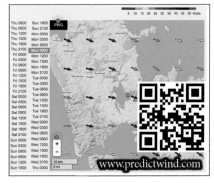

Predict Wind

ClearPoint Weather

With ClearPoint Weather you first download the number-crunching software onto your computer. The software then pulls in raw data from the Internet each time you want updated conditions or an updated weather prediction for a specific area. This type of service can allow you to get incredibly accurate conditions and predictions. The advantage here is that only small amounts of data are coming in for each prediction. If you're racing, doing a crossing or any multiday coastal navigation,

ClearPoint Weather

this is the serious power that you need. The package also includes weather routing for fastest times or storm avoidance. Considering the nature of weather, a small investment like this is worth it.

Observing a Weather Map

You can gain a lot of knowledge about imminent weather conditions by learning to read a weather map.

Here is a typical situation in the northern hemisphere.

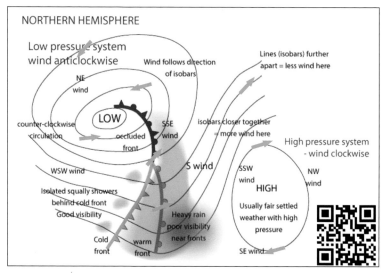

Northern Hemisphere Weather Systems

And here is a typical situation in the southern hemisphere.

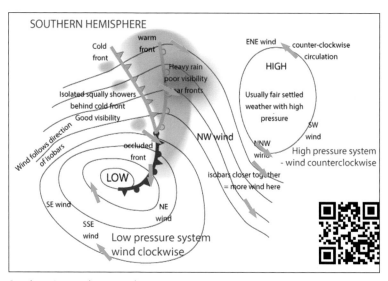

Southern Hemisphere Weather Systems

The bottom line is that the weather we sail in is seldom stable, forecasts are becoming more predictable, but sailors need to use the technology and also be constantly alert to changes.

Weather Warnings

Weather services will also provide **weather warnings**, such as small craft or gale warnings for a certain area, as well as fog predictions. These warnings are very accurate and should be heeded. Small craft advisory and gale warning pennants (flags) may be flown in some marinas and other official locations alerting day sailors to be wary of conditions as they leave a sheltered harbor.

For any country and/or local area, it is a good idea now to search around for your local warnings issued via web interface.

For the USA, you can use the National Weather Service.

National Weather Service

Or for any country including USA wunderground.com is a good reference to search for severe weather warnings.

Weather Undergroud

Major storms also get major media coverage. But knowing a storm is coming is not enough. You must also know how to get out of its path in adequate time. Heavy weather should be avoided at all costs by inexperienced sailors, regardless of how strong the vessel may be.

Today there is little excuse for sailors not knowing quite specifically what kind of weather they will encounter if they simply use the weather services freely available on board a vessel, such as handheld VHF radios or apps.

Heavy Rainstorm in Anegada, BVI.

In summary, before beginning any sailing adventure, be it a short day sail or an extended journey, check the weather and sea conditions at your destination and monitor your weather throughout the voyage.

If you have major trepidations about weather or sea, the prudent thing is to stay in your slip until you are convinced your sailing skills are capable of handling the existing weather and sea conditions.

Clothing

Dressing appropriately for weather conditions is an important but often overlooked topic. Weather in the marina may be considerably different from weather beyond the marina and conditions can drastically change during your venture. Preparing for the worst is always prudent.

New Zealander Sir Edmund Hillary and Nepalese Tenzing Norgay were the first to summit Mount Everest in 1953. Compared to today, clothing technology had not even been invented. In 1958, Sir Edmund went on to the South Pole in a Ferguson farm tractor. Can you imagine a wool jumper, nylon jacket, and leather boots with wool socks?

Wet and cold are not your friend. Nowadays, clothing technology is amazing and will do the job of warm and dry. There are many companies producing very high quality sailing gear well worth your investment. Gill, Helly Hansen, Henri Floyd, Musto are a few to name. And compared again to the 1950s, some of it can look quite stylish.

Stylish Clothing

Here is a good description of layering. Tap on each layer. Courtesy of Gill.

If you own a boat, here's a tip: Take a bag, put a complete change of clothing of various sizes in the bag, zip it up, and stow it on the boat. Then every season, take out the bag and wash all the clothing to get rid of any musty smell. Why? Man overboard! That's why. Last time we had a man overboard I was very impressed with the owner. Out came the bag and back into the race we went with a very grateful crew member.

Also, keep on board a bottle of sunscreen, spare sunglasses, a few different size jackets hanging up in a closet, spare hats, and a blanket including a hypothermia blanket. As a captain, you are responsible for the crew at all times. This includes being prepared for the unprepared crew member.

Chapter 2
Electrical Systems

Introduction

Modern yachts depend heavily on electrical energy, from starting a diesel engine, powering communication devices, turning on navigation lights, and providing creature comforts like a cold refrigerator. It is essential that today's sailors have a fundamental understanding of electricity, batteries, circuit breakers, wiring, and charging systems for troubleshooting, efficiency of use, and safety.

A Hard Swim

Battery failure once forced me to tow my 28-foot boat back to the dock by swimming with a dockline tied around my waist—at 2 in the morning. Fortunately, it was Lake Travis in Texas in the summer.

Alternating Current and Direct Current

In your house, your wall outlets deliver alternating current (AC) electricity. The electricity provided to your house and your marina from the national electric grid is AC. Most all of the devices in your house consume AC power.

In contrast, on a sailboat (and in your car), most of the electricity consumed by the devices on board is direct current (DC) and comes from the onboard battery.

There is a distinct difference between AC and DC electricity, and there is a very good reason why your house and your sailboat differ in this respect.

DC

While anchored up at night in a gorgeous cove, your only source of electricity is from the batteries on board. Thus, batteries are an essential element of a modern-day yacht. Batteries power essentials such as lights, the GPS devices, alarms, bilge pumps, and creature comforts like the refrigerator, fans, electric toilets, and the frozen concoction blender (some might argue that those are also essentials).

Batteries only store electric energy in the form of differently charged plates, one positively charged and the other negatively charged. When these plates are connected via a circuit (through a light bulb for example), electrons flow consistently in one direction. This unidirectional flow of electricity out from a battery is called direct current (DC). Thus, almost all of the devices needing electricity on a boat are designed to consume DC electricity because DC is readily available from the batteries. To charge a battery, which means to place positive and negative charges on opposing plates inside a battery, you must also push DC current into the battery.

AC

Some sailboats are fitted with air conditioning units and microwaves. By their own nature, they require AC electricity and a lot of it.

There are two sources of AC on a sailboat:

1. While you are docked at the marina you can pull AC electricity from the marina via your shore power cord—the "yellow dock line." This is called shore power because it comes from the shore. In the USA and Canada, the AC voltage is a potentially lethal 110 v AC. In most of the rest of the world, the AC voltage is an even more lethal 240 v AC.
2. Your boat might have an onboard marine generator. These are large fuel-driven engines specifically designed to create enough electricity to power an air conditioning unit, microwave, and hair dryers, for example, while you are away from the marina. They weigh in the range of 300 pounds (140 kilograms) and are typically only on larger yachts greater than 40 feet (12 meters). Generators will typically also power the onboard AC outlets.

Creating electricity is fairly simple: You spin a shaft carrying copper wires between two magnets. As the wires cut through the magnetic field lines, electrical current is created in a direction through the wire. When the shaft rotates 180 degrees and cuts the magnetic field in the other direction, the current is reversed. This is the same process used in hydroelectric power station, where the mechanical energy of

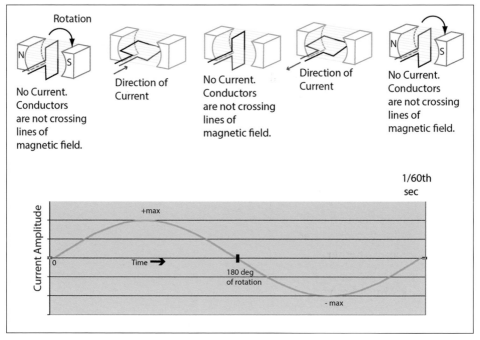

Creating Electricity

the spinning shaft in a turbine is converted to electrical energy and distributed to the electric grid in AC form.

AC, by its own nature is dynamic, and thus, it is not possible to store electrical energy in AC form in a static battery. So, you will never see a thing called an AC battery. To store electrical energy, you must convert AC to DC and then pump it into a battery.

Electrical Measurements

To be prepared and understand electrical power usage on a modern vessel, it is important to learn a few basic terms and concepts. These are all applicable to a modern vessel's electrical energy usage, as well as our daily use on land. Since we cannot directly see electricity, we will use an analogy with water to help illustrate.

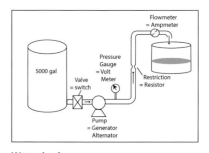

Water Analogy

Charge

Consider a tank of water just sitting there. It is ready to flow, but for now, since the valve is closed, it just sits there. This is akin to the electric charge in the plates of a battery; electrons are all gathered around just sitting there waiting to flow.

Voltage

The strength of both AC and DC is measured in units called volts, named after the Italian physicist Alessandro Volta, who also invented the battery.

As electrical voltage increases, so does the propensity for the electric charge to flow. Voltage may be likened to water pressure in a tank: the higher the pressure in the tank, the more water flows out when you open the valve.

Every sailor who uses electricity for any purpose is well advised to know the voltage level and whether it is AC or DC. Volts can burn, maim, or even or kill if improperly handled.

If your sailing takes you to other countries, you will want to be aware of these differences as they will influence your electrical devices, plug converters, and shore power hookup.

The voltage in most automobiles and boats globally is 12 volts DC.

Ampere

The ampere, or better know as the amp, is named after the French mathematician and physicist André-Marie Ampère. An amp is the measure of current. It is the flow rate of electric charge.

Amps may be thought of like water flowing through a pipe. The faster the flow, the more cups per second of water drains out of the tank. Similarly, the higher the number of amps (the current), the more charge drains from your battery.

Starting an engine requires a lot of current—upward of 100 amps. In contrast, operating a simple GPS unit takes very little current—less than 1 amp.

Ohm

An ohm is a measure of how much resistance there is to the flow of charge. The ohm is named after the German physicist Georg Ohm who realized there was a direct linear relationship between the amount of voltage applied and the amount of current that flows for a given resistance.

Going back to the water analogy, resistance is akin to a restriction in the water pipe. When you kink your garden hose, the kink adds resistance and the water flow rate slows. Likewise, adding resistance to an electrical circuit reduces the current flow.

Ohm discovered that, like water, when you double the pressure with a constant resistance, you double the flow. Or if you double the resistance with constant pressure, you halve the flow.

Ohms law states: Current (in amps) = Volts / Resistance (in ohms)

This relationship is particularly important when it comes to safety. Our human body has a certain resistance to the flow of charge being passed through it. As the voltage increases, more charge per second (current) will pass through. As we get up to the 110 volt to 220 volt range, the current becomes lethal. But even 12 volts can give you a nasty burn across a wet finger.

Watts and Joules

The watt, named after Scottish engineer James Watt, is the electrical unit used to measure the consumption rate of electrical energy. Energy is expressed in units of joules, named after the English physicist James Prescott Joule. When energy is being consumed at the flow rate of 1 joule per second, then the consumption rate is 1 watt.

A battery holds energy in the form of electrically charged plates. When you drain all the energy from the battery, the battery is deemed flat. The flow rate that you drain the energy out is expressed in terms of watts. The bigger the flow rate of drain (wattage), the quicker the energy stored in the battery is drained.

Energy and the flow rate of energy is cool stuff. Follow it from the source to its use in the following example. In a hydroelectric dam, the water held in the lake is called potential energy. As the water begins to race down the surge pipes to the turbines, it converts its own potential energy to kinetic energy. The faster the water travels in the pipes, the more kinetic energy each liter of water holds. The water then imparts its kinetic energy into the turbine, causing it to spin. The spin energy, as in the alternator discussion above, then converts into AC electrical energy expressed in wattage and delivers it to the electric grid. Power stations are thus rated in megawatts. This is a measure of how many million joules per second the power station delivers to the electric grid.

The energy travels along the electric grid to your house where light bulbs are rated in watts. A 60 watt bulb consumes 60 joules of energy per second.

Relate this to water in the hydroelectric dam: 1 liter of water in a hydro power station falling at 120 mph through the turbine has 1460 joules of kinetic energy. If you use 60 joules per second in your light bulb, the 1460 joules will be consumed in 24 seconds.

Think about this: in your house, if you accidently leave a 60 watt bulb glowing in your closet for the day while you are at work, you will waste about 200 liters or about 50 gallons of water out of a hydro-dam lake (not accounting for inefficiencies in the generation and transmission systems). As sailors, we are naturally conservationists and so this calculation above will surely remind you to turn off lights and other energy using devices.

More importantly, however, it is a reminder to conserve your battery energy on a boat because of the limited charging ability or the need to start your noisy polluting diesel engine just to charge the batteries.

Batteries are rated in amp-hours. This is the amount of energy it holds and the ability to deliver an amount of current over time. A typical marine battery holds 100 amp-hours. This means it could ideally deliver 1 amp of current for 100 hours before it is completely flat. Or it could power a 60-watt 12-volt bulb for only 20 hours. It is not really that much. In the hydro power station model, that amount of energy is about equivalent to 3000 liters of water imparting its energy to the turbine. Take note and conserve.

Multimeter

A multimeter can measure AC and DC volts, and ohms. Those with a clamp attachment are able to measure current as well. This tool is valuable for assessing many electrical problems that might occur on a vessel. They are inexpensive and readily purchased in most electronic and home supply stores. They take minimal training to use.

Batteries

The source of DC power is usually one or more marine grade batteries, normally 12 volts each. They are similar to automobile batteries, except sturdier—and of course more expensive.

These powerful DC batteries can be classified into three major categories:

- Wet or flooded batteries that contain lead plates in a mixture of distilled water and sulfuric acid. These have been the most common for many years, and must be serviced regularly. Unless they are sealed, you will need to inspect the acid levels. If they are low, top up with distilled water or collected rainwater only.
- Batteries containing a gel material, instead of liquid, that allows them to be sealed, thus minimal service is required.

- Absorbed glass mat (AGM) that use micro fiberglass. These represent the latest state of the art and are generally the most expensive but tend to last the longest.

DC Battery

Since batteries are often networked together, it is suggested that you use only one category type of battery above on your vessel. This will aid in extending the life of your batteries.

All batteries tend to be heavy, and so they should be firmly secured low in the vessel, under a settee near the vessel's center.

Sometimes, in order to double the amount of overall available energy to the boat, two batteries are wired together. If you wire two batteries together, you must do so "in parallel." This means positive on one battery to positive on the other battery and negative to negative. This keeps the output voltage at 12 volts. Wiring "in series" will result in 24 volts, which will blow up your circuits and bulbs and bilge pumps and who knows what else.

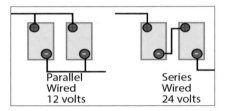

Parallel and Series Wired Batteries

Engine and House Systems

Perhaps the most important use of DC power on a vessel is for starting the engine. Considerable power is needed for this task and if the engine does not start immediately, you will drain even more energy from the battery.

Thus, it is prudent to always assign one "isolated" battery or bank of batteries for the sole purpose of starting the engine and assign another battery or bank of batteries to "the house"—all the other systems and creature comfort devices such as the stereo and refrigerator needing electrons for themselves. In this manner, you always have enough battery power for starting the engine even after running the stereo, refrigerator, lights, windlass, and all the other energy sucking devices all day and night.

A variety of switches are available for this purpose. One of the most common has four positions:

- Off
- Battery 1

- Battery 2
- Both

Battery Switches

The system is usually cleverly set up so that once the engine is started, both engine battery and house battery systems are being automatically charged.

This allows flexibility in distributing your DC battery power. Often Battery 1 is designated as the battery for starting the engine and Battery 2 for all other purposes (house). The occasion for using "Both" occurs if the engine does not start immediately from Battery 1. By using both batteries, you may be able to get the engine started.

In the event of an electrical fire, you should turn the battery switches to the off position as quickly as possible.

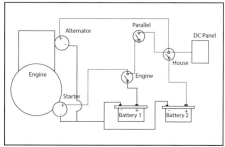
Electrical Diagram

Battery Charging

Batteries are limited in their storage capability and must be recharged.

The batteries are typically charged when docked in the marina via the AC shore power. The AC electric distribution panel will more than likely have a switch labeled "Battery Charger." When on, it will direct current to the battery charger.

The battery charger converts the AC shore power voltage to DC electricity and pumps it into the batteries. The standard procedure is to keep the charger activated at all times, even when hooked up to shore power. This will ensure that you will always have adequate 12-volt DC power. Modern DC battery chargers are designed to not overcharge your batteries even when left on

Battery Charger

indefinitely. Check your model to make sure this is the case.

When away from the dock, the batteries must be charged from onboard devices. Most commonly the batteries are charged from a device called the alternator, which is connected to the engine crankshaft via rubber belts and pulleys. This means the engine must be running for the alternator to produce electricity. The alternator creates electricity in the same manner as the generator (rotating a wire through a magnetic field) except the alternator has a built-in diode. The diode blocks the reverse flow of current so that only DC current flows out of the alternator. This is then pumped into the batteries. For the alternator to be working properly, you should engage the throttle to bring the engine to at least 1500 rpm.

Generator

Another use for the generator on board is to charge the batteries. The AC current from the generator is fed to the battery charger.

Solar Power

Solar panels produce DC power and are used to charge the batteries. A relatively small solar panel such as 1 square foot (0.1 m²) can produce about ½ an amp at 12 volts during daylight hours. It is not practical to charge a battery from completely drained to full using a small solar panel. This would take approximately 30 hours. However, a solar panel is excellent for keeping the batteries "topped up."

Solar Panels

Boats that spend an extended time away from the marina often are fitted with a large array of solar panels which produce enough electricity to keep up with the daily demand of energy from the crew.

Wind-Power Generators

Wind-power generators are typically installed only on ocean crossing vessels, where the vessel is away from the marina for extended periods of time and where there is a need for conserving onboard fuel.

The wind spins a blade attached to a generator that creates AC electric current. The AC power is quickly converted to DC power using diodes and used to charge the batteries.

Spinning Propeller

As you sail along, the water flowing over your propeller will cause it to spin. Some sailboats are fitted with a special alternator that will create electricity from a turning propeller shaft.

Charging Notes

You must be constantly vigilant to keep your batteries charged with whatever form electric energy available. In the electrical age, flat batteries on the ocean are a precursor to disaster.

Batteries do not like being constantly cycled from fully drained to fully charged. They typically stay in better health if they are constantly kept full of charge and a solar panel mounted permanently on a cabin top is good at doing this.

Regularly inspect your alternator, and its belt and pulleys, otherwise your only sign of failure will be a flat battery when you are out on the water. To test the alternator, you need to check that it is pumping about 13.5 to 14 volts into the 12-volt battery. Start the engine after the battery has been drained a little. Check the voltage across the terminals of the battery. If the voltage is in the 13.5 to 14 volt range then it is likely that you alternator is functioning properly. If the voltage reads the same as the battery when the engine is off, you may have a problem. Likewise if the voltage is reading too high around 15 volts, you may have also have a problem.

Battery Load Testing

Multimeters are not ideal for testing the health of an automotive or marine battery. For this you need to use a load tester, which puts a heavy current drain on the battery and analyses the output. Virtually all automotive stores and marine chandleries have a load tester and will test your battery for free. Thus it is not necessary to invest in one as they cost several hundred dollars.

Battery Usage

Batteries are a vessel's major source of power for many essential functions both when in the slip and while sailing. These include:

- Engine starting
- Bilge pump(s)

- Running lights required for nighttime sailing
- Cabin lights
- Raising anchors—although most anchor winches require that the engine is idling at about 1500 rpm
- Power winches
- Windlass
- A wide variety of navigation and communication instruments
- Refrigeration
- Entertainment devices such as stereo, TV, and DVD player
- Electric flushing heads
- Water pump
- Cabin fans
- Macerator
- Starter solenoid for the gas oven
- Electric outboard engine for the dingy
- Small battery chargers

Modern vessels are loaded with many appliances that consume electrical power, even when turned off. Before adding any appliance to the vessel, it is essential to know the impact it will have on your systems to ensure power consumption viability, function, and safety. For example, if you have a 12-volt DC refrigerator that you wish to keep running at all times, you must maintain a charged battery for it.

By far, one of the bigger energy draining devices on a boat is the windlass (the anchor winch), which can can draw upwards of 100 amps at 12 volts. Thus, it is a good idea to run the engine anytime you are using the windlass. Some boats are wired so that the engine must be running.

Inverters

Inverters are devices used to convert 12-volt DC battery electricity to AC 110-volt or 220-volt electricity. Special electronics in the device take constant level current and turn it into an alternating sine wave shaped current. Kudos to the engineers who invented them.

Inverters come in a variety of sizes and capacity. Small ones are simply plugged into a 12-volt DC outlet (formerly called cigarette lighters) and produce a

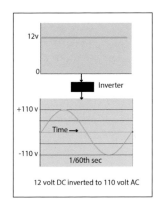

12 volt DC inverted to 110 volt AC

Inverting Current

modest AC power supply for running small devices like computers or small battery chargers for a cell phone or camera, for example.

Larger capacity inverter units will convert DC power from banks of batteries into AC power capable of powering a microwave oven or hair dryer. However, running devices like the microwave using energy derived from the batteries can deplete the batteries rapidly.

On a boat, if a large inverter is present, there will be a specially labeled AC outlet plug denoting it is an inverter outlet.

Bilge Pumps

An emergency bilge pump(s) is a very significant electrical device on any vessel. This pump is used to pump out water that may collect, for whatever reason, in the bilge.

The bilge pump has a dedicated circuit that is always on. This ensures that if a leak occurs and water begins to fill the bilge, the bilge pump will automatically engage and pump out water until the bilge is dry or the battery is exhausted. Usually, you can not turn off the automatic engagement of the bilge pump at the DC circuit breaker panel. The switch on the

Bilge Pump

panel is reserved for manual on and off. This is a good thing!

Since the bilge pump will automatically empty overboard any liquid in the bilge, it is imperative that no oil or other chemicals are allowed to drain into the bilge.

Bilge pumps are rated by the number of gallons they pump per hour. However, this requires that adequate electric power is available. Should there be a significant amount of water entering the bilge, the pump will drain

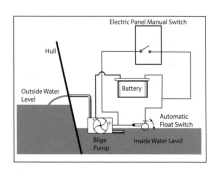

Bilge Pump System

the batteries unless the batteries are being constantly charged.

The diagram above shows the typical electrical wiring diagram for a bilge pump.

Electrical Panels

The electrical panel, located at the navigation station, normally has two distinct and separately marked sections; one section is devoted to 110-volt or 220-volt AC

Typical AC Electric Panel

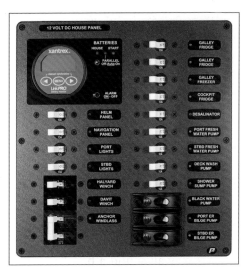

Typical DC Electric Panel

power and the other section is devoted to the 12-volt DC power. Learn the location and operation of all circuit breakers on both panels before using your vessel. These panels may be hinged and can easily be opened to inspect wiring or to add or replace circuit breakers.

Circuit Breakers

On the electric panels, circuit breakers and switches serve the same function. That is, they act both as a manual on/off switch for both AC and DC circuits as well as a safety automatic shutoff when they detect a problem that could ruin a piece of equipment or even start a fire. Fuses are out, circuit breakers are in.

Circuit breakers are indeed your electrical friends and should be treated with respect. Trying to override, or wire around circuit breakers, can be very dangerous. Breakers may not be rocket scientists, but they know their job and do it well.

The DC power system starts at the battery and passes through a main DC circuit breaker before the current is distributed via the DC electric panel. The two largest DC circuits are usually the engine start and the windlass (anchor winch) circuits. However the engine start circuit typically does not go through the electric panel. Its switch is on the key-start panel in the cockpit.

Circuit Breaker

The windlass circuit breaker is often located not on the DC electric panel but, for some reason unbeknownst to anyone, in a very hard to find location. When you get onto a new vessel, always ask where the windlass circuit breaker is.

This is a typical windlass circuit breaker.

The AC shore power enters your vessel through a plug on the stern of the vessel. It then passes through an AC circuit breaker (also usually located in an obscure place on the vessel) before going to the AC electrical dis-tribution panel located at the navigation station. Current is then distributed to the various circuits, each with their own circuit breakers, which are rated in current size appropriate to that circuit.

Windlass Circuit Breaker

This may all sound a bit like overkill, but be assured these safety devices are there for you and your vessel's safety. Study and know each of their functions.

Marine-Grade Appliances

A word of caution whenever using any home AC appliances on a vessel. Generally, these devices will work fine at first, but in a marine environment they are subject to corrosion due to the salt air. In addition, many are not designed or built for the tumbling they may face when sailing. Always be cautious when using home appliances on a vessel. Check with experts at marine stores if you are uncertain.

Shore Power Connection

One of the more common sources of fire on a boat is a loose connection of the shore power to the receptacle plug on the stern of the boat. Always make sure this is fitted tightly when leaving the vessel.

If you are not getting power to your boat via the shore power, check the circuit breaker panel box on the dock. Yes, there are circuit breakers there too.

Take care with the shore power cord after you have disconnected it from the boat. If it falls into the water you will trip the circuit breaker in the panel box on the dock. You probably will not be able to reset it because the water inside the plug will continually trip the breaker. Make sure there is some means to stow the cord so that no one accidently (or purposefully (*kids arhhh*)) can knock it into the water.

The shore-power cord should never dangle in the water. If it does the electric field in the water sets up an electrolysis reaction that tends to eat anything metal on your boat and surrounding boats.

Chapter 3

Auxiliary Power—Diesel Engines

Introduction

Modern sailboats rely not only on wind for power, but also auxiliary sources, most commonly diesel engines. These engines provide propulsion and generate electricity. The engine can get you out of trouble and help you maneuver in marinas, and if need be, get you home in time.

Fun sailing occurs when the winds are flowing smoothly across properly trimmed sails as the vessel moves steadily through the water. It is quiet time when sailors and their sailboat are in perfect harmony with nature and their inner selves. It is a glorious feeling for crew, passengers, and the vessel.

But then comes the moment when:

- The winds suddenly die
- You need to maneuver your vessel smartly into its slip
- Your DC electrical power supply is running low
- You decide to motorsail to meet a schedule
- An emergency requires the engine's use

The Famous Golden Gate

My Dad always talked about the relief he felt as he returned from WWII, sailing in under the Golden Gate Bridge on a troop carrier. Thanks to the brave souls of that era, 60 years later, I was able to sail free and recreationally under the same bridge. Thanks Dad!

Except, while I personally was free from totalitarianism, the current ebbing from the San Francisco Bay was not releasing me from its bond. On each tack across the channel under the bridge we passed exactly the same place as on the previous tack. Eventually, we gave up and turned on the engines. Cook, Magellan, Drake, and others had no such luxury. Additional note: when sailing outside the bridge, check the tide tables. Durh!

Diesel Engine

Thanks go to a Mr. Rudolf Diesel who years ago in Germany cleverly invented an engine that today bears his name (luckily, they chose his last name)—the diesel engine. It is the ideal engine for a sailboat because of high reliability, good torque, relatively inexpensiveness to operate, and low maintenance cost factors. Diesel engines are now standard auxiliary power plants on most sailing vessels.

Diesel engines have mechanical similarities to a gasoline engine except for the fuel they burn, called diesel fuel. This fuel requires high compression instead of a spark for ignition. However, this requires fuel injectors and a heavier engine block to handle the higher compression.

Earlier diesel engines were large and heavy. Modern diesels are more compact, and some models are quite small by previous standards. Their output is expressed in traditional horsepower terms, and comes in a wide range.

When using a diesel engine on a sailboat, you do not have to worry about distributors and spark plugs because there are none. Instead, you have highly reliable fuel injectors that seldom require maintenance.

Since diesel fuel is less flammable than gasoline, it is much safer to store in closed containers on board.

Reliability and efficiency are the hallmarks of diesel engines. If you keep diesel fuel clean, a diesel engine will run for up to 5000 hours before any major overhaul is required.

Diesel Engine Fluids

Diesel engines make use of a variety of fluids, including raw and coolant water, diesel fuel, and lubricating oil. A problem in the flow of any one of these fluids can cause further problems. Diesel engines produce a lot of heat due to high compression and this heat must be efficiently dissipated.

Knowing the purposes and flow routes of diesel engine fluids is simple and useful if the engine has a problem. You are not required to be a diesel mechanic, but you should be familiar with these fluids, their operational levels, and of course, flow.

A prudent suggestion is to visually inspect the engine every time you go sailing. This visual inspection may provide clues to any potential problems, and will establish a baseline of knowledge. Specific information for inspecting the type of engine you have is readily available in your owner's manuals. Location of filters, dipsticks, and hoses is dependent upon the engine size and is also found in your owner's manuals.

Diesel Water Systems

Diesel engines run hot because of high compression and therefore need to be cooled. Fortunately, ample cooling is readily available from the water the vessel is sailing in; however, since ocean water is highly corrosive due to salt content, ocean sailing must be given special attention.

First a brief overview of a diesel's two water systems.

To keep it "cool," a diesel engine uses two water systems.

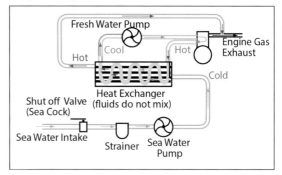

Diesel Cooling Water Systems

The raw-water system and the (internal) closed-coolant system. The internal coolant contains fresh water and antifreeze, similar to an automobile. This mixture flows around the cylinders and draws heat away from the combustion, making the water hot. This hot water mixture is then pumped to a device called a heat exchanger whereby it exchanges heat with the raw water-system. It is called the closed water system because it never exits the engine area.

The raw-water cooling system pumps ambient water from outside the hull into a second part of the heat exchanger where it drains off heat from the internal water/coolant system and then exhausts this raw water out into the lake or ocean. This heat exchanger functions much like the radiator on an automobile, except it uses raw water instead of air.

These two water systems needed for cooling a diesel engine are almost foolproof. A problem may occur if the raw-water intake in the hull becomes clogged due to kelp or other clogging material. Your engine temperature gauge and horn will alert you to the fact that you have a water temperature issue. Stop the engine immediately in this sound occurs.

Diesel Raw-Water System

We begin with a list and pictures of typical elements in the raw water system. You should visually study your engine to insure you know their location and how to repair them, if necessary:

- Through-hull fitting with seacock valve—capable of being turned on and off. Ensure that it is open whenever the engine is running.
- Seawater strainer—check for cleanliness.
- Impeller pump—essential to keep raw water flowing. Easily replaced.
- Heat exchanger
- Exhaust

Raw water enters the engine through a through-hull fitting and seacock valve. The seacock is a ball valve; the handle should be in the open position any time the engine is running. Normally the valve handle runs parallel with the pipe housing when it is in the open position. Locating this valve handle may sometimes require exploration. Consult your owner's manual.

Next, the raw incoming water flows through a sea strainer, which is designed to strain out any large particles that may be sucked up from the outside through the seacock. Most often debris is small bits of seaweed or waste.

After the strainer, the raw water flows through the impeller pump. This pumps the raw water forward to the heat exchanger. The pump is usually belt-driven, which needs to be inspected often to insure proper tension with no fraying.

The raw water flows out of the boat through the engine's exhaust to provide a last bit of cooling to the exhaust. It is important to check for raw water outflow in the engine's exhaust every time the engine is started. This spurting of exhaust water ensures that hot raw water is flowing through the heat exchanger and effectively cooling the closed water system.

Good advice is to include a replacement rubber impeller in your spare parts kit. Preventive maintenance means checking the sea strainer, working the seacock, and replacing the rubber impeller once a year.

Diesel Closed Water System

The second cooling system fluid is called the closed or coolant water system. And some elements of this system include:

- Water
- Antifreeze
- Heat exchanger
- Thermostat
- Cycle to the hot water heater
- Water circulating pump
- Reservoir

Antifreeze is added to the water in this system to lower the temperature at which the water will freeze. This is imperative because should the water freeze and expand inside the closed system, things will break.

The engine's thermostat opens and closes, much as in an automobile, to maintain optimum water temperature for efficient engine operation.

A circulating pump moves the coolant mixture throughout the closed system. This pump is belt-driven and often not easy to access or service. Because the antifreeze water mixture is not corrosive, this pump should remain trouble-free for a long time.

It is important to check the closed water system fluid level in the reservoir and via the cap located usually on top of the engine. However, as with a car, only crack open the cap when the engine is cold. When hot, the system is under high pressure and thus extremely dangerous. Also during inspection, look for chaffed or damaged hoses that can cause leaks.

Standard maintenance also includes checking the tension of the belt that drives the pump. A belt that is either too loose or too tight can cause problems. See your operator's manual for recommendations. Spare parts to have on your boat include belts, hoses and clamps, antifreeze, and a thermostat.

Diesel Fuel

The search, discovery, refinement and resource control of fuel has a rich and very sordid history. But just like conversation on a boat, let's not delve into politics.

The Human Imagination

After the discovery of liquid fuel, can you imagine then sitting down with a pencil and paper and designing an engine? One with contained explosions in a cylinder pushing down on a rod connected off-centered to a shaft to cause rotation? Would you have foreseen the world change though your mind's eye?

Caution: Never Mix Fuels

Almost invariably, your inboard mounted engine will run on diesel fuel. Whereas, if you have an outboard engine, it will most likely run on gasoline (petrol). Never ever, as the saying goes, mix drinks—engine drinks that is: gasoline and diesel fuels.

Each type of fuel is produced for use in a specific engine and should never be mixed. If a mixture should happen by mistake, obtain professional help to remove the mixture before running the engine, else your engine will not be running for long.

Filling a fuel tank with the wrong kind of fuel can easily be done if you do not pay attention to what is happening at the fuel dock. A bit of advice: before allowing the fuel dock attendant, or yourself, to fuel your diesel powered vessel, always ensure—double ensure—that the supply hose is pumping diesel fuel into the diesel fuel tank and not into your vessel's holding or fresh water tank. This sounds really simple but not paying attention can cost you a lot of money.

Also note that names of fuels vary by country. In Europe, diesel is called Gasoil or Gasole. In British-speaking countries petrol is the term used for gasoline. It's important to know your fuels and local names of fuels when visiting other countries.

The elements of the diesel fuel system include:

- The fuel fill cap. Located somewhere on the outside of the vessel. This is where you fill the tank(s) at a fuel dock or from a can.
- Fuel tanks. Commonly plastic or metal.
- Shutoff valve (aka petcock valve)
- Primary fuel filter (aka water separator)
- Fuel lift pump (aka supply pump)
- Secondary fuel filter
- Injector pump
- Injectors
- Return line
- The diesel fuel itself

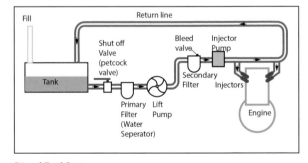

Diesel Fuel System

Fuel purity and cleanliness is vital for proper operation of the engine. Thus make it a habit to check the fuel filters often.

Note that diesel fuel is diesel fuel and *nothing* should ever be used as a substitute. There is however, such a thing called biodiesel that can be used if the manufacturer allows. Fuel for all engines have their own characteristics such as lubricity and energy output. Lubricity affects the engine wear. The energy output determines the heat generated in the cylinder; too high energy output can lead to premature burnout of the engine.

Contaminated fuel is the source of 90 percent of diesel engine problems. If possible keep the tank full to help prevent condensation and water from getting into the diesel fuel. If fueling from a dock or barrels that you are not familiar with, special precautions are in order.

When metal fuel tanks are not full, there is the possibility of condensation forming because of temperature variations, and thus there is condensation dripping into the fuel. This may lead to the formation of bacteria and degradation of the fuel. There are several additives used for retarding this formation, but in general, these are not necessary. Check with local fuel docks for recommendations in your sailing area. Most modern fuels are treated and do not need additives. In addition, tanks are now often made of non-metallic plastic materials that are less likely to create condensation. Check your tank; it will either be stainless steel or plastic.

For safety, there is always a shutoff valve—called a petcock valve—right at the fuel hose leading from the tank. Again, be advised to study your owner's manual for its location and proper usage.

From the petcock shutoff valve, the diesel fuel flows to a primary or water separator filter that is designed to remove any water. Water in diesel fuel can be very disruptive, from making the engine run poorly to stopping altogether. Whenever your engine sputters or seems to lack power, you should immediately suspect faulty fuel.

Next, a lift pump aids in priming the diesel fuel. It is a small low pressure pump sending fuel through the secondary filter and on to the high-pressure fuel injector pump.

Diesel fuel exits the injector pump through high-pressure hoses to each of the injectors where it is compressed in the cylinders by the rising pistons. There is also a return line, where unspent diesel is returned to the diesel tank.

Troubleshooting a diesel fuel problem includes checking the water separator filter and ensuring there are no leaks in the system. Spare parts should include filters and an up-lift pump.

Don't Run Your Engine Dry of Diesel Fuel

Running out of diesel is a big hassle. Since the diesel injector pump needs to create high pressure for the injectors, any air in the line can cause major problems. If there is air in the line, not enough pressure is created and thus no fuel flows to the combustion chamber. In this case, you will need to bleed the line of air. It's a simple but arduous task. You'll need to release a value atop of the secondary filter and work a lever up and down attached to the lift pump. Once air bubbles stop exiting the secondary filter, tighten its valve. You may need to further release air from the pipe flowing from the secondary filter to the injector pump. All this requires bending into places you may not be able to bend depending on your age and last time you did a yoga class.

Consumption

Fuel consumption is a big advantage with diesel engines. Below is a graph of fuel use for some typical engines for typical boat sizes. A typical engine for a 25-33 ft (7.6—10 m) sailboat consumes about 1.9 liters (0.5 US gal) per hour operating at 2400 rpm.

Diesel Lubricants

The last fluid we consider is the engine's lubricant: oil. Just like in an automobile engine, oil helps prevent heat from developing as the result of piston friction. A diesel's oil system consists of the following components:

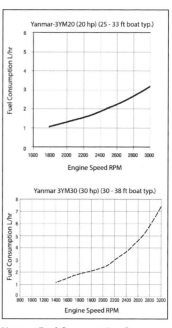

Yanmar Fuel Consumption Specs

- Oil—varieties available for various conditions
- Oil filter—for cleanliness
- Dip stick—for measurement
- Oil receptacle—tank

Oil in a diesel engine is under more stress than in a gas engine due to higher temperature. Thus make sure you use oil designed for diesel engines when refilling or changing. When checking the oil level with the dipstick, do not be alarmed by blackened oil; this is normal.

If the oil is milky or bubbly, there is a breakdown in the system and either water or fuel is mixing with the oil. Troubleshooting includes checking the level and color of the oil. Maintenance includes recommended scheduled oil changes, often every 100 hours. Spare parts include oil and filters.

Disposal

As sailors, we have an inborn desire to be Earth-friendly. But just in case you're switching over from a stinkpot (what non-sailors call power-boats) and don't know any better, disposing of diesel fuel and oil is strictly controlled by law, and violations are punishable. Your vessel must have a placard indicating what is legal and what is not legal. This sign must be displayed next to the engine. Putting it simply, these two flu-ids must be disposed of in properly designated

Discharge of Oil Prohibited

The Federal Water Pollution Control Act prohibits the discharge of oil or oily waste into or upon the navigable waters of the United States, or the waters of the contiguous zone, or which may affect natural resources belonging to, appertaining to, or under the exclusive management authority of the United States, if such discharge causes a film or discoloration of the surface of the water or causes a sludge or emul-sion beneath the surface of the water. Violators are subject to substantial civil penalties and/or criminal sanctions including fines and imprisonment.

Discharge of Oil Plaque

containers, never in trash receptacles or toilets. Scan the QR code for a PDF you can turn into a plaque at your local office supply store.

When you replace your engine oil, simply take it down to the local vehicle oil change garage. By law, they are required to provide oil dump stations for the pub-lic and are only too happy to accept your old oil. At home, save a few large plastic bottles around for this purpose. And please make sure you properly recycle the plastic as well. We believe that as sailors, we've got a responsibility to lead a green example.

Refueling

Fueling up your boat can be a bit tricky if you're using 5-gallon (20-liter) containers and carelessness invariably leads to spillage. While you think a few drops here and there are a necessary evil, it is not. Have you ever seen the rainbow film on the water produced by even one drop? It's not good; and with a whole marina of people doing it, even a few drops can jam up the waterways and make a wasteland of life in the marina and beyond.

Siphoning Fuel Easy

Instead, there is a most awesome device called a Super Siphon. It's got a one-way check valve so that when you push the tube down into the container, diesel flows into the siphon hose. By vigorously shaking it up and down you fill the hose and siphoning becomes the easiest job ever.

Watch this video.

You can buy a Super Siphon from Amazon or many other places.

Super Siphon Refueling

Diesel Engine Operation

As noted earlier, diesel engines are sturdy and highly reliable and operating them today is straightforward. New diesel engines operate much like gasoline engines and the days of "glow plugs" (electric fuel warmers to heat the air before it passed into the combustion chamber) have passed into history.

There are usually very few problems associated with diesel engines.

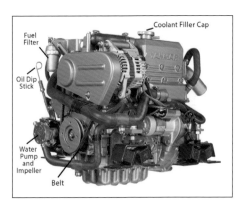

Diesel Engine Essentials

- If an engine is turning over but not starting—it is probably a fuel problem.
- If it will not turn over—it is probably a battery issue.
- If it starts but stalls when shifting into gear—there is a line caught around the prop.
- If it is overheating—the fresh water pump is not working properly.

A few additional pointers:

- Unless you are operating in extreme cold conditions, diesel engines do not need a long warm-up. As soon as they are running smoothly after starting, they are good to go.
- Each diesel engine has its range of optimum rpm (rounds per minute). These operating conditions should be observed. Typically, you'll find that 3000 rpm is the max short-term operating speed and 2500 is the max long-term operating speed.
- Engine noise is usually adequately muffled by soundproofing materials.
- On many vessels, the diesel throttle, whether in forward or reverse position, also engages the transmission. There is typically a button of some sort to pull next to the throttle/gear lever to disengage the gears whilst still throttling the engine. This is most often used to charge batteries or during the anchor windlass (winch) operation.

One symptom that may require professional help is a smoking diesel engine. This may be due to a wide variety of causes, including overfilling the oil receptacle, faulty injectors, or corrosion.

The reason for these somewhat detailed explanations is to ensure proper attention is given to maintaining your diesel engine. It is a vessel's primary source of power for getting in and out of slips, for providing essential electronic services and creature comforts, and most importantly, in emergency situations.

Here is a simple but essential prestart checklist:

- Diesel fuel tank level
- Engine oil level between the min and max on the dipstick
- Fuel filter
- Water filter
- Coolant water
- Belts
- Engine pan—no collection of oil or fluids
- Hoses

Lastly, we leave you with this: Avoid stowing the keys to the engine in someone's pocket. If that person goes overboard, you've got problems.

Chapter 4
Hulls, Rigging, and Sails

Introduction

An easy way to think of a sailboat is that the hull keeps us afloat and the rigging and sails keep us moving.

Let's do a flyby over a typical cruising sailboat, naming a few of the essential parts.

Rigging and Sails

Flyby Video Animation

Sailboat Design

Surely, the first sailboat was invented by a five-year old child with a block of wood. He or she stuck a twig through a piece of animal skin and down into a knothole in the wood. A fascinated father sat by amused at the child's ingenuity. The distracted father was then eaten by a saber-toothed tiger and sailboats were not thought of for another 10,000 years. Perhaps!

As humans, we just can't stop wondering what is over the horizon and it was sailboats that first quenched that thirst when a large body of water was encountered. The same yearning you feel for harnessing the wind and travel was felt by the Phoenicians, the Egyptians, and the Chinese, thousands of years ago. Paddles were all fine and dandy but that took energy from manpower and consumed lots of food. Wind is a free and abundant source of energy—what was needed however was to develop the skill to harness it.

Over history, design of boats and sails has evolved empirically. Small improvements were made century by century. Today, we use computers to design for hull strength and slipperiness through the water (yes, slipperiness is a technical term in sailing). We use finite element analysis computer models to optimize compressible wind flow around sails and vertical standing wingsails. Composite materials are purpose-designed for optimal directional strength and light weight. We pop boats out of the water on hydrofoils to make them s go at speeds in excess of 50 knots. Hundreds of millions of dollars are invested in America's Cup boats that push the envelope of sailing technology. It's exciting stuff!

Mostly gone however is the use of sailboats for commercial trade. Today, most sailboats are designed for day cruising, sailing vacations, racing, or to satisfy the yearning for the blue horizon.

Regardless of its use, however, there are several features common to most sailboats. They are:

- **Keel.** The weight and location of a vessel's keel keep the vessel from tipping over and helps stabilize forward motion. While the keel is vital to a sailboat, we only infrequently see it, usually when the sailboat is heeled over in strong winds or hauled out for maintenance.
- **Hull.** This is perhaps the most important feature of a sailboat. When all else is lost: rigging, rudder, engine, sails—an intact hull will save your life.
- **Rigging, standing, and running.** The rigging, standing, and running consists of all the devices needed to control the sails.
- **Sails.** Sails are the beautifully and cleverly designed synthetic materials that grab and control the wind.

To maximize sailboat efficiency and stay within production cost limits, boat designers cleverly integrate these components. The result has been an incredible evolution due to creative ideas, new construction materials, and better science.

Some common parts of the boat at the stern are shown here.

Common Names Animation

Hull and Keel

A sailboat's hull and keel receive considerable attention from a sailboat designer since they determine the capacity of the vessel, how fast it will go, and the degree of safety and comfort.

The hull is the essence of all boats. It is carefully designed for water flow. Some hulls are designed to go fast across the top of the water. These are called planing hulls because the velocity of the water under the hull provides lift so as to lift the hull upward. This reduces the amount of hull in the water and thus less water needs to be moved out of the way. This reduces the drag and consequently the boat can go even faster. Many smaller dinghy sailboats plane on top of the water.

Most larger sailboat's hulls are called displacement hulls. This is because there is no appreciable lift provided to the hull from the boat's velocity. Thus, the boat will always displace the same amount of weight of water as the boat's weight. This is the essence of the ability to float.

Still, you can imagine there is considerable thought invested in designing a displacement hull to make it slippery. Reducing resistance from the water make the boat go faster. Think of the resistance of a knife slicing through water versus the same knife turned sideways.

Keels are a sailboat's stabilizer and provide the ability to sail in directions other than directly downwind. Their weight and design provide resistance against the heeling power of the wind and determine a sailboat's ability to stay upright. On very rare occasions when keels have dropped or been ripped off—not a fun experience— the vessel will capsize and sailing is over for a while, sometimes forever. Additionally, as the keel slices through the water, the keel also provides resis-

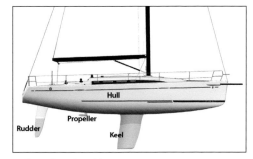

Hull, Keel, and Rudder

tance to the sailboat from being pushed completely sideways through the water from the wind.

Monohull and Multihulls

Historically we are used to thinking primarily about monohull sailboats. However, in the past 20 years stronger materials have led to multihull (catamarans and trimarans) sailboats entering the sailing market. Each configuration has its own features.

Multihulls, usually catamarans (two hulls), are popular among charter companies because of their ease of use, stability, and creature comforts. Due to the catamaran's width, slips are sometimes difficult to obtain and if so, are usually at twice the price. But for those who are willing to pay, the tradeoff can be worth it.

Hull Protection

It is vital to protect your hull from the harshness of the water environment. Algae and barnacles are not your friends. For this reason, serious amounts of research have gone into various types of paints for the section of the hull that sits below the waterline. No matter what paint technology you use, serious blistering and damage can occur if you do not maintain and recoat the hull every three to five years, depending on the environment.

Some environmental considerations depending on the water include:

- Barnacles
- Temperature of the water; higher temperature water spawns faster growth of algae
- Algae count
- Salt: salt water is a harsher environment

The more often you brush the unwanted nasties off your hull, the longer you can extend your paint job. But that usually requires a swim or paying someone to do it for you. Keep several brushes and masks/snorkels on your boat; make your guests pay their rent by helping you brush the bottom when anchored in a nice cove in warm water times. Chuckle chuckle! Guests are often only too happy to help.

Rigging

At boat shows, we see folks huddled down in the vessel's salon oohing and aahing at the leather cushions to sit on, and at the electronic gadgets for navigation and entertainment. But the real sailing excitement takes place where the wind streaks across sails and transmits its energy through the vessel's powerful rigging and onto the hull.

Rigging is commonly divided into two categories:

Standing and Running Rigging

- Standing Rigging
- Running Rigging

Standing rigging is just that; it does not move and is a generic name for masts, spreaders, and stays, many of which are now made from exotic materials. It was only a few years ago that trees provided the primary source for these stationary objects.

Running rigging is rigging that moves, including "ropes" with crazy names. The halyards, sheets, cunninghams, reefing lines, blocks, fairleads, winches, and miscellaneous hardware all make up the running rigging. These items work in conjunction with the standing rigging. Some are flexible and can be adjusted to meet a variety of conditions.

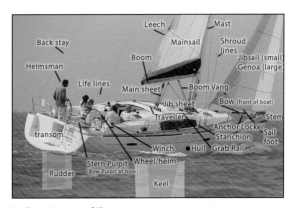

Sailboat Names of Thingies

The image above shows most of the nomenclature of the rigging on a modern sailboat.

Standing Rigging

To keep the mast from toppling over, an array of rods, cables, ropes (lines), and wires are attached at various spots on the mast and run down to the bow, stern, and sides of the vessel. Professional riggers using highly specialized tools and standards are required to adjust all rigging properly. The process is called tuning the rig.

Cables, wires, or rods running from various points on the mast to the vessel's deck are stays. Stays are identified as forestay, backstay, port, and starboard sidestays depending upon where they are attached to the deck. Sidestays are also known as shrouds. Stays ensure that the mast remains upright as well as assist in the transfer of energy from the mast's sail to the vessel's hull. Vessels currently produced by some manufacturers have eliminated the backstay by shifting the connection to the deck of the sidestays to a more aft position. This rigging design is called the B&R rig. Some argue that the B&R rig reduces performance and prefer to stick with a backstay. The advantage of the B&R rig is that without a backstay in the way, an arch over the top of

Standing Rigging

the cockpit can be used to house the traveler for the main sheet. This is typically done on cruising boats. Sailboat racers frown at this design.

Whatever your preference, the standing rigging is all the stuff that provides support to the sails but do not move.

Masthead and Fractional Standing Rigging

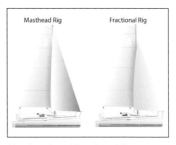

Masthead and Fractional Rigs

There are two variations on the standing rigging set up: Masthead and Fractional.

On masthead rigs the attachment point for the sidestays (shrouds), forestay, and backstay (if it exists) is at the top of the mast.

On fractional rigs, only the backstay reaches to the top of the mast, whereas the attachment point for the sidestays and forestay is near the top of the mast but not all the way at the top. Tensioning the backstay will bend the mast, which provides an additional means of controlling the shape of the sail.

The strength of the mast material is relied upon to prevent it from flexing too much or breaking past the point of forestay and sidestay attachment.

See the animation and watch the sail flatten when the backstay is tensioned.

The Mast

The mast is simply a strong spar, or "stick," that reaches upward into the air to hold the sails. The

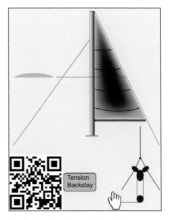

Backstay Tension Animation

mast is attached to the vessel, sometimes through the top deck and down to the keel, though sometimes it sits on the top deck and is supported by compression posts underneath.

When the mast goes directly to the keel the sailboat is said to be "keel-stepped," but if it attaches to the deck it is called "deck-stepped." Most vessels in the 30- to 50-foot range are deck-stepped.

This deck-stepped arrangement allows for a variety of sail designs and opportunities for diversified salon designs.

Masts are often aluminum extrusions or made of carbon and/or fiberglass composite materials. Their shapes are sometimes complex because they house electric wires going to the top of the mast. In some cases there is a vertical rod in which the sail furls around inside a cavity in the mast. This is called a roller furling mast.

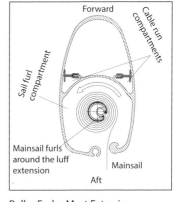

Roller Furler Mast Extrusion

The Spreaders

Spreaders, rigid structures attached perpendicularly to the mast, strengthen the mast in conjunction with standing rigging. You will note that on some vessels spreaders are swept back, while on others they are not. There may be several sets of spreaders on larger vessels.

As stronger and lighter materials are being created, masts and their spreaders are modified to better support sails and provide for different rigging configurations.

Spreaders

Running Rigging

A sailboat's running rigging consists of those items controlling the sails and helping the sails to capture the wind's energy.

Here you find a fascinating array of hardware, all with specialized functions and unique names. Most tend to be quite expensive. They are expensive because they must be uniquely designed and made of reliable materials that will not fail under stress.

Running Rigging

The main running rigging names you should know are shown here below.

- The main halyard, is used to hoist the mainsail up the mast.
- The cunningham is used to provide downhaul tension on the sail. It usually has multiple blocks so that extra tension can be applied over the ability of the main halyard.
- The boom vang controls the downward tension on the boom, which acts to flatten the sail.
- The mainsheet allows the boom to swing out to capture the wind at various boat angles to the wind.
- The reefing lines allow the sail to lower a little, which decreases the area size of the sail.
- The boom topping lift holds the boom up when the mainsail is not up. Care must be taken to not allow the boom topping lift tension to act against the main sheet or boom vang. Under sailing conditions, the boom topping lift should be slack.

Running Rigging Names Animation

If you are lucky, most of the rigging lines run back to the cockpit for easy access.

The Boom

The boom is a horizontal pole (spar) attached to the mast and capable of swiveling. In addition to holding the sail out in its classic triangular shape, the boom also provides a means for multiple controls of the mainsail. The sail's leech (trailing edge) can be tightened by tightening the main sheet. Letting out the mainsheet allows the boom to rise and swing out. The traveler can pull the boom to windward without changing the shape of the sail. The boom vang pulls down on the boom, which can flatten the sail. The outhaul flattens the foot of the sail.

You'll find a more in-depth discussion on controlling the sails in Chapter 7. (Also see the NauticEd Sail Trim Clinic for a very technical lesson.)

Hardware

A few words about the plethora of running rigging hardware commonly found on sailboats. They are made from a wide variety of materials, each with its own set of characteristics and problems. Stainless steel is good looking and resistant to corrosion but expensive and it will in fact corrode in the presence of oxygen and chlorine in ocean water (from the salt NaCl). Thus freshwater wash down is prudent.

Plastic materials have a tendency to dry out and become subject to cracking. Some sail materials will often be degraded by sunlight. Hulls may blister. Corrosion is ever present. And so on.

The bottom line is that all the materials on a sailboat have limitations. While in general problems are infrequent, the sailboat materials, like sailors, do occasionally exhibit a weakness.

There are many items that need periodic replacement or can be easily lost. Every vessel should have an adequate store of spare items. Be careful not to buy cheap replacements. Cheap ends up being expensive.

Department of Redundancy Department

As a guest on a Mediterranean sail between Cannes and Corsica, I asked the captain why he seemed to have replacements for every part of the boat stored somewhere down below. The Captain said merely, "Experience, boy. Experience." He'd sailed the boat around the world for over four years.

Winches

Using a winch is fundamental to most of us but the first time you see one it may not be obvious. You use a winch to wind in the sheets (lines-ropes) nice and tight. It provides hundreds of times the mechanical advantage over what you could apply with your hands and it will hold the sheet long after you get tired.

The essence of the winch is the number of wraps of the line around the winch cylinder. The winch cylin-

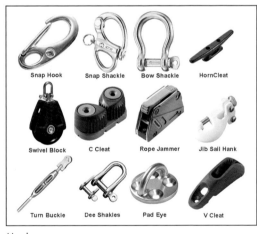

Hardware

der is knurled with a rough surface to help prevent the line from sliding back around. The wrap provides back-tension in the form of friction from the winch cylinder on the line. The more wraps the more friction and thus back-tension. A line with a thousand pounds of force from the sail can be held with only a few pounds of pull by your hand when there is 3-4 wraps around the winch. But when pulling in by hand you don't gain the mechanical advantage. Thus, to pull in the line, you must turn the winch using the winch handle. The mechanical advantage to pull in the line is gained by the gearing inside the winch. The person winding the winch is usually backed up by another person "tailing" the line as it comes off the winch. The tailer must keep tension on the line. If they cannot provide enough tension to keep the line from slipping in the winch then you should put another wrap around the winch. In light winds usually 2 wraps is fine. In higher winds add 1 or 2 more. After the line is wound in, the line either held by hand for constant trimming purposes or set into a cleat.

Self-tailing winches have a slot around the top. A self-tailing winch does not require anyone to pull on the sheet as it comes out of the winch. The slot automatically clamps the sheet in so it cannot pull out backward. You'll need to notice the stainless steel tab that drops down over the slot. Use this tab to bring the sheet up into the top slot. Many people make a mistake of just winding the sheet up into the slot without the tab. This will cause the sheet to undo. Use the tab! Self-tailing winches also have the advantage in that the cleat for holding the line after it is wound in is built into the winch.

Many winches go in both directions; one for faster winding in and the other direction for slower winding. The slower direction applies more mechanical advantage. So use the fast direction until it gets too tough, then switch to the other direction to wind in the last bit.

Here are the quick secrets:

- No matter what you think, you always wrap the sheet (line/rope) around the winch in a clockwise direction (even in the southern hemisphere).
- The more times you wrap the sheet around the winch, the more friction is applied and the more pulling power you can apply.
- If the sheet is not moving as you turn the winch, wrap it around the winch one more time.
- Usually, most winches are limited to about 4 wraps.
- Under most circumstances, 2 wraps will do.
- If the wind gets above 12 knots, you'll need 3 wraps.
- Use the tab to get the sheet up into the top slot.
- Keep your fingers clear.

Winch Use Animation

The animation shows the line being wrapped clockwise around the winch and then up onto the tab and into the self-tailing slot.

Locking Cleats

Locking cleats are simple. They simply lock the line from moving back out once you've pulled it in. The trick to unlocking the cleat is simple: the lever has to be ALL THE WAY BACK, not halfway up. An important safety item: **NEVER JUST FLICK OPEN THE LEVER**. If there is tension on the line, you or the person holding the line will experience rope burn, which is not a pleasant thing. We

Locking Cleats

all learned this as a child. ALWAYS wind the line around the winch at least two times and cleat it, then flick the lever all the way open, now slowly release the tension on the line. Once the tension is gone, you can remove the line from around the winch.

Watch this video on how to manage the winch handle.

Sailing Tip

Lines and Knots

Sailboats seem to be awash in "ropes," which are properly called lines by sailors. These lines come in a wide range of materials from some that stretch easily (nylon) to others that are less elastic.

Selecting lines is not simply a matter of what color or thickness you like; these lines serve specific purposes calling for unique characteristics.

Here is a partial list of common lines and their functions.

- Halyards—Used to raise and lower sails
- Sheets—Used to control the set of the sail
- Furling lines—Used to furl main and head sails

Some lines might pass through various blocks (pulleys) and adjusting devices, like travelers, and some may end up being controlled by winches. Lines that are subject to abrasion should regularly be inspected and replaced if it appears they have been compromised.

Contrary to many a crusty sailor, there are, however, at least three ropes on a boat. This piece of trivia can be used to win libations at the local marina bars.

- **The Bell Rope:** The small rope attached to the ball on a bell.
- **The Bolt Rope:** The sewn-in rope at the leading edge of a sail to hold it in its track.

- **The Bucket Rope:** About 6 ft (2m) long attached to a bucket used for deck washdown.

Caution: After you are under way use of the bucket rope may require the use of a Man Overboard throw line.

Knots

The art of using lines (rope) to perform many sailing tasks often requires tying knots. Many of these knots are clever indeed and have a long rich history. Sheet bend knots dating back to 7,000 BC have been found in Finnish fishing nets.

Learning to tie knots is both fun and challenging. The bowline, which is a loop that will not close, is well known, but many other knots are equally important; e.g. the half hitches, sheet bend, splices, and figure eight. Some knots tend to be purely decorative, while others may be essential for survival.

Animated Knots
iPhone App

The website http://www.animatedknots.com is by far the best source reference for learning to tie knots. The knots are shown in an animated format so you can easily learn the progression. They also have iPhone, iPad and Android apps that you can use to take with you on a sailing trip and make challenges for the kids (adult kids too).

Animated Knots
Android App

Below are the knots you need to at least know. By clicking on the image you will be taken to the animated knots specific knot page.

Bowline

A bowline is typically used to tie the jib sheets to the clew of the jib sail.

Bowline

www.animatedknots.com

Reef or Square knot

The reef knot also known as the square knot is mainly used when reefing the sail. This knot is not very secure and it can easily slip undone.

Reef (Square) Knot

www.animatedknots.com

Round Turn and Two Half Hitches

A round turn and 2 half hitches is typically used to tie to a pylon.

Rolling Hitch

A rolling hitch is used when you need a knot that won't slip when pulled at an angle. This knot is ideal for taking strain off another rope.

Clove Hitch

The clove hitch is quick to tie and easy to adjust; it is ideal for securing fenders (and horses).

Cleat Hitch

The cleat hitch is used to make fast to a cleat

Figure Eight

The figure eight knot is easy to tie and stops rope from escaping through a jammer, block, or pad eye. It is also very easy to undo when needed.

Sails

Sails are sophisticated objects. It is not only the materials they are made from that is important, but also, the way they are cut and sewn. They are made mostly from a wide variety of synthetic materials, primarily Dacron, which is a homogeneous material that has the same strength in all directions. But since stresses from the wind come from different points and angles on the sail, some sails are designed from more high-tech materials such as carbon and Kevlar fibers. These have unidirectional strength designed into them to provide strength at specific points and angles. This reduces stretch in the sail and helps maintain sail shape where it is critical. Critical as in winning the race.

Mastering sail design and sail handling is a lifelong learning experience that involves practice and knowledge, as well as intuition. Adjusting sails while trying to anticipate wind shifts is fun indeed.

Because, That's Why

In a race in Auckland Habour on a Beneteau First 45, I asked our highly paid professional racer sail trimmer to explain exactly why he gave the mainsail a half turn on the winch since everything looked fine and trimmed to me. His answer—"Because I felt it needed it." I guess that is why he is paid a lot of money for his job.

Every sail on a vessel represents a compromise involving the kind of winds the vessel will encounter, the vessel's displacement, racing or cruising configuration, and finally, and perhaps most importantly, the depth of the owner's pockets. Most sailors are initially quite content with the basic main and headsails provided by the manufacturer, but to win races, a deep pocket is required.

A Sailing Regatta

Sail Nomenclature

The following illustration shows the parts of the sail and associated control lines. Of note is the bolt rope, which is one of very few actual ropes on a boat. (Remember the other two? Bell rope and bucket rope.)

- The bolt rope is usually sewn into the luff (leading edge) of the sail. It provides strength to the luff of the sail and is used also to slide into the track if there is one. On a head sail, the bolt rope provides strength to the luff of the sail when "hanks" are used.
- Hanks are basically sliding clamps that slide up the forestay and are clamped onto the bolt rope at the leading edge (luff).

- The main halyard is attached to the head of the sail and is used to pull the sail up the mast.
- The gooseneck is a swivel connection from the boom to the mast.
- The reefing points are points where the sail can be pulled down in order to reef the sail if a roller furling system is not used.
- The topping lift holds the back of the boom up.
- The boom vang holds the boom down when beating to wind. On downwind legs, the boom vang can be loosened to provide more shape to the sail.
- The cunningham pulls the sail down tight and is used also when reefing.
- The outhaul line is attached to the clew to pull the sail out along the boom.

Names of Sail Thingies

Click on a letter to show the part name; click again to hide the part name. Then test yourself.

Types of Sails

Headsails:

These are genoas and jib sails attached to the forestay. Genoas are by definition large enough whereby and the clew (bottom aft point of the sail) extends back behind the mast. A jib is smaller whereby the clew does not reach behind the mast.

Mainsails:

These sails are large and attached to the mast and boom. They fly behind the mast. These sails generally provide the primary propulsion force.

Additional commonly used sails are the spinnaker and gennaker. These are the classic gorgeous colorful sails you see used for capturing air to push the boat in downwind directions.

Furling Headsail

Furling headsails are more common than not these days. They unfurl (unroll) and furl (roll up) around the headstay in a matter of seconds. They provide ease of sailing for cruisers because there is no need to go up on the foredeck to bring the sail down or raise the sail. There is also no need to change to a small sail size when encountering higher wind conditions because the roller furling sail can simply be rolled up incrementally to reef the sail (make the sail smaller). Some efficiency is lost because furling sails lack the battens that provide shape to the sail, making it more like the shape of an efficient airfoil. Some sailmakers have provided vertical battens for roller furling systems. This helps some with efficiency although not 100 percent. Still, the trade-off in ease of handling versus loss in efficiency is an obvious choice for most. Unless you're wanting to win races, the roller furling headsail is a good choice and the cost of installing such a systems is also inexpensive.

Right is a video by Harken who manufactures roller furling systems. It's about 5 minutes long and is a good introduction to using a headsail roller furling system.

Harken Video

Here is another headsail furling video by Profurl who also builds furling systems. This is a more technical explanation on the components of a furling system.

Profurl Video

Sail Trim

Sail trim is the essence of being a sailor. It involves understanding fundamental physics to make judgments about the conditions in which you are sailing. This topic is never exhausted and often the source of warm to heated discussions.

Contrary to the thought that the wind pushes the sails, sails actually provide "lift." If this were not the case, how could the wind push the boat in upwind directions? When a sail is providing lift, the windward side of the sail has a higher pressure than the leeward side. This difference in pressure is the force that propels the sailboat. This is the same aerodynamic force that keeps a plane flying using its wings.

Trimming sails for maximum lift is a sailor's primary challenge. This trimming is done using lines called sheets (jib and main) and these lines are often tensioned using winches, manual and/or electric.

As the sailboat turns to a more downwind angle, the sails begin to be pushed by the wind while also maintaining some lift. The overall object of trimming the sails is to understand and optimize the lift and push forces on the vessel. Good sail trim balance results from constantly being aware of wind flow over the sail and then making prudent adjustments of sails.

Chapter 7 discusses sail trim in detail.

Summary

The following shows the major parts of the boat that you will refer to on every outing. These names will become second nature to you after a while and you'll then be able to stop referring to them as "the thingy over there."

Chapter 5

Rules of the Nautical Road

The Rules

The Rules are the Rules are the Rules. Called the International Rules of Prevention of Collision at Sea, they are internationally agreed upon. They are absolute essential knowledge for a skipper. Built into the rules is the requirement to be a responsible seaman (seaperson is more of a PC term, but we're not sure if this is a word; it should be). This means knowing them and understanding them completely. Lack of knowledge is not a defense. And neither is just keeping out of the way. In fact, merely keeping out of the way can be dangerous because the other boat is expecting you to behave in a certain way—according to the rules.

The biggest reason people don't study the rules is that they perceive that the study would be incredibly dry (isn't the idea of sailing to get slightly wet?). Thus there is a temptation to put this knowledge off. But what is often misconstrued by those not completely studying the rules is that a person who seemingly had "rights" during a crossing situation is not exonerated from liability if a collision occurs. How is that possible?

Since all of the rules are important and relevant to a sailor, it would be irresponsible for us to just touch on the rules and give you some basics in this book. Fortunately, NauticEd has an excellent and engaging and interactive course on the rules online. As a benefit to this book, we offer and encourag you to take and pass the NauticEd Navigation Rules course online for free. Scan the QR code and sign up for free. The Rules course will automatically be dropped into your curriculum.

You'll find that the study of the rules is rich in history and interest. For example, why do you think that a port tack boat must give-way to a starboard tack boat? Could it have equally been the other way around? No—there is a specific reason that was forged in history. Take the FREE online rules course now and learn why.

Signup for a Free
Rules Course

Some Common Sailboat Rules

There are about 20 or so really important Give Way rules that you absolutely must know to be a responsible sailor. And guess what? One of the rules is that you must be responsible.

All the rules apply the same everywhere in the known universe.

Not to trivialize any rule, but here we present 5 basic rules for instant knowledge. As stated above, we are relying on you to round out your complete knowledge by taking the FREE online course offered.

Sailboats on Same Tack

The Rule

12 a (ii) when both have the wind on the same side, the vessel that is to windward shall keep out of the way of the vessel which is to leeward.

In the image right, from the set of the sails the wind is obviously coming from the bottom of the image. Thus the blue sailboat must Give Way to the red sailboat since blue is in a windward position relative to red.

Two Sailboats on a Port Tack

Sailboats on Opposite Tacks

The Rule

12(a) (i) when each has the wind on a different side, the vessel that has the wind on the port side shall keep out of the way of the other

In the image right, from the set of the sails the wind must also be coming from the bottom of the image. Thus the red sailboat must Give Way to the blue sailboat since blue is on a starboard tack

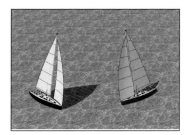

Two Sailboats on Opposite Tacks

(wind from the starboard side of the boat) and red is on a port tack (wind from the port side of the boat).

Overtaking

The Rule

13 (a) Notwithstanding anything contained in the Rules, any vessel overtaking any other shall keep out of the way of the vessel being overtaken.

In the image right, the sailboat is overtaking a powerboat. From the rules, any vessel overtaking another must Give Way. Therefore the sailboat must Give Way in this instance to the powerboat. This is also the case if the powerboat was lying adrift in this position.

Sailboat Overtaking Another Vessel

A similar rule applies when two sailboat overtake each other. The image right presents an interesting situation. The trailing sailboat is on starboard and is overtaking the leading sailboat who is on port. In this case the sailboat on starboard Gives Way to the sailboat on port.

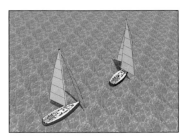

Sailboat Overtaking Another Sailboat

Sailboats Under Power

The Rules

3 (c) The term "sailing vessel" means any vessel under sail provided that propelling machinery, if fitted, is not being used.

15 (a) When two power-driven vessels are crossing so as to involve risk of collision, the vessel that has the other on her own starboard side shall keep out of the way and shall, if the circumstances of the case admit, avoid crossing ahead of the other vessel.

In the image right, the sailboat is under power and meeting another vessel under power. Since both vessels are defined as power driven vessels, the sailboat must Give Way to the powerboat, that is, the sailboat has the powerboat on its starboard side.

Sailboat Under Power

NOTE: Regardless of whether a sailboat has its sails up or not, if it is being propelled by machinery then it is defined as a power-driven vessel.

Rule 14(a) is pertinent when you are maneuvering under power in the marina. If you are approaching another power-driven vessel head to head, turn to starboard and pass port side to port side.

14 (a) Unless otherwise agreed when two power-driven vessels are meeting on reciprocal or nearly reciprocal courses so as to involve risk of collision each shall alter her course to starboard so that each shall pass on the port side of the other.

Action to Avoid Collision

The rules specify throughout that it is your responsibility to take action to avoid collision regardless if you are the Give Way vessel or not the Give Way vessel. It means that if you enforce your "rights" to stay on course and a collision happens, you will be held accountable. For this reason, the rules do not define "right of way." They merely state that all vessels shall avoid collision.

We encourage you to take the FREE Navigation Rules Course online.

A Quick Test

Scan the QR code for a quick 6 question test on who Gives Way.

Navigation Rules
Test

Chapter 6

Leaving the Slip, Maneuvering in the Marina, and Returning Safely

Introduction

Leaving and returning to slips, moorings, or anchorages are essential skills for every sailor. It is simply not good enough to be good at sailing. Being a good sailor, by its own nature, means that you are also confident and competent at handling the boat in tight quarters in a marina and around other boats in all wind and current conditions.

Our book, *Maneuver and Dock Your Sailboat Under Power,* details how to become an expert and we highly recommend picking up a copy. Here we will cover the main topics and keep you out of trouble. We'll also cover here how to prepare your crew and vessel, maneuvering in forward and reverse, and effective use of spring lines.

The Magic Moment

The magic moment on any outing is right as you pull out of the slip. You're going sailing—yay! But there are some responsibilities bestowed on you as the skipper that will keep your crew safe and the gelcoat on your boat.

Maneuvering in a Marina

Crew

It is important to know how much experience your crew has before you embark on any sailing adventure. Can they handle the worst-case scenarios? As a captain and good leader, you need to give a proper safety briefing each and every time. You also need to create an environment in which your crew and guests feel comfortable asking rudimentary questions.

In Chapter 11, Safety and Emergencies, we provide an excellent crew briefing checklist and how to prepare your crew.

Vessel Preparation

Sometimes it is a good idea to get nasty stuff out of the way first.

The Head

The marine toilet is called the head because in olden times it was at the front of the boat. Basically, it works like this: the head pump brings water in from outside the hull, which flows into the bowl. Some deposits are made and the resultant mix is flushed away into a holding tank or back overboard. After the exit pump, a "Y" valve mounted close to the head in the bathroom cabinet or under the floorboards directs the wastewater to either holding tank or the outside. Various valves must be turned or buttons pushed to direct the flow of inbound water and outbound effluent.

Nasty Nasty Job

The worst things about a marine head is that it because of the size of the pipes and delicate pumps, guests unfamiliar with how things work will more than likely flush things that should not be flushed. This blocks up the head. Your game plan around the head needs to be education education and more education or you will be stuck with a very nasty job.

The Head Pump

Some systems have a manual pump, some are electric. With electric systems, there will be a macerator, an electric grinder, after the bowl. It chops everything into small pieces before moving it overboard or to the tank (as if your own body hasn't ground it up enough—actually it is mostly for the toilet paper).

For manual pump handle systems, the physical pumping smushes the "stuff" good enough before sending it to the tank or outside.

Scan the QR code on the next page for an animation of a manual pump system. Tap #1 or #2 on the animation depending on your body function.

If you want your regular crew to know this, below is a link to our blog post on this nasty topic. Send the link on to your crew.

Somehow, seawater makes the smell of the entire system very unpleasant. So some boats are fitted with a fresh-water supply to the head pump. If this is an option to

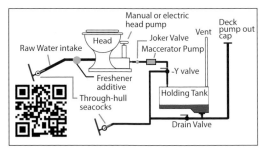

Head Animation

purchase for your new boat, go for it, but be aware that it will use up your onboard water supply quickly.

How to Go to the Potty

Some systems have an inline freshener for the supply water. This is a really good idea.

For manual pump systems, use a head pump lubricator oil every now and then to keep the manual pump from squeaking and becoming overly tight.

The Holding Tank

In the United States and most countries, it is illegal to pump out your head directly overboard anywhere within three miles from shore, in certain wildlife areas, and most definitely in all inland lakes and rivers. Consider our precious environment and use your holding tank. Only when way off shore should you consider dumping.

The holding tank has a vent that releases potentially dangerous gas. Thus when someone does the do, there is usually a brief unpleasantness outside.

You'll find many charter companies overseas do not even have a holding tank or they falsely tell their clients that the tank is inoperable; shame on them for being environmentally irresponsible. In this instance, it's best not to swim in the marinas where they operate.

When approaching land, always switch the "Y" valve to the "Holding Tank" position.

Chandleries (or Amazon) sell a tank freshener, which is a must. Keep plenty on board and pour it into the bowl and flush after each outing.

DO NOT use any bleach products, which will degrade the rubber components very quickly. Don't keep bleach products in the head area cabinets, as guests will tend to think they are doing you a favor and pour them into the head.

It is a good idea to pump out the tank often. When you do this, flush lots of water back into the tank and then pump it out again.

Given that your entire game plan around the head is to not have people flush anything that should not be flushed, you need to supply a means to deal with those non-flushable things: Make available small plastic disposal bags in a dispenser mounted in the head area.

Head Instructions

Here are some useful links for sign postings for your head. Scan the QR codes, save the PDFs, print them out, laminate them, and stick on the wall.

Manual pump handle instructions	**Electric pump instructions**	**Here is a link to a funny Do Not Flush This Stuff sign**

Crew Briefing Regarding the Head Use

Each marine head has unique operational characteristics, so making sure the crew understands your head is an absolute must. "Head indoctrination" is sometimes a bit embarrassing but unless you do it, you will inevitably find yourself later unbolting the head and cleaning out the nasties.

Here are some tips that will help you in regards to briefing the crew on the use of the head.

- Make certain everyone understands what kind of stuff may be deposited in this unit, and what kind of stuff may not. The general rule is that only things that you have first eaten or small amounts of toilet paper can go in the head. Large cleanup jobs require lots of flushing. Four squares of TP each flush max.
- Make sure to at least demonstrate how to rid the bowl of the nasties and how to the pump or flush the bowl dry.
- Be cognizant of kids who somehow find large volumes of toilet paper fascinating.
- Encourage a lot of swimming.

Make Ready Your Boat for Safe Sailing

Stowing Items

"What is not on the floor will be on the floor." I make this announcement to the crew each and every time as we go below to ready the vessel. A bag placed on the settee will not remain there for long after the boat heels over. Drinks and food items not stowed properly in the galley will quickly turn into floor stew. Thus prior to pulling out of the slip, do a final check around to make sure everything is heeling immunized.

PFDs (Life Vests)

If not worn, PFDs need to be made accessible.

Horn

Your sound device needs to be readily accessible.

Ample Fuel, Water, and Food Supply

Of course.

Weather

Weather should be checked prior to sailing. You should also verify your ability to gather weather updates while on board.

Safety Equipment

See Chapter 11.

Lights

Ensure all navigation lights are in working order before heading out.

Engine

Check that you have sufficient fuel, oil, and coolant water.

Sails

Despite your eagerness to get out on the water and sail, it is a lot easier and safer to remove sail covers and prepare the sails while in the calm waters of the marina rather than in a rocking swell.

Food and Water

You must have enough based on how long you plan to be out. Don't forget to bring extras for contingencies plus sufficient cooking gas. Refrigerators also need to be inspected.

Communications

Before heading out be sure you have working communication devices including a working VHF, cell phones, radar reflector.

Hatches Closed

Always.

Don't Wet the Bed

A car ferry passed us once while sailing in Greece. A few moments later two crew members came upstairs looking for the jokester who threw 15 buckets of seawater into their cabin through the side hatch. Rather, they found out that it was the wake from the ferry that perfectly (or imperfectly) did a crescendo through their open hatch and into their cabin. Sheets, blankets, clothing, bodies, and the mattress were soaked.

Plan

Make a basic passage plan considering such things as intermediary dangers, current, wind direction, and approximate waypoints, charts ready, filed a float plan with friends or relatives.

Electrical and Instruments

On and working.

Starting the Engine

Prior to starting the diesel engine:

- Become familiar with how and when a vessel's transmission gear shift and throttle are engaged and disengaged. Most vessels combine the throttle with the gear shifter. There is usually a small red button to push or pull to disengage the gear shifter so the throttle can used separately. Make sure that the gear is in neutral and the throttle is set to idle.
- Some diesel engines (most don't) require that you heat the "glow plugs" prior to starting. This preheats the combustion chamber of the engine so that starting is easier. Heating the glow plugs requires that you push and

hold the preheat button (identified if it exists) for probably 20 seconds. Learn about your engine in the owner's manual.

- Check for lines in the water.
- After starting the engine, check to ensure that cooling water is coming out of the exhaust. It is easy to see. It is not a constant flow like a hose pipe but more like spitting with exhaust fumes and water mixed together. This is important. If there is no cooling water flowing, the engine will overheat and cause damage.

Good Practice

Get in the habit early in your sailing career to always check for lines in the water before starting the engine. You can guarantee that the time you need the engine the most will be the time a line gets wrapped around the prop. If your engine starts but immediately stalls when you engage it into gear, you can be sure a line is wrapped around the prop.

Dock Line Release

The moment is near.

Have a dock line untying plan based on the wind and the current direction and then communicate this to the crew. Depending on which is stronger, leave windward or up-current dock lines tied until last.

CHECK TO ENSURE THAT THE DOCK SHORE POWER LINE IS DETACHED FROM THE VESSEL AND PROPERLY STOWED. We call this "the yellow dock line." It should be released prior to any dock line. Forgetting to detach the yellow dock line is not only an expensive mistake but also one of the most embarrassing.

The best way to release the dock lines is to reset them so that they go from the vessel to a half turn around the dock cleat and back to the vessel. In this manner, your crew is able to be on the boat and release a dock line by just untying one end from the boat cleat and pulling the line from around the dock cleat. There is no last-moment jumping aboard which, many times, ends in providing entertainment to the diners in the dockside restaurant. This manner also allows you, as the skipper, to use your crew rather than random dock people who tend to release lines too early.

One point of note is to make sure that lines are not allowed to linger in the water and possibly get wrapped around the prop at a very inconvenient time.

And this bears repeating: whenever starting the engine (regardless of whether you are returning to the dock or heading out), make sure all lines are clear of the prop.

Just before releasing lines, ensure you will be clear of traffic as you pull out. This is really important; tangling with traffic in the marina slipway is not a good idea. There is limited space to maneuver and other traffic will have speed and momentum, which works against your desire to keep gelcoat on your boat.

Returning to the Slip

Time flies when you are sailing. But sadly, the moment comes when you must return and put your vessel back in its slip. Much of what has to be done to return is simply the reverse of what was done to go sailing, but there are some differences and therefore you need a plan.

Considerations:

- Wind and current direction
- Crew assignments
- Docklines ready and none dragging in the water
- Fenders placed appropriately and the right height off the waterline
- Dinghy positioned, either brought in close behind or alongside
- Fishing lines reeled in (funny haa haa right? No, we are speaking from the experience of many lost lures)
- Check for traffic conditions that might jam up the entrance and the slipway

It is imperative that you as the skipper give clear directions to your crew to set the boat up correctly. Many times the crew will not know the correct height of fenders or which length dock lines go on which cleats. Also, don't assume that your crew can tie a decent knot. If you set your boat up well, you are going to have fewer issues at the crucial moment of "touch down." Before entering the marina, give the helm to someone else and take a walk around the boat to ensure it is set up as you prefer.

View this video on how to quickly tie a fender using a clove hitch. Pass this on to your crew.

How to Tie a
Clove Hitch Fast

A word of caution: Attempting to sail a 30- to 50-foot vessel into a slip invites serious problems. This should not be attempted by a new sailor. If you are unable to motor into your slip because of engine problems, you might try sailing onto a clear tee head (the end of the dock) where the landing will possibly be a little easier. Performing this maneuver into the wind is a little easier than downwind because stopping the boat in a downwind situation will tend to make you overshoot. Whatever the case, have plenty of dock lines available and call for assistance from people on the dock. Most are quite willing to help.

Contingency plan: There is always the possibility that space is not available where you thought you were going to park your boat. If this is the case you may find you need to swap sides of fenders and dock lines. Sometimes when going into an unfamiliar harbor, it is prudent to set dock lines to both sides.

Docking Article

Here is a really good blog we wrote about docking. It has some gems.

Securing the Vessel

Securing the vessel is an art.

Use separate lines for each function. Attach them to the dock cleat then bring back on board so that the lines can be adjusted independently from the boat, especially if you are staying on the boat.

The following are recommended placements for dock lines, depending on the manner in which you are docked.

Notice that there are no lines that run straight to the dock. Instead, all lines are run at angles. Dock lines are typically made of slightly stretchable nylon rope. The longer the line the more

Dock Line Placement

stretch there is in a line. Thus, dock lines at an angle are called spring lines. In this manner any waves that come through from wakes allow the boat to rise up and down and back and forth without harshly yanking on the cleats and thus saving potential damage to the boat (and dock). Make sure there are adequate fenders and they are tied at the correct height.

Lines around pylons are best tied with a round turn and two half hitches. To a dock ring, you can simply go through the dock ring and back to the boat cleat or use a bowline knot with an extra round turn through the ring to prevent chafe. A round turn with two half hitches could also be used for a dock ring.

When tying two boats together, whether at the dock or under anchor, stagger the boats so that the cleats do not line up. This allows you to set spring lines at angles.

Dock Line Placement Two Boats

When a tide exists, ensure you allow for the dock lines to be long enough to go with the tide. Length of dock lines should be at least 4 times the height of the tide. Scan the QR code here:

Docking with a Tide

Many marinas have outer pylons. Capture the windward pylon and the marina tie ring first.

After securing the boat, relax for a few minutes to decompress and rejoice that you landed without any problems. Following that perform a shut-down procedure. It's a good idea to develop a standard written checklist that you follow each time after docking so that you do not forget vital close-down procedures.

Docking with Pylons

Here is one that you can print out, put into a large Ziploc plastic bag, and stow in the chart table. Feel free to personalize. This list is great for sharing boats also.

Check On Check Off List

Maneuvering Topics

Maneuvering a boat requires expertise. You gain this from learning the theory of the skills and applying many times in practice. You cannot assume that because you can drive a car that you can expertly drive a boat. The differences are substantial.

Considerations:

- Prop walk
- Wind direction and current
- Water flow over the rudder and how that affects responsiveness
- Your rudder is at the aft of your vessel. Unlike a car where the turning wheels are forward.
- Momentum of the vessel and how long it takes to stop when in forward and when in reverse. There are no brakes.

Motoring in Forward

Force on the rudder from water flowing over the rudder acts to turns the boat. The effectiveness of the rudder is proportional to the square of the water flow rate over the rudder. If there is no water, there is no turning. Double the flow rate will give you 4 times the turning force.

When sailing, the speed of the boat is the speed of water flowing over the rudder. When engaging forward gear, the propeller pushes high-velocity water over the rudder. This greatly enhances your ability to turn the boat. This picture illustrates how this happens.

Thus even when the boat is standing still, you can turn the boat by turning the rudder and engaging forward gear for a very short time. This becomes a very effective tool to maneuver your boat without gaining any appreciable velocity.

Maneuvering in Forward

When moving forward through the water and using forward gear, more water is flowing over the rudder, making the rudder even more effective.

Motoring in Reverse

Backing a sailboat is rather easy but seems intimidating. You must realize that when reversing, the water flow over the rudder comes only from the movement of the boat through the water, None comes from propeller wash. Thus you actually have to be moving backward before the rudder can be effective.

Additionally, keep in mind that the curves on the blades of the propeller are designed to operate most efficiently in forward. Therefore, stopping a boat moving in reverse takes only a little touch in forward. The complete opposite is true when moving forward and trying

Maneuvering in Reverse

to stop the boat. Significantly more time is required to stop the forward movement of the boat when reverse is engaged. The best way to get used to this is to try it out yourself in open water. Practice makes perfect.

Other factors to consider include current and wind flow and directions relative to the boat. These factors greatly affect your ability to maneuver in reverse.

Wind always wants to push the bow of the boat downwind. Thus the best way to gain control of your boat when starting from zero speed and desiring to go backward is to face the stern of the boat to windward. This prevents the wind from pushing your boat around until you gain steerage control by water flow over the rudder.

Prop Walk

Prop walk is caused by the tilt of the propeller shaft and occurs when the propeller is turning prior to the vessel making headway or sternway. Without going into too much theory about how the prop walk phenomenon occurs, it is suffice to say that prop walk moves the stern of the boat sideways to port every time reverse is engaged (this is true for most boats). A full explanation of how the non-incident angle of water flow through the propeller creates a longitudinal torque (prop walk) is described in the NauticEd's *Maneuver and Docking Your Sailboat Under Power.*

Dealing with prop walk is relatively easy. We call it a preemptive strike. Prop walk is only a nuisance when you start from zero speed. Once the boat starts gaining sternway (moving backward) the effectiveness of water flow over the rudder takes over and you now have full control of the boat. Thus, if you know your boat will turn 30 degrees clockwise when you engage reverse from a standstill, then start a further 30 degrees off your desired track. It's as simple as that.

When reversing into a slip, be aware that if you stop the boat's movement because you screwed up the docking maneuver, when you go to start again in reverse, the boat will screw clockwise again, which will further screw up your docking maneuver. Thus, don't stop your momentum and expect to recover. Instead you will need to do a "go around." That's pilot talk for abort the landing and circle the airfield for another try.

Using Spring Lines

Right now, pull out your phone, place it on your desk and do this exercise.

Hold the top right corner down with a finger then push the bottom middle of the phone in the direction shown. You'll see the phone turn. It's kinda obvious when you do this but, needless to say, this is how you can apply this process to your boat to get you in to and out of some really tight places.

Below we show some common scenarios you will encounter and how to use a spring line to your advantage.

iPhone Spring and Moment

First however, understand the dynamic of the thrusts from the propeller and the rudder. The propeller pushes water backward, whereas the rudder directs the flow direction of the water. Thus the rudder changes the direction of the water flow by applying a force to the water flow. To balance the universe and make sure we all don't just spin off into space, the water pushes back on the rudder in an equal amount in the opposite direction.

When springing on and off docks, we apply this directional force of water on the rudder at the middle stern of the boat and combine it with force from a dock line at a cleat to create a turning moment. Turning "moment" is the desire of the boat to spin, not a "moment" in time. The magnitude of the turning moment is equal to the force multiplied by the perpendicular distance between the forces.

Thus, each spring maneuver is purposefully designed understanding the placement and direction of forces. In many cases you don't need to spring on or off. In those cases, the wind or current is helping you get in or away. Thus you only need spring on or spring off when the wind or current is not being your friend today. Friendly directions in the images below are marked in gray.

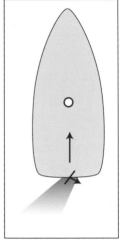

Thrust Over the Rudder

Spring the Aft Out from a Tee Head

Use this in any wind direction but take note to be careful if the wind is coming from forward. A strong wind could push your bow down before you gained enough speed to get out and away. To do this maneuver, place a spring line on a forward dockside cleat and run it aft to the dock. Use a fender to protect the bow against the dock. Turn the wheel into the dock and apply forward thrust. The aft of the boat will turn out. Once the angle is clear of other boats, engage reverse.

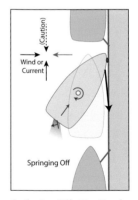

Springing Off a Tee Head

Spring the Bow Out from a Tee Head

Using forward: See scenario A. Use this when winds are not coming from behind. Place a spring line on the non-dockside aft cleat and run it aft behind the stern of boat to the dock. Turn the wheel away from the dock and apply forward thrust. The aft quarter of the boat will be squashed into the dock, so make sure you use a fender. The bow will turn out. Once the angle is clear of other boats, release the spring line.

Using reverse: See scenario B. Use this when winds are not coming from forward. Place a spring line on dockside aft cleat and run it forward to the dock. Center the wheel and apply reverse thrust. The aft quarter of the boat will be squashed into the dock, so make sure you use a

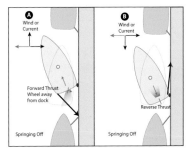

Spring Lines

fender. The bow will turn out. Once the angle is clear of other boats, release the spring line. And engage forward thrust.

Spring onto a Tee Head

Come in at a fairly high angle with a dock line ready on the forward dock side cleat. Have a crew member cleat the dock line aft wards to the dock. Turn the wheel away from the dock and apply forward thrust. The stern will move in toward the dock. Take care when doing this maneuver downwind. You would be better off pointing the boat into wind.

You could also back upwind placing the stern into the dock and then spring the bow around. Perform this by having a dock line cleated to the dockside aft cleat. Run the dock line aft wards to the dock. Turn the wheel into the dock and apply forward thrust. Only do this method when backing upwind—the reason being that the turning moment is reduced because the distance between the thrust force and the dock line force is small.

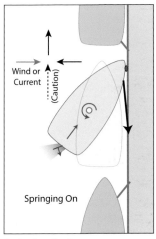

Springing the Stern onto a Tee Head

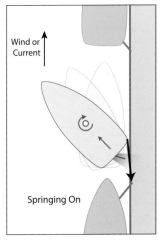

Springing the Bow into a Tee Head

Springing Out of a Slip

Most of the time it is easy to get out of a slip except when the wind is working against your turn into a tight slipway.

Spring Your Boat to Windward

Here is a neat trick to use when in a Mediterranean mooring situation with your boat stern to the dock. Many times, you want your boat to move sideways to windward. Simply turn your wheel downwind and apply forward thrust. The thrust on the rudder pushes the boat to windward. The aft or midships spring line prevents the boat from moving forward.

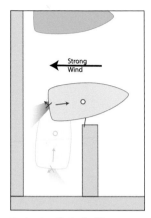

Springing Out of a Slip

Maneuvering and Docking Experience

Farmboy

I grew up on a sheep farm in New Zealand. My dad had me driving the Land Rover by the time I was four. He'd set the hand throttle and all I had to do was to steer the truck around the paddock while he jumped off, ran back to the trailer, and tossed out hay to the sheep. My instructions were to not hit water troughs, trees, or fences. By nine, I could back the trailer through six inches of mud into the hay shed. It's all about experience.

Spring Your Boat Upwind

In sailing, the wind is your friend, but too much wind can quickly become your nightmare. Maneuvering your boat under power in the marina is similar. Albeit, zero wind is your BFF (*best friend forever—haa, now you know what your daughter's acronym means*).

It is important, then, that you become an expert at maneuvering in all wind conditions and directions. In the NauticEd's *Maneuver and Dock Your Sailboat Under Power* book we provide you with a comprehensive set of exercises that lead you through every docking scenario: side, stern and forward winds, going backward and forward into slip and Tee heads, using spring lines, and Mediterranean mooring situations. We highly recommend that book.

Chapter 7
Sailing

Introduction

This is the chapter you've been waiting for. As you've seen so far, there is a lot more to learn than raising the sail and having the wind take over. But for now, the waiting is over—let's learn the finer points of sailing the boat.

Beneteau First 40

A benefit to this book is the FREE online NauticEd Basic Sail Trim course.

The course will take you about 2 hours to complete. It is loaded with interactive animations and is a great way for you to gain additional knowledge on sail trim. Please enjoy this additional benefit.

Free Sail Trim
Course

The Art of Sailing

The secret of artful, efficient, and safe sailing consists of many things, but some primary factors emerge. They include:

- Understanding directions of your boat, wind, and things that get in the way
- Knowing how the wind angle on your boat determines the set of the sails
- Understanding the forces of the wind on your rig
- Understanding the dynamics of wind strength versus the heel of your boat and being confident it won't flip

- Knowing the specific maneuvers of your boat
- Managing your sails
- Managing fine points of sail trim and reefing
- Knowing your instruments and boat systems
- Expressing your skills as a leader of the crew

Please pay close attention. This chapter is the crux of the points above.

Rubber Ducky

Did you know that at a young age we were all sailors? Even if you can't remember, we bet you had a rubber ducky; while the real job was supposedly to get clean in the bathtub, you were happy playing for hours with your yellow friend.

Now your former bathtub has become a river, lake, or ocean and your ducky has grown into a fiberglass marvel.

Beneteau 38 Movie

There is a rush that comes from sailing that you never get over. The feeling is one of freedom, adventure, and enthusiasm.

The video below is a Beneteau 38 going through its paces. It's just to get you in the mood.

Directions

Directions are super important because while sailing, you will always be in communication with others regarding directions of obstacles, wind changes, your destination, water current, and other boat traffic. Directions are stated in many ways, and so it is important to not only understand them but to communicate them to others in the proper manner. The terminology is important to learn now or else you'll be ultra-confused on the boat.

Port and Starboard

When facing forward, the port side is on the left and the starboard side is on the right. If you look at the front of any boat, you will see a red light on the port side and a green light on the starboard side. These colors are by convention and are the same on every boat in the world. To remember this, use the mnemonic:

"Is there any red port left?"

Besides the reference to delicious after-dinner drinks from Portugal—the country whose sailors invented world discovery—the phrase reminds us that red is on the port side and the port side is the left.

Upwind and Downwind

You'll see and hear the terms "upwind" and "downwind" a lot and some confusion can set in.

The term "upwind" can mean ANY direction that is toward the direction that the wind comes from. It does not have to be directly into the wind. Thus, 45 degrees upwind means 45 degrees off from where the wind is coming from. "Downwind" can mean ANY direction that is toward where the wind is going. Thus, 135 degrees downwind means 135 degrees off from where the wind is coming (and it is toward a downwind position). 180 degrees downwind is directly downwind.

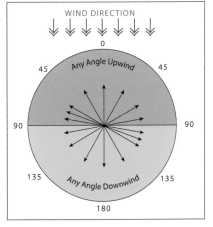

Upwind Downwind

Angles to the wind are stated as zero through 180 (many times the word "degrees" will be omitted). Zero is into the wind directly. 180 is directly downwind. Any angle less than 90 degrees is "sailing upwind." Any angle that is greater than 90 is "sailing downwind." There is no angle greater than 180 in this form.

Heading Up and Bearing Away

- Heading up or coming up means turning the boat upwind.
- Bearing away or coming down means turning the boat downwind.

Thus, a skipper may say "I'm bearing away to 135 degrees downwind" or "I'm bearing away to 135 degrees off the wind." This would mean that the skipper is turning the boat so that it is sailing downwind 135 degrees away from where the wind is coming.

Head-to-Wind

Head-to-wind is a direction directly into the wind.

Luffing

When the boat is headed too far into the wind for the set of the sail, sails will start to flap at the leading edge (the luff edge of the sail). This is called luffing. When you are head-to-wind, the sails will be flapping wildly like a sheet on a clothesline. To fix this, bear away to fill the sail. If the sails are set too loose for the wind angle to the boat, a tactician might say "Bear away, you are luffing." Or the skipper might say "Come in on the mainsheet, the main is luffing."

Luff-Up

Luff-Up means to bring the boat head-to-wind. Consequently the sails will luff. A crew member might ask the skipper to luff-up so that a tangle in the jib sheet may be released. Or a tactician might ask the helmsperson to luff-up to slow the boat before a race start to gain an advantageous position.

Now you know what this means: "You luffed-up head to wind. Your sails are luffing. Bear away to 40 degrees to starboard off the wind."

Angles Relative to the Boat

Often angle directions are given relative to the boat. Zero degrees is always toward the front of the boat. A skipper might say "Watch out for that rock 60 degrees off our port side." In this case, the direction has nothing to do with the wind direction. It means that if you are looking forward toward the front of the boat and then turn left 60 degrees you will see the rock.

The tactician might say "Come up 10 degrees." This means relative to the boat heading now, turn the boat

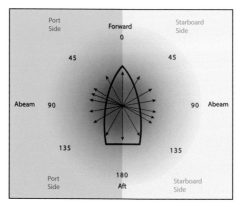

Relative Angles

in an upwind direction 10 degrees. "Bear away 30" would mean turn the boat 30 degrees downwind from where it is now but keeping the wind on the same side of the boat (that is, no tack or gybe for this). To get a feel for these degree changes just think about how 90 degrees would be off your shoulders when looking straight forward—30 degrees is 1/3 of that. See the clock positions on page 93.

To make directional changes, ALWAYS pick a spot on land or something (a cloud, a boat, a buoy) that is approximately where the direction change is to be, then after you have picked it make your change toward that or relative to that. Otherwise, you will begin your turn and not accurately know where to stop turning. Getting your direction changes wrong is a good way to get the helm taken from you by someone more competent.

In addition, a tactician may give you an angle in an o'clock manner. For example, "do you see that boat at 3 o'clock?" These angles are also always stated relative to the front of the boat no matter what direction you are headed, 12 o'clock being the front of the boat (bow) and 6 o'clock being the back (stern) of the boat.

While pretty obvious to most, we'll show a graphic for the benefit of those brought up in the digital age only.

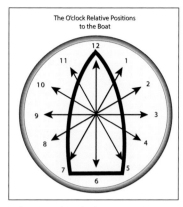

Relative to the Clock

The o'clock description of directions is highly convenient and often used. There is no need to state port or starboard and for most of us, it is intuitive.

In all other cases, angles and directions are given with the label distinction "upwind" or "downwind" OR "port" or "starboard" so that you can distinguish if the angle is measured from where the wind is coming from or relative to the boat.

These are examples of valid angle commands or observations using port or starboard relative to the boat.

- "Turn 90 degrees to port."
- "A boat is at 130 degrees on our port."
- "A rock is abeam to starboard" (abeam is 90 degrees).
- "There is a buoy in the water at 1 o'clock 100 meters out."

These are valid directions commands or observations using wind angles.

- "Come up to 30 degrees off the wind."
- "Bear away to 120 degrees off the wind."
- "There is a boat downwind of us."
- "Tack and then bear away to 45 degrees off the wind."

Compass Directions

Another set of directions used is compass directions. This is more fully covered in Chapter 9, Navigation.

A skipper may tell the helmsperson "make your course 270 degrees on the compass." This is

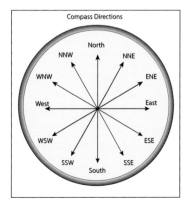

Relative to the Compass

referring to sailing the boat in a compass direction toward 270 degrees (270 degrees is west).

Compass directions are all about the compass and nothing to do with the current boat heading or the wind or the clock.

Windward and Leeward

Windward refers to any direction toward the wind. Leeward (sometimes pronounced *loo-ward*) refers to any direction downwind. Thus, a lee shore is a shore that is downwind. The windward side of the boat is the side closer to where the wind is coming from. A boat to leeward means a boat that is in a more downwind position from you (though not necessarily directly downwind). Remember this from the Rules: a leeward boat is the stand-on vessel when both boats are on the same tack.

The High-Side and the Low-Side

When the boat heels over it creates a high-side to windward and a low-side to leeward. Typically the helmsperson sits on the high side of the boat to help balance the heeling force from the wind. Many times the crew are placed "on the rail" (the high side) and told to think of fat thoughts of hot dogs and hamburgers to further counterbalance the heeling force.

High and Low Side

Sailing and Wind Forces

A sailboat moves in upwind and downwind directions. Downwind is intuitive; it just gets blown downwind. But just how does a sailboat move into the wind? To understand how a sailboat moves, let's think about an airplane wing. Most of us know that a plane lifts off the ground because the wings provide lift. It does this in the following manner: The wind moving across the top of the wing has farther to travel and thus must move faster. According to some mathematical equation (who cares; but it is Bernoulli's Equation in case you really want to know) faster moving air has lower pressure. A wing with low pressure on the top side and higher pressure on the bottom side will move up thereby dragging the plane and passengers with it.

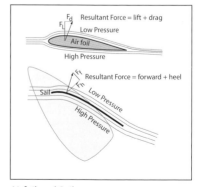

Airfoil and Sail

The interesting point on this is that the wind pressure on the sail helps make the shape of the sail like a wing.

Another comparison can be made with a hair dryer. Rather than make you take out a hair dryer to see the effect of fast moving air creating low pressure, here is an animation of exactly what happens. Turn on the hair dryer.

Hair Dryer Animation

When sailing, a sail is just a vertical wing. Instead of lifting the sailboat up to the sky, it lifts the sailboat forward upwind. It can't be any other way. If the wind was always just pushing on the sails, how could the wind push the boat in an upwind direction?

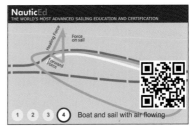

Wing and a Sail

Wind Vane

Just like a speedometer on your car, your boat has an instrument you must check often (very often) to see how you are doing in relation to the wind. Over-speed in your car at the wrong place and you get a ticket. Sail at non-optimal sail set with respect to the wind and your crew are going to admonish you. If you're racing and you are the sail trimmer or helmsperson, you're going to get a tongue-lashing from the tactician.

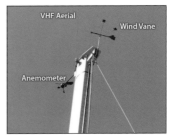

A Wind Vane at the Top of the Mast

You will be checking this instrument every 4 to 10 seconds depending on what the wind is doing—varying, gusting, changing direction: veering (changing clockwise) or backing (changing counterclockwise).

Here it is—it's called a wind vane. It sits on top of the mast and points to where the wind is coming from.

Looking directly down onto the wind vane from the sky, if you are pointing

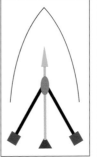

Head to Wind   Sailing at 45 Degrees

directly into the wind it will look like the drawing on the left.

Or if you are sailing along and the wind is coming from say 45 degrees off your starboard side, it will look like the drawing on the right.

The arrow always points to the direction of the apparent wind. The two bright red tails are stationary and indicate that if the darker red tail of your arrow is in this zone you are sailing too close into the wind. You can only sail your boat efficiently if the red tail of the arrow is outside the two red stationary tabs.

Now hear this: Just like steering your car, you would NOT keep looking at your speedometer while you accelerated to 60 miles per hour (100km/hr). You'd be off the road in a ditch. What you do is glance at your speedometer for 1/2 second or so as you approach your target speed.

The same principle applies: DO NOT look at your wind vane for any longer than 1/2 second each time. Keep your eyes on the water and land so that you are sailing in a straight line. When you want to make a direction adjustment, check the wind vane first (1/2 second), then bring your eyes back to the land. Now make a relative adjustment to the land and then check your wind vane for 1/2 second to see if you made the correct adjustment. Repeat if necessary. You simply cannot make direction adjustments while looking at the wind vane. You will overshoot your mark EVERY time no matter how experienced you are.

Because every novice makes this mistake, we will just repeat it. DO NOT look at your wind vane for any longer than 1/2 second and do not watch the wind vane while you are making direction changes. Just don't do it: EVER.

Points of Sail

Points of Sail is a term used to describe the angle the boat is headed relative to the wind. Initially as a novice, it is not that easy for you to determine; but it becomes easier with experience. At all times, you must know your Point of Sail because this determines how you set your sails.

Novices can tell you that the wind is coming from the left side of the boat or the right side. But if you ask them to state the angle relative to the boat, they clam up. That's okay—this is all new.

Fortunately, the wind vane tells you almost exactly what is going on at all times. And now, armed with the knowledge of the wind angle and thus the Point of Sail, you can set your sails almost perfectly.

For every angle to the wind you wish to sail, there is a name for that heading. These names relate to the angle the wind hits your vessel and each has its own distinct personality and characteristics due to wind factors. Words like broad reach, beam reach, close reach, close haul, and running are quite intuitive and will soon become part of your nautical lingo.

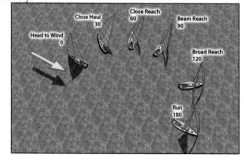

Points of Sail

Below is a diagram depicting the "Points of Sail" of a sailboat. Study and enjoy it and you will see how truly simple it is, except for learning a few new terms. The number is the degree angle the boat is sailing off the wind.

Sailing a Course Video

Also note that sometimes some sailors will refer to a close haul as a "beat." It probably originates from the point of sail where you will feel the most beat up. In a close haul, you're heading relatively close into the wind and the waves.

Now watch the video of a sailboat as it sails around a course.

The animation right helps you see what the wind vane is doing and how the sail should be set for each Point of Sail. Tap on any and all of the Points of Sail and you will see what is happening. Start with close haul on starboard.

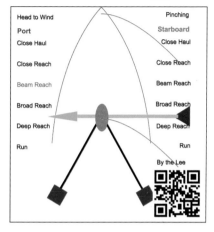

Point of Sail Animation

Head-to-Wind

Head-to-wind means your boat is headed directly into wind. The sails are "luffing" or "flogging" back and forth and the jib sheets are whipping dangerously. The boat is not moving and you're basically stuck. It's called "stuck in irons."

To get out of "irons," tighten up on the headsail sheet to one side. Turn the rudder so the tiller is parallel to the headsail. Since the boat will begin to go backward slightly, both the sail and rudder act in unison to turn the boat. In the image below the boat will turn clockwise.

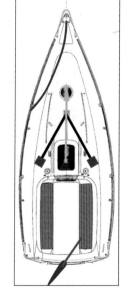

Getting Out of Irons

Pinching

In pinching, you might sort of be sailing but not really. The angle is too close to the wind to create any sail shape. Your speed will be extremely slow and the sails are lightly luffing. The front of the sail is collapsed in on itself and is considered "back winded." To get out of this, bear away from the wind until the wind vane arrow tail matches one of the stationary tails; a close haul.

Close Hauled

Close hauled means the wind is as close to the bow as possible while still being able to provide efficient sail power, about 30-45 degrees off the bow.

- Sails are sheeted in as tight as possible
- Boom is positioned at about the vessel's centerline
- Boom vang is tight
- Headsail should be close to, but not touch, the spreaders
- As the vessel heels, there is slight weather helm* on the tiller, you feel lots of wind in your face
- Telltales* are streaming back on both windward and leeward sides

Close Haul

*more on weather helm and telltales soon

Close Reach

With close reach, the wind is a bit farther around toward the side of the boat than a close-hauled point of sail, somewhere between 50 to 75 degrees off the bow.

- Sails are eased more than close-hauled
- Main boom is off centerline and the headsail is not as tight
- The boom vang can be eased to help fly the top telltales
- The vessel heels but not excessively
- Telltales streaming smoothly on both windward and leeward sides

Close Reach

Beam Reach

On a beam reach, the wind angle is approximately 90 degrees off the bow; across the beam of the boat. It is a very efficient point of sail.

- The sails are eased further, seemingly almost all the way out

- The main boom extends over the side of the vessel. The spreaders may just begin to indent the mainsail. This should be monitored carefully to prevent chaffing
- The headsail telltales will follow the curve of the sail on both windward and leeward sides
- The boom vang can be eased further to allow the mainsail to twist out at the top

Beam Reach

Many sailors tend to oversheet the sails on a beam reach; let it out. Oversheet means you have pulled in the sheet too far for an efficient set of sail.

On a beam reach, the vessel is relatively flat and has excellent speed.

Broad Reach and the Deep Broad Reach

On a broad reach, the wind angle is 120 degrees or so off the bow. On a deep broad reach, the wind angle is 150 degrees or so off the bow.

At anything more than about 140 degrees off the wind, you are being pushed by the wind. You no longer have lift to contend with so the telltales are not going to give you much information.

- The traveler can be eased down to leeward
- The boom vang can be adjusted to help the top of the mainsail be perpendicular to the wind
- At this position, the vessel is simply being pushed by the wind
- The apparent wind decreases and so furled reefed sails can possibly be unreefed
- The outhaul and cunningham can be eased to create bagginess to the sail. Don't do this in high wind conditions
- The luff of the headsail may curl forward of the vessel's forestay
- The broad reach and deep reach are very comfortable points of sail

Broad and Deep Broad Reach

For downwind sailing angles, there are many special sails available to capture more wind. The most noticeable being the spinnaker and gennaker. These huge colorful and billowy sails capture lots of wind for fast sailing. A spinnaker is used for deep broad reaches through direct downwind angles. It blows way out the front of the boat and uses a pole to windward to stabilize it. A gennaker is sometimes called an asymmetric spinnaker. It is a larger headsail made of light sail material used for sailing in downwind angles from a beam reach to a deep broad reach. It does not do well in a direct downwind point of sail.

A furling gennaker is used as the head sail while the jib is furled (rolled in around the forestay).

Running Downwind

The final Point of Sail is when the wind is directly behind the sailboat. This is called running downwind. Now the mainsail totally blankets the headsail. The mainsail can be let out to its maximum, but be aware of spreader interference.

On this heading, there is no lift on the sails. The headsail can now be positioned

Running Downwind

on the opposite side of the main. This configuration is called "wing and wing." Sometimes a "whisker pole" is used to hold the headsail out from the mast. More often however in a race, the headsail is doused and the spinnaker is used.

Running directly downwind with sails positioned on opposite sides can be a little dangerous because without constant attention, the mainsail and thus the VERY HARD boom can gybe across and injure a crew member. Besides this, there is not too much advantage to heading directly downwind even if your destination is downwind. You'll find that gaining some apparent wind by coming back up to between 140 and 160 degrees gives extra boat speed. Heading off your downwind direction will require you to gybe back and forth, however the extra boat speed over-accounts for this. For this reason, you seldom see a professional sailing directly downwind.

Sail Set for Each Point of Sail

Now view the sail set animation again to see how the sails should be set of all the Points of Sail.

If you merely follow the set of the sails shown in this animation for each Point of Sail, you will probably be sailing better than 90 percent of sailors out there, unless of course they have read this book. Finer settings of the sails come from the finesse of sail trim skill whereby you make small adjustments based on telltales and "just a feeling."

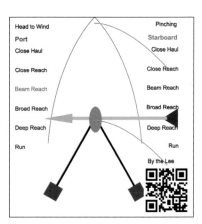

Points of Sail Animation

Wind: Velocity and Direction

Velocity

A sailboat moves through the water because of the pressure the wind projects against your sails. It's imperative that you understand this pressure because it can overpower your sails and your rigging, causing catastrophic damage. Pressure from the wind creates the force on your sails. The mathematical formula is Force = Pressure × Area. So the greater the area of the sails presented to the wind, the more the force on the rig and the boat. Halve the sail area and you halve the force; this is the basis of reefing in high winds, which will be discussed in the following pages.

While it's good to understand the linear relationship between pressure, force, and sail area, there is a far more imperative mathematical formula you must understand. Pressure = 1/2 air density X velocity^2. Since air density is a constant given the conditions, it means that if you double the velocity, the pressure and thus force goes up by 4 times. Or more dramatically, if you go from 4 knots of wind speed to 16 knots, the force goes up 16 times. Or even more dramatically, if you go from 4 knots to 32 knots, the force goes up 64 times.

Given this, you can understand the inherent danger of sailing on a windy gusty day before you are properly experienced. If you're not prepared or do not know exactly and instantly what to do, a sudden gust can knock you over and break a lot of things.

Wind Directions and Angles

Wind when expressed relative to the compass is called the wind direction. When it is expressed relative to the boat, it is called a wind angle. For example, the wind direction is out of the north and the wind angle is 30 degrees off the port bow. This seems like a minor language point but accurate communication on a sailboat is important.

It's also important to distinguish between apparent wind and true wind. Here is a small recap of this topic, more fully covered in the FREE Basic Sail Trim course.

(If you have not taken this FREE Basic Sail Trim course yet, now is a good time to take it. Everything makes more sense and it is a prerequisite to receiving a passing grade for this course.)

True Wind

True wind is the direction the wind is indeed blowing on the planet, as witnessed by flags, smoke, or trees bending. If your vessel were standing still, at anchor or securely in the slip, you would measure true wind speed and direction.

The weather report will tell you the true wind speed and direction (at least it tries to).

However, as we know, true wind is always fluctuating depending upon weather conditions and the things that affect it, like landmasses, tall buildings, cliffs, and mountains, among other things. Use true wind speed forecasts as an approximation, but be aware that it can change (shift) dramatically.

Apparent Wind

Apparent wind is the result of the true wind and your boat speed. Here is an explanation that you can easily grasp because it relates to something you experience almost every warm summer's day.

Apparent Wind Animation

Play with this animation by sliding the slider to speed up the car. Then read the below text and replay this animation.

Put your hand outside the window of your car traveling at 60 miles per hour (100 kph) on a still warm summer day and your hand will feel a 60 mph wind coming from the front of the car. That's apparent wind; yet the true wind is zero. What if the car was driving into a 20 mph head wind? Your hand would feel 80 mph. Or if the wind was blowing from behind at 20 mph, your hand would feel 40 mph.

Now, what about a crosswind of 20 mph? Well, we need to do a little Pythagorean Theorem work on this. What is the square root of the sum of 60 squared plus 20 squared? Your hand would feel 63.24 mph and mostly from a direction in front of the car. If the car accelerated to 100 mph your hand would feel 102 mph, again mostly from the front. If the car decelerates to 10 mph your hand would feel 22 mph, mostly from the side of the car (and if the car stopped you'd feel the full true wind of 20 miles per hour from the side of the car). Whatever your hand feels is the apparent wind. The apparent wind equals the true wind when your car is not moving.

When determining direction of the apparent wind, the faster the car goes the more the apparent wind direction comes from the direction of the travel of the car. Again imagine the crosswind. At 1 mph forward speed in your car and a 20 mph crosswind, the apparent wind feels almost like the true wind from across the car. As the car accelerates the wind feels more and more like it is coming from the front.

This is similar to a boat. The faster the boat sails into the wind, the more the apparent wind speed increases and the more it feels like it is coming from the front of the boat.

So now that you understand the difference—let's put the practical application to work for you on a sailboat.

The minute your vessel is no longer standing still, it creates a wind vector of its own and thus the wind you feel (speed and direction) is altered from the true wind speed and direction. When sailing, apparent wind information is needed for efficient set of the sails and the information required includes both velocity and direction.

There is fun mathematics associated in determining apparent wind speed, but at this time in your learn to sail quest you are luckily spared this computational exercise. Sorry. Or perhaps you're glad!

One more time for repetition purposes: the apparent wind speed and direction is the resultant determined by the angle and speed the vessel is sailing and the actual true wind speed and angle; it's the wind that you feel on your face, or the back of your neck, and the one that makes you smile when you're out in it.

Apparent wind is also the wind that the boat and the sails feel—just like your hand feels when it's outside the car. Thus, any telltales on the sails, wind vanes, and wind meters are working with the apparent wind direction and speed. Wind meters with an anemometer will also tell you apparent wind velocity. A wind meter can also tell you the true wind speed and direction from a set of computations that the wind meter does inside its electronics. But again—as you're sailing, you're mostly likely concerned with the apparent wind. True wind knowledge comes in handy when you begin to do navigation, plotting, and course planning.

Imagine four sailboats:

- "A" stopped and pointed into wind.
- "B" is heading upwind on a close haul at 30 degrees off the wind.
- "C" is headed across the wind on a reach.
- "D" is headed almost downwind on a broad reach.

As you now know, the true wind condition is independent of boat speed or boat direction and remains unchanged for each boat but the apparent wind varies widely for each boat.

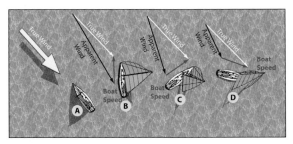

Apparent Wind vs. Point of Sail

"A" is pointed to wind and is therefore stopped. People on "A" feel the wind unaffected by boat speed and so they feel the true wind.

"B" is more like a car headed into the wind. Thus on an upwind course, the apparent wind is higher and alters in direction to feel like it is coming more from the front of the boat.

Traveling across the wind, "C" would feel the largest change in direction. Again, the apparent wind direction feels like it is coming more from the front of the sailboat than the true wind.

"D" feels a reduction in apparent wind speed. Think about a car driving downwind at 20 mph with a tailing wind at 20 mph. You'd feel nothing. However, "D" also feels the direction of the apparent wind become more from the front of the boat than the true wind.

Thus people on A, B, C, and D feel completely different wind speeds and velocities, even though the "true wind" is unchanged. In "D," imagine the boat going a lot faster—the "apparent wind" vector would get much shorter and swing more to the front of the boat.

As a general rule of thumb, when on a boat, if you point toward where you feel the wind is coming from (the apparent wind) then move your finger 15 to 20 degrees toward the stern of the boat, that is where the true wind is coming from. This rule is more so going across the wind and less so heading into or away from the wind.

Next time you're on a boat with an electronic wind meter, toggle between true wind speed indication and apparent wind speed indication. Except standing still, going dead downwind, or headed directly into the wind, in every case, going from apparent to true, the needle will flick more toward 180 degrees—guaranteed. If you're headed into the wind the true wind speed will be less and if you're headed downwind the true wind speed will be higher.

Here is another way to look at it. Tap the buttons to make the boat turn.

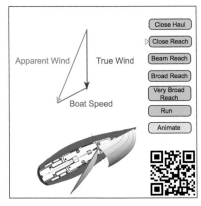

Apparent Wind Animation

Don't Be Scared

Why a Sailboat Does Not Tip Over!

Below is an animation that shows the balance of forces: actually it is technically the balance of a concept called "moments." First off then, we'd better explain moments. Simply explained: if you hold your hand out straight and someone puts a pound weight in your hand, that is harder to hold than if they put the same pound on your elbow. Even easier—if they put the pound weight right by your shoulder. It's the same pound weight, but it was the "moment" that was straining your muscles, not the weight. Moment (nothing to do with moment in time), then, is weight multiplied by distance.

- What tends to tip the boat over is the moment of the wind force high up in the sails.
- What tends to right the boat back is the keel weight and the distance it is heeled over away from the vertical center line.

So now watch the animation 10 times over or so and watch each dynamic as it is happening. Then refer to the text below, which will further explain.

Use the green "incr. wind" button.

The force on the sails is the pressure multiplied by the area on the sails on which the wind is acting. The pressure is proportional to the velocity of the wind squared. Why? It just is! It's one of those formulas that make up the universe.

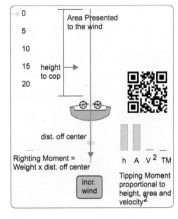

Balance of Moments Animation

And from above, the moment is the force multiplied by the height of the position where the wind is considered to singularly act. This position is called the center of the pressure (COP). The center of pressure is the position on the sail whereby if we replaced all the wind all over the sail with an equal force at some position that would be the position called the center of pressure. On a right triangle sail the point is 1/3 of the way up the mast starting at the boom.

So the tipping moment is proportional to area, height, and wind speed squared.

So what really happens is this: the wind tips the boat over a bit and this shifts the keel weight off centerline a bit. The boat will continue to heel over until the tipping moment by the wind is equal to the moment from the keel being off center. At this point the boat will stop heeling over further and the moments are balanced.

Now the wind picks up again, and again the boat heels over farther and the keel does some righting. But also notice that the area of the sail presented to the wind has reduced and the height to the COP has also reduced. So as the boat heels: area and height decrease on the tipping side of the equation.

At all times, for the boat to not continue to heel farther, the moments of tipping and righting have to be balanced.

This equation must balance: keel weight x distance = area X height x velocity^2

(Note to the puritanical: ok, ok, well not quite. There is the factor of ½ density of air but that is constant. We're trying to make it simple here.)

The only dynamic input to the system is the wind. Everything else in the equation is just working to balance the velocity squared.

So the heel angle of the boat is purely a mathematical balance of the wind force on the rig versus the keel weight off-center. Durh! While you knew that, perhaps you had not seen it in equation form.

Now go back and run the animation some more. Notice that the two moments are always in balance.

To further extrapolate: when the boat heels way way way over, there is almost no sail area presented to the wind and the height (h) has reduced also. Additionally the keel distance off center has moved way out, which is acting to pull the keel down (boat upright) again.

So next time you're out there and the boat heels way way way over, don't worry; every little thing is going to be all right. You've got mathematical equations working in your favor. Area and height are reducing and keel distance off center is increasing.

Best you check the keel bolts every now and again however! Yup, the keel dropping off would be a problem!

Tacking and Gybing Maneuvers

Tacking

When you want to sail in a direction from exactly where the wind is coming from— guess what—you can't! The best we can do is to follow a zig-zag course by sailing at about 30 to 40 degrees off the wind on one side for some distance then turning the boat to sail 30 to 40 degrees off the wind on the other side. Then repeat as necessary. Each time we turn so that the bow goes through the point where the wind comes from is called *tacking*. After the tack, since the wind is on the other side of the boat, the sails must also change sides of the boat.

Tacking is usually performed when you are sailing at angles into the wind: that is, on a beam reach up to a close haul. If you feel the wind on your face, you will probably tack. This means turning the boat toward the wind, through the point of where the wind is coming from and then back downwind a little so that now it is hitting you on the other side of the face/boat.

Gybing

When you're wanting to sail in a direction to exactly where the wind is going—guess what—you can! But . . . it has its difficulties because the sails must be held on opposite sides of the boat lest the mainsail "shadows" the headsail from the wind. They are thus balanced somewhat tenuously. Often the headsail is lowered and a spinnaker or gennaker is deployed. We've all seen the gorgeous site of the big colorful and sometimes fun sail blowing out over the front of a boat as the boat sails downwind. These sails are either a gennaker or a spinnaker sail used exclusively for sailing in downwind directions.

Sailing Downwind with a Spinnaker

Usually, however, smart tacticians do not sail directly downwind even if that is the direction of their destination. From the Sail Trim course, you understood that the boat and thus the sails feel only the apparent wind. A smart tactician usually will "crack" off the downwind course a little and aim up at about 140 to 160 degrees maximum angle sailing downwind. By doing this, the boat picks up more apparent wind and thus boat speed than what it loses in angle when sailing directly downwind. Similar to tacking, the skipper must zig-zag the boat from one tack to another. But this time, since the maneuver means the boat is aiming downwind and the aft of the boat transverses the wind, the maneuver is called a gybe. Some people call it a jibe. Either way is correct. For consistency we will use gybe.

Gybing is usually performed when you are sailing at an angle away from the wind, that is on a beam reach to a run. If you feel the wind on the back of your neck or around to the side of your face you will probably gybe the boat. This means turning the boat farther downwind, through the point where the wind is blowing to and then a bit more, so the wind is hitting now you on the other side of the boat.

Tacking and Gybing

The following diagram shows a typical race course a skipper must maneuver around. Careful study of this diagram will reveal all the secrets of sailing in one go. Notice the tacking and gybing maneuvers where the sails shift sides.

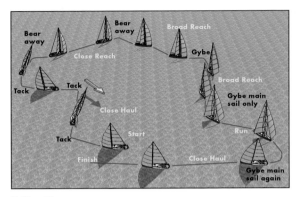

Sailing Maneuvers

The following is a video representation of the same sailing course.

The animation shows the distinction of a gybe over a tack.

Whether you tack or gybe depends entirely on circumstances. Select carefully. Gybing has more potential for accidents, including equipment failures.

Sailing
Maneuvers Video

To perform either of these maneuvers efficiently, you will need to practice and get the "feel" of your vessel and establish rapport with it.

Gybe versus a
Tack

How to Tack the Boat

Alert the crew and passengers to this maneuver by announcing, "Prepare to tack." or "Prepare to come about." The crew begins by wrapping the non-working jib sheet (i.e. upwind sheet—also called the lazy sheet) 2 to 3 times clockwise around the upwind winch drum to prepare it for becoming the working jib sheet. Make sure the working jib sheet (about to become the lazy sheet) is ready to run clear.

The helmsperson then asks "Ready?" When the crew replies with "Ready," the helmsman begins turning the vessel's bow through the wind. There are a variety of nautical announcements that may be issued, the most common of which is "coming about," but also heard are "helm's alee," "hard alee," "tacking," "helm's over" or "lee ho." All work just as effectively as you move the tiller or the wheel. The key is to have all the crew understand what is happening.

At the moment the headsail begins to fold in on itself at the forestay, the crew should ease the taut "working" headsail sheet, then unwind it off the winch completely, allowing the headsail sheet to easily run free. Watch and make sure this sheet does not catch on anything such as mast cleats or hatches.

An Expensive and Often Amateur Mistake

A new and overly eager crew member wanted to winch in the jib sheet as we tacked. He neglected to chase the sheet with his eyes as he cranked (and cranked). $500 and a few weeks later we had a new hatch.

As the headsail comes across the vessel's foredeck, a crew member begins taking up slack on the other headsail sheet, previously prepared and wrapped loosely around the winch. Speed is of the essence here. The faster the crew member brings in the slack the less the crew member will have to use the winch to tighten the sheet when the load comes on. For this reason, it is a good idea for the helmsperson to tack slowly. Time spent tightening the sheet by the crew is time lost.

Trim both sails for the new point of sail, starting with the headsail first because the headsail controls the flow of wind (slot effect) over the mainsail. If you are tacking from one close haul to the other then there is little need to trim the mainsail. Concentrate instead on the headsail.

There is one refinement on the note above to tack slowly: An aside—when tacking, the vessel's bow should be turned through the wind, fast enough to maintain forward momentum, but:

- If the rudder is turned too quickly, it will act as a brake and the boat may stall in low winds.
- Turning the rudder too quickly creates eddies in the water—not too much of a problem but it is energy you are taking out of the boat and giving to the water. Best leave the energy (that is, speed) in the boat.
- Turning the rudder too quickly gives the crew no time to properly get the headsail trimmed before the load comes on. This slows the boat.
- Turning the rudder too slowly may prevent the bow from completely coming through the wind. In this case, you may get stuck in irons or simply stall. You will need to turn back downwind, gain some speed, and try again.

Satellite Signature and Old Habits

I used to sail with an ex-submarine captain. He hated turning the boat too fast during a tack. When I asked him why he muttered something about leaving eddies in the water that the Russians could see.

When tacking from one close haul to another close haul on the other side of the wind, the boat will turn through about 90 degrees. This means that before you tack you should pick a point (a house, a tree, a landmass, a cloud, something) that you will end up sailing toward once you come out of the tack. "Ninety degrees?" you say. "How is that possible when a close haul is 30 degrees off the wind? It should be 60 degrees total for the tack? Aha, gotcha." Sorry, you forgot the (approximate) 15 degrees between true and apparent. Thirty degrees apparent is really about 45 off the true: 45 plus 45 = 90.

Safety concerns: The jib sheets whip quite violently with the sail as the boat is pointing head to wind. The new working sheet must be tightened as fast as possible to minimize this whipping, which can snap at crew members at speeds close to 100 miles an hour (160 km/hr). Anyone standing in the way of these whipping sheets can be severely hurt. If you think a whipping wet dish towel in the kitchen hurts then stay away from the jib sheets.

How to Gybe the Boat

Gybing is one of the things that new sailors find slightly intimidating. Gybing is the act of changing sailing directions when you're sailing downwind, so the stern of the sailboat passes through the wind and one or more sails change sides. This is the functional opposite of tacking where the bow of the sailboat turns through the wind.

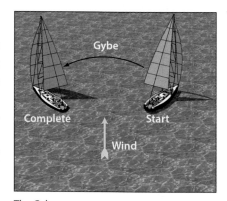

The Gybe

During the gybe procedure, the sails are switched to the other side of the sailboat automatically by the wind.

When proper precautions are taken. gybing is easy and safe. But potential problems can arise if the boom is permitted to swing rapidly and unrestrained from one side of the vessel to the other. This can be dangerous to crew and boat, so do it carefully.

The boom's swinging can be violent during a gybe because the wind is blowing from the back end of the mainsail and once it gets on the other side of the mainsail the boom swings quickly across. (During a tack, the wind blows from the leading edge and so this tends not to happen.) A chicken gybe, discussed later, is actually tacking instead of gybing to avoid the potential dangers of gybing when high winds exist.

To help visualize the dangers of gybing, imagine you are a mast and you attach a piece of plywood to your back so that it extends away perpendicular to your back. Now go outside on a really windy day. Imagine what happens as you turn your face through the point of origin of the wind. Nothing too violent as the plywood is being blown downwind through the turn. That's a tack. Now keep turning around so that your back goes through the wind. When the wind catches the other side of the plywood you'll probably be launched over so hard you'll be glad this is only imagination. That's a gybe! Ouch!

On top of all that, since you're probably flying a headsail as well, you've got to deal with that at the same time. Left unattended during a gybe the headsail will first fly forward then come around on the wrong side (the downwind side) of the forestay. You'll have a real problem trying to get it back into a sailing position as the boat straightens out on the other side of the wind. And for a new sailor trying to impress their crew, it's totally embarrassing.

So here are the tricks to gybing that make it simple and easy on your sailboat rigging and crew.

1. Begin by alerting crew and announcing: "Prepare to gybe."
2. Ensure loose items below decks are stowed and drinks and gear above decks are secured.
3. Check all around for traffic.
4. Ensure no crew are in harm's way of the swinging boom or lines changing over on the foredeck.
5. Prepare the headsail by hauling in taughtly on the lazy headsail sheet (the upwind sheet that is not doing anything) and cleating it off around the winch. This will prevent the headsail from wrapping around the forestay during the maneuver and will place the sheet almost in position for fine-tuning after the gybe maneuver is complete.
6. Prepare the mainsail by hauling in on the mainsheet bringing the mainsail toward the center of the sailboat. This will be relatively difficult since there is a lot of pressure on the mainsheet. As you become better at gybing and your crew become more finely tuned, you can begin turning the vessel and simultaneously haul in the mainsheet until it is amidships. Turning reduces the pressure on the mainsail and makes it easier to haul it. But take note that timing has to be perfect. So, until you and your crew are finely honed at gybing, the best practice is to pull in the mainsail before you execute the turn. Bringing the mainsail close into the center of the sailboat prevents the boom from swinging through a large arc. This in turn prevents the boom

from building up a great speed as it swings across. It's the speed of the swing that causes the damage on rig and crew.

Of biggest concern is the crew. If the boom is allowed to swing dangerously across at speed, crew can be hit in the head quite possibly killed—it has happened. Many crew have been slung overboard and drowned while unconscious. Take heed!

Of secondary concern is SERIOUS damage to the gooseneck—the connection point of the boom to the mast—or other parts of the rig.

7. The next trick is vital, or your sailboat will be violently heeled over and rounded up into the wind. As the boom flips across because the wind is now on the other side, QUICKLY ease the mainsail out to its desired position. If the mainsail is not eased fast enough, the center of pressure of the wind is aft on the rig as the boat completes the gybe. But aft COP pushes the stern of the boat downwind, which rounds the boat up into the wind. W^2NW^3 (which was not what was wanted).

The best way to do this is appoint a crew member to manage the mainsail. Ensure they have the mainsheet wrapped around a winch (clockwise) with the clutch released or uncleated. As the boom flicks over to the other side, immediately release the mainsheet out in a controlled fashion.

8. As the headsail is coming across, another crew member should now release the old working headsail sheet completely allowing the new leeward working headsail sheet to take the load.

9. Now you have successfully gybed and the only matter is for the crew to observe the new heading of the vessel and trim both sails accordingly.

10. Phew!

The Accidental Gybe

The accidental gybe occurs when the helmsperson is not paying close attention. It is a rookie mistake that can cost dearly with injuries (death) and damage. **You must avoid an accidental gybe**.

When sailing directly downwind, a rookie helmsperson takes his eyes off the wind indicator and allows the boat to drift into a positon where the wind is coming from the same side on which the mainsail and boom are positioned. This happens after a shift in wind or a slight course change. The wind, now on the other side of the sail, pushes it over quickly and with it the head-knocking boom. Bam!

If you are sailing at any angle close to downwind, you must keep a diligent eye on the wind angle and keep rookies off the helm. If you are a rookie—don't be.

Sailing by the Lee

Sailing by the lee is possible and done BUT it is dangerous because you are extremely close to the accidental gybe position above. Sailing by the lee means that the wind is coming from behind (you are sailing downwind) and anywhere from 0-30 degrees off to the same side as the mainsail. If the mainsail is let all the way out, the wind will still hold the mainsail out rather than swinging it over. But you are riding on the edge.

Sailing by the Lee

When sailing by the lee, make sure a crew member is assigned to the main sheet and is ready to—at less than a moment's notice—quickly haul in on the main sheet to capture the boom before it SLAMS all the way across. Tell all crew members to keep their eyes up and their heads down.

Here is a video from Wichard, manufacturers of a good device called a Preventer, which slows down a gybe—accidental or otherwise.

Wichard Video

And here is another product that actually stops the boom from swinging across in an accidental gybe.

Take care using this device. If the gybe is continued through accidently and if the clutch is not released there will be a lot of force on the sail/rig and your boat will heel over dangerously. Like any gybe, make sure when you release the clutch, you control the mainsheet, otherwise the boom may swing violently across. This is not a problem if you have an experienced crew.

Stopping the Gybe Video

Here is a great video by *Yacht World* magazine also on gybe preventers.

When sailing downwind, a good safe rule of thumb is: if moving between the foredeck and the cockpit, walk on the same side as the

Yacht World Magazine Video

boom. In this manner, the boom will only swing away from you during an accidental gybe. It's particularly important to teach your crew this as early as possible. As skipper, be wary of turning the helm over to an inexperienced helmsperson when the boat is going downwind.

Important safety concerns:

- Be aware of the boom coming across quickly
- Be aware of whipping jib sheets

- Tighten the lazy jib sheet prior to the gybe to prevent the jib flying forward and around the forestay
- Let out the mainsheet quickly after the boom comes across to prevent excessive heeling

The Chicken Gybe

In high winds, 15 knots and above, we don't recommend gybing. Instead, use the "chicken gybe," which is essentially a 270-degree tack. Instead of turning the boat downwind, you turn the boat up into the wind and perform a normal tack then bear away from the wind to the desired point of sail.

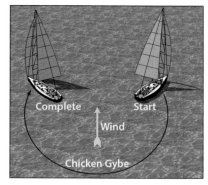

Chicken Gybe

The chicken gybe is mostly performed when the skipper is uncomfortable because of high winds. The chicken gybe is much safer. And the end result is the same. You are merely tacking the boat from a broad reach on one side over to a broad reach on the other side. It's simple, easy, effective, and safe. The only thing to watch out for is that the jib sheets will whip back and around quite violently. So, it's a good idea not to have anyone near the jib sheets (that is, on foredeck).

Here is an animation of the sails as they go through the gybe and chicken gybe maneuvers.

Below that is another animation of the boat as it moves through the gybe/chicken gybe maneuvers.

Gybe and Chicken Gybe

Also in high winds, a gybe will tend to round the boat up into wind very quickly and cause excessive heeling. This is usually upsetting to the crew. To prevent the excessive heeling, once the mainsail gybes over, you've got to let out the mainsheet as quickly as possible. Getting the mainsheet out will stop the rounding up and heeling over.

Gybe and Chicken Gybe

Hence, before you go gybing in high winds, become an expert in lower wind conditions first and use the chicken gybe method until you've gained the confidence to gybe correctly every time.

Unfurling or Raising the Sails

You have motored your vessel from the slip into open water and are now ready to either unfurl or raise the sails, depending on your setup. The procedures for deploying the sails are reasonably standardized, though every sailor will, over time, develop his or her own routine.

On modern sailboats, mainsails are commonly stored ("stowed") either by being:

- Lowered and lashed onto the boom.
- Lowered into a stack pack (a long bag permanently mounted above the boom).
- Rolled into the mast (mast-furled mainsail).
- Rolled onto the boom (boom-furled mainsail).
- Removed and folded into a sailbag for stowage below.

Sailing is rife with opinions that add greatly to the excitement of this sport, and there are many opinions as to which is the preferred method, but for now, you will find that each has its pluses and minuses.

A Furled Mainsail

If a mainsail is rolled into the core of the mast it is called a "mast furled mainsail." If it is stored rolled up into the core of the boom, it is called a "boom-furled mainsail."

Unfurling: In preparation to unfurl the mainsail, head the vessel into the wind. Depending on wind conditions, you may wish to keep just enough speed, from the engine, to maintain steerage.

Just for fun, unfurl the mainsail from the mast now.

The mainsail is usually unfurled first. Unfurling is done by either raising the sail from out of the boom using the halyard, or hauling the sail out from the mast using the outhaul.

The following steps provide a guide when the mainsail is furled in the mast:

Mast Furling Mainsail

1. Motor into the wind maintaining steerage.
2. Release mainsail furling inhaul line.
3. Release tension on the boom vang and mainsheet (very important).
4. Pull (haul) on the outhaul line—this brings the mainsail out of the mast along the boom.

5. Tighten the mainsail against the boom by tensing the outhaul line. On light wind days, don't tension the outhaul so much. Allow about 10 inches (26 cm) of draft. Draft is the distance that the sail curves out and away from the boom. On windy days, use more outhaul tension, say 4 inches (10 cm) of draft.

6. Bear away to the desired heading and trim the mainsail with the mainsheet (the line/rope that brings in or lets out the boom)

A Good Whipping

Once when unfurling the mainsail, we didn't keep the outhaul line taut. The clew of the mainsail started whipping violently, which prompted the outhaul block to break free and join in. A Doc-in-a-box visit later, my friend exited with five stitches to his face.

Don't let lines whip. People and things break!

If you are unfurling the mainsail from the boom, first attach the halyard to the "head" of the sail and then raise the mainsail by hauling on the mainsail halyard.

Here is a video by Leisure Furl using a boom furling mainsail. It shows the boom furler in use as well as showing how to reef the boom furling mainsail while under sail.

Leisure Furl
Boom Furling

Raising the Mainsail

Many boats these days still do not have an in-mast roller-furling mainsail and you must raise the sail up the mast by pulling on the main halyard. The luff (leading edge) of the sail will most likely fit into a track and thus will need guiding up. During this process, it's important that the helmsman keep the boat facing directly into wind. Any side force on the sails will make it very difficult to raise the sail. You can alleviate the force on the mainsail if you are not directly into wind by further letting out the mainsheet. Be careful, though, because the boom will now "flog" (oscillate) from side to side with possible head injury consequences.

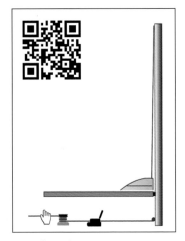

Raise the Sails

The helmsman is also responsible for keeping an eye on traffic and obstacles. It is easy to become distracted by the sail going up.

Just for fun, let's raise the mainsail now. Scan the QR code.

Often the mainsail is stored in a stackpac, which is a long bag permanently mounted to the boom. Lazy jack lines extend from the mast down to the sides of the stackpac bag. The lazy jacks ensure the mainsail drops easily into the stackpac at the end of the sail. However, battens are always getting caught in the lazy jack line as you hoist the mainsail. Take care when hoisting and look aloft as the sail goes up.

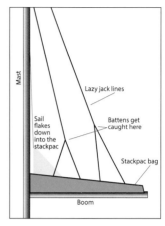

Stackpac

Once the sail is all the way up, cleat off the halyard and tighten down on the cunningham if one is available. The amount of tension you put into the leading edge (luff) of the sail through the halyard or cunningham is proportional to the wind strength. Light winds require slight tension to keep the sail baggy and giving it plenty of shape. High winds require high tension to reduce the curvature of the sail.

The outhaul is another line to help make the sail more efficient. The outhaul is the line that is attached to the clew (bottom aft connection point) of the sail. When you tighten this it flattens the sail against the boom. On high-wind days, you want to tighten the outhaul as much as possible to keep the sail flat thereby reducing the curvature and lift. Don't worry about losing curvature, you already have an abundance of lift from the high wind; at this stage you want to get rid of lift to reduce the heeling of the boat.

In low wind, loosen the outhaul to make the sail baggier and curvier thereby increasing the lift.

Halyard tension and outhaul adjustments also apply to in-mast roller-furled mainsails.

Turning Off the Engine

Before you switch off the engine, bear away from the wind and get the boat sailing so you have maneuverability. Once you are sailing you may turn off the engine. It is important to not have the engine on if the boat is heeling because the cooling water intake may be out of the water and the engine could overheat.

Sailing at last! Is this real freedom or what?

Setting a Course

Next decide where you want to go. Select a destination, such as a compass heading, a scenic spot in the bay, a distant idyllic island, or maybe a channel marker. When this decision has been made, you will next unfurl/raise the head (jib or genoa) sail.

Unfurling the Headsail

Before starting to unfurl the headsail (jib or genoa), it is best to have the downwind jib sheet already wrapped 2 to 3 turns around its winch. Once the sail goes out, if the wind is strong, you will not be able to hold the sail by hand without the help of those wraps.

The Headsail

Make certain the jib furling line is laid out so it can flow out without tangling. Now you simply pull (haul) on the downwind jib sheet to unfurl the headsail. As the headsail begins to fill with wind, it will want to unfurl rapidly by itself. Therefore, you should control this as well by wrapping the jib furling line around a winch or cleat to slow its rate. Uncontrolled furling lines create bird's nests in the furling drum that

Headsail Furling Drum

you will regret. As a precaution, always check the furling drum after deploying the jib sail.

Be careful: More than often, the loose furling line laid out in the cockpit will tangle. The crew member hauling on the jib sheet must watch to make sure this does not occur. Otherwise the crew member cranking the winch is just pulling against the furling system.

Look Aloft

An early sailing mentor would slap me on the back of the head (like Gibbs in *NCIS*) and pronounce: "Look aloft young man, look aloft." It meant that I was not chasing every line its full length with my eyes as I winched in. Something was jammed and I wasn't seeing it. Thwack!

Furling the Headsail

You'll find that if you head the boat downwind, furling the headsail will be much (much) easier. To furl the headsail, have one crew member slowly release the jib sheet while another crew member hauls in on the furling inhaul. Keep a slight tension on the jib sheet so the headsail rolls reasonably tightly around the forestay. Often enough tension can be created by having the jib sheet wrap once around a winch as you pull in on the furling line.

Be careful also that the crew member hauling the furling line keeps an eye on the amount of line remaining in the furling drum. Otherwise you will reach the limit of the line and continuous hauling can cause damage. For this reason, when using a winch on any furling line, if the tension gets high, start looking for the problem.

In some circumstances, you'll need to drop a furling type headsail to the deck for maintenance. This is simple because the luff of the sail usually contains a bolt rope that slides up into a track on a plastic extrusion, which is slid over the forestay. The sail will need to be unfurled. Simply release the headsail halyard and pull down on the leech of the sail. To raise the headsail back up again just guide the bolt rope into the track in the forestay extrusion and tension the halyard.

Raising the Headsail

Many boats do not have a roller-furling headsail. In this case you'll be raising the headsail up the forestay. The headsail is usually stowed neatly in a bag below decks. Depending on the wind you'll want to select the appropriate size headsail. High winds dictate a smaller sail; low winds require a bigger sail.

A Hank

The sails will be labeled with numbers #1, #2, or #3, with #1 the largest, usually the genoa; #3 is a jib sail for high wind conditions and #2 is for midrange wind conditions. (The larger the number the smaller the sail. Why?—Just is.)

The luff (leading edge) of a headsail often has "hanks," which are small clips permanently attached around the bolt rope about every 2 to 3 feet (0.6 to 1 m). The opening slider of the hank will clip around the forestay as the headsail is hoisted.

Prior to leaving the marina, you will want to prepare the headsail for deployment. First, lay the headsail out on the foredeck. Then, attach the headsail halyard to the head (top connection point) of the headsail, the tack of the headsail to a clip mounted at the base of the forestay, and then the clew of the headsail to the jib sheets. Run the jib sheets back through the appropriate fairleads that will guide the jib sheets back to the cockpit. You'll need to know the bowline knot since this is the recommended knot for the jib sheet to attach to the clew. Now clip the hanks onto the forestay. Use sail ties to tie the sail down to the foredeck so that it is secure until you want to raise it once you are out in the bay.

After you have deployed the mainsail and the boat is sailing, untie the sail ties as another crew member pulls on the headsail halyard. Once this is complete it is advisable to move back to the cockpit as the flapping headsail and jib sheets can be very dangerous in high winds.

Finally, trim the leeward headsail sheet with the headsail sheet winch. There you have it—you're now fully under sail.

Dousing the Headsail

To douse (bring down) the headsail at the end of your sail is also pretty simple. It is best to douse the headsail first. For roller furling headsails, bear away downwind since this will make furling far easier.

For headsails that you drop to the deck, turn on the engine and head up into wind. This allows the headsail to drop to the deck and not into the water. Make sure you use sail ties again to tie the sail to the foredeck or lifelines to stop it from self-deploying.

> **Pay Attention**
>
> Leaving North Sound in the British Virgin Islands, we saved another sailboat from crashing by sounding five blasts on our horn. The inattentive helmsman had been watching the crew trying to get down a jammed mainsail instead of looking where he was headed.
>
> The helmsman's job is to keep the boat clear of obstacles and traffic.

Dousing the Mainsail

Dousing the mainsail is done by heading into the wind with the engine on. For furling systems, maintain a small amount of back pressure on the outhaul for mast furling or halyard for boom furling. This is essential so that the mainsail is rolled tightly around its core.

For sails that are lowered into a stackpac (long bag along the boom) there is not too much to do except help to flake the bolt rope from side to side as it lowers into the stackpac. Watch this quick video as a sail lowers into a stackpac

Video of a Sail Dropping into a Stackpac

Many mainsails are lowered and tied along the mast, then a mainsail cover is zipped over the sail to protect it. Watch this video of a mainsail being flaked along the boom.

Video of Flaking a Mainsail

Sail Trim

While setting the sails to general rules of thumb will get you really close to a good sail set, the true finesse in sailing is understanding sail trim.

With sail trim knowledge, you use the telltales to observe the flow of air over the sails to perfect the sail set and maximize the efficiency. Telltales are pieces of ribbon or wool threads where the leading edge is glued to the sail. By observing the flow of the telltale, the sail trimmer can visualize the flow of the wind over the sail at that point.

As a benefit to purchasing this book, you have access to a FREE interactive Sail Trim Course online. Now is a good time to remind you that if you have not already visited the FREE Basic Sail Trim Course online, do so now. There is no better introductory course than the NauticEd FREE Basic Sail Trim course.

A Special Interactive Learning Tool: NED

A special interactive learning tool is embedded into the Basic Sail Trim course online. It is called NED. With NED, you can adjust your heading and adjust the set of the sails. NED will automatically give you a sail efficiency and boat speed accordingly. You get to practice exactly how the sails should be set for each boat heading. It's a really cool tool. Unfortunately, the tool is built using a technology that does not work on mobile devices. Thus you'll need to do the course online on a computer.

Play with NED online on your computer by signing up for the FREE Basic Sail Trim Course at www.nauticed.org.

Reefing

Before heading out, check forecasted wind conditions to see if you might need to reef at some point during the day. If so, make appropriate preparations in the calm marina and ensure your crew know the procedure.

It is important to realize that you are not necessarily going fast when heeling excessively, though you might think you are. To the contrary, you will slow down under such conditions. The following image shows a boat being excessively heeled over. It is uncomfortable for the crew

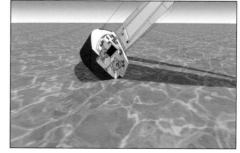

Over Heeling

and it puts excessive strain on the rig and makes the boat go slower because the wind is stalling on the backside of the sail. To speed up the boat you need to reef the sail.

Airflow

The following illustrations show how smooth flow of air (called laminar flow) over a sail creates a forward force and heeling force. Smooth airflow is created when the sails are trimmed correctly. As the wind flows around the leeward side of the sail it bends and "stays attached" to the sail shape.

When you ask the wind to bend too much, it will spawn and create turbulence. This reduces the effect of the sails and slows the boat. The higher the velocity of the wind, the less the wind tends to bend. This is one of the reasons why in high wind conditions you need to reduce the size of the sail. Since the sail is smaller when reefed, the wind is required to bend less over the distance from the front (luff) of the sail to the back (leech) of the sail, and therefore the wind will not break away from the sail as much. Once the wind breaks away from the low pressure side, as in the diagram at right, you're reducing efficiency. In the same way, an airplane will stall. When the flow of air breaks away from the top side of the wing, lift is lost and the plane quickly aims itself at the ground. In sailing, the result is less dramatic. Simply let the sail out and the wind will reattach to the leeward side of the sail.

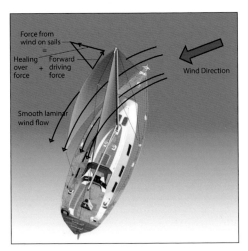

Laminar Flow Attached

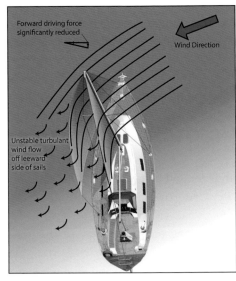

Turbulent Flow Detached

Reefing—reducing sail area—should begin at or around 12 to 16 knots of wind. Reefed sails reduce the heeling over force from the wind and helps the wind stay attached to the leeward side of the sail, thus reducing turbulent inefficient flow of wind.

Reefing Roller-Furling Sails

Reefing using roller-furler sails is by far the easiest way of reefing. You simply wind up the sail until you are satisfied with the sail size. Here is a basic animation.

Roller Furling Reefing

In general, for your first reef at about 12 to 16 knots you should furl up the sail about 18 inches (45 centimeters). Around 18 to 22 knots, you'll need another reef; for this second reef, you should furl in the sail another 18 inches (45 cm). As you gain experience with your boat, you'll get the feel for how much to reef in. Essentially, if your boat is heeling over a lot, you'll need to reef in more.

So which sail do you reef first? The headsail or the mainsail? The answer is pretty complex and involves the design of your boat and rig. When you reef a sail you are moving the center of pressure point that the wind acts on the sail relative to the boat. That is, making the triangle smaller moves the center of that triangle forward on the boat. This affects the dynamic relationship between the rudder, the keel, and the sails.

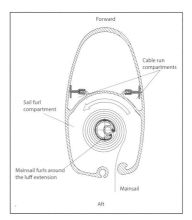

Roller Furler Mast Extrusion

In a practical sense then, test out your boat's behavior by reefing the different sails in different orders on a windy day (with minimal gusts) and feel the changed pressure on the rudder. As a novice sailor, this is going to be hard. As you gain more experience you'll feel the difference. We say all this to ward off the concept of a formula of which sail to reef first. The process is dynamic. Given all that, if you are just starting out, primarily all you are trying to do is reduce heeling and reduce the forces on the rig. So start by reefing the mainsail, then move onto the headsail.

The center illustration shows the mast extrusion and how the sail is rolled up into the mast.

Roller Fuller System

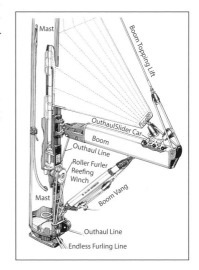

The next illustration shows the Selden roller furler ratchet system. By turning the reefing winch, the sail winds up inside the mast. The endless furling line allows the crew to turn the reefing winch from the cockpit. The ratchet lever will prevent the sail from unwinding. Thus, to unfurl the sail, the ratchet level must be set to "free."

Both illustrations are courtesy of Selden.

Traditional Reefing Systems

A traditional mainsail system does not have a mast furling mainsail. Rather, the mainsail must be hoisted up with the main halyard to begin sailing. When reefing, the mainsail must be lowered to reduce its sail area.

Here is a basic animation. It shows replacing the number 1 headsail with a number 3 headsail, which is smaller. It also shows lowering the mainsail to the predetermined reefing points. From the above discussion on which to reef first, the order in the animation is not showing the order of reefing. Like we said above, this depends on the boat and rig.

With headsails that are hoisted as opposed to furling, you can't reef. Rather, you change out the sail for a smaller one.

Reefing Animation

To Reef the Mainsail

At the front (luff) of the sail there are usually two reefing points, the first and second (aka primary and the secondary). The primary is the first reef you'll put in for wind speeds of approximately 12 to 16 knots. The secondary reef will need to be put in at about 18 to 22 knots.

You can reef the mainsail while sailing with just the headsail. Here is the procedure:

1. Decide if you are going to use the primary or secondary reefing points.
2. Check the boom topping lift so that when you ease the halyard down the boom does not drop completely into the cockpit.
3. Ease the mainsheet so there is no load on the sail from the wind.
4. Optionally, over-tighten the headsail sheet so as to back-wind the mainsail. This reduces wind loading on the mainsail.

5. Ease the main halyard so that the reefing point is just higher than the boom.
6. Place the cunningham hook into the reefing point and tighten so that the reefing point is brought down to the boom level (lowering the sail).
7. At the leech of the sail the corresponding reefing must also take place
8. Trim both sails.

Single Line Reefing System

The leech reefing lines may be secured at the aft of the boom or they may run down to the boom, travel forward inside the boom, down the mast and back along the deck through a series of pad eyes to the cockpit. Pulling in on the appropriate reefing line will lower and thus reef the leech of the sail.

A convenient set-up on some reefing systems is a single line reefing system. With a single line reefing system, one line acts to pull down both the luff and leech of the sail simultaneously. Here is a video from Selden Masts showing a single line reefing system. If you have one installed on your boat, you will love how easy it is to reef.

Whenever you are reefing the mainsail, observe the boom topping lift line and the main sheet and ensure that they are not tight, otherwise these will interfere with your ability to tighten the leech reefing lines.

The holes in the sail at the reefing points are called cringles. In some cases there are additional cringles in the center of the sail between each reefing point. Small reefing tie lines go through these cringles to secure the sail to the boom when it is reefed.

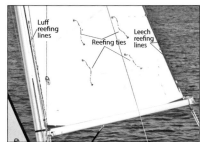

Reefing Ties

"Shaking Out the Reef"

Releasing the reefing lines and raising the sail back up fully is called "shaking out the reef." Here's how:

1. Ease the mainsheet
2. Undo any reefing ties in the center of the sail
3. Ease the cunningham completely and remove the hook
4. Ease the leech reefing lines
5. Raise the mainsail halyard
6. Trim the mainsail
7. Check topping lift is loose

The following illustration shows many of the components of the sail and the traditional reefing system.

The following shows the same sail reefed to the secondary reefing position.

When reefing, you do one sail at a time. You can reef the boat while still under sail with the other sail still propelling the boat. A close haul is best. Heading to wind is an option but all the sails begin to flap wildly, which can be dangerous because of the whipping sheets.

In heavy weather, reefing usually requires someone to go forward of the cockpit. Ensure this person is harnessed to the jacklines, safety lines connected to the deck running the length of the boat.

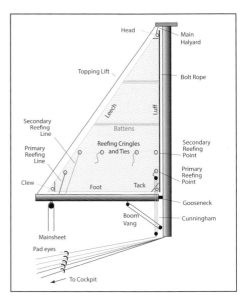

Sail Components

Heave-To

What Is Heave-To?

When you have successfully hove-to (heaved-to), your sailboat will be in a stable situation with the mainsail and headsail still up. Your forward speed will be minimal and you'll be sliding downwind slightly. Essentially you're under full sail but nearly stopped! Cool eh?

This makes it an ideal strategy for the following situations:

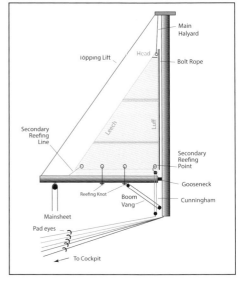

Sail Reefed

1. Lunch, simply taking a rest, or instructor debriefing
2. Storm tactics and reefing
3. Conditions are too rough and you need a break
4. Man overboard recovery
5. Boarding by another vessel (crew change during a race, or law enforcement safety inspection)

How to Heave-To and Its Mechanics

The books say that to heave-to, you tack the boat and leave the headsail cleated to windward and the tiller all the way to leeward (wheel to windward). While that is technically correct, there are a lot more things to consider and understand in order to correctly heave-to.

In a heave-to, the mechanics dictate that the forward speed of the boat has dropped to a minimum because the headsail is back-winded and the mainsail has been eased out far enough to reduce nearly all of the forward driving lift on the sail. The back-winded headsail creates a large turning moment on the boat to turn it downwind. However, as the boat turns downwind, the boat tends to pick up a little speed. As the boat picks up a little speed, the windward locked wheel causes the rudder to turn the boat back upwind, killing the speed. It creates a little see-saw action. You can adjust the see-saw by adjusting the set of the headsail, the mainsail, and the rudder angle. Each boat will see-saw a little differently in differing wind conditions. Once the boat is settled, by making small adjustments to the angle of the rudder, the amount the mainsail is eased, and by the "depth" or flatness of the headsail, a skilled operator can make very useful adjustments to the exact way in which the boat is lying to the wind

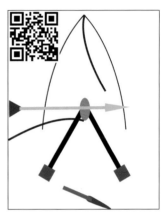

Heave to Animation

and seas. Practice practice practice! When that storm comes, you'll be glad.

Watch the animations and hit pause throughout to read the explanations.

While the animation period above is about 12 seconds, in real life the see-saw cycle takes about 30 seconds to 1 minute.

A Cool Trick about Heaving-To!

Try to lie in a heave-to position that your boom is on the port side. Why? So that you're technically sailing "on starboard tack," putting you in a more advantageous stand-on position with regard to the Navigation Rules vis-a-vis other sailboats' "on port" tack. Wouldn't want to disturb our lunch now would we? It's not a big deal but just something most people may not have considered.

How to Heave-To

You'll enjoy having this little skill under your belt once you've mastered it. But you've got to practice it a few times. To enter into a hove-to position, if practical, start out on a on a port tack with the headsail sheeted in tight. Tack the boat slowly onto a starboard tack (bleeding off some speed while head-to-wind) but leave the headsail cleated (i.e., don't tack the headsail). Turn the boat so you're on a close reach (60 degrees off the wind) and let out the mainsail most of the way out so it is luffing. Now wait until the rest of the boat's headway speed bleeds off. Once the speed has bled off, turn the wheel all the way to windward (tiller to leeward) and lock it and leave it in that position.

Heaving-To in a Storm

It's really important to realize the wisdom of heaving-to in a storm. With one huge caveat; since you slowly slide sideways through the water, make sure you have plenty of sea-room distance to leeward to avoid rocks, shoals, or the other hard stuff (like land!). Heaving-to in a storm gives you and your crew a rest from the elements. And it can be a safer means of riding out a storm rather than trying to sail it out. In a heave-to position, the boat is in a completely stable position. You should probably lower or deeply reef the main or raise a storm tri-sail (very small mainsail) as well as a small head-sail to reduce loads on the rig. Here's a really cool

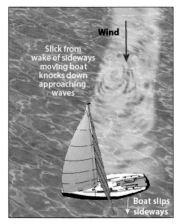

Heave-To in a Storm

kicker: Since the boat will be slipping sideways, a wake is left to windward. Any breaking waves hit this "slick" and flatten out, thus reducing the wave action on your vessel. Now that's really cool.

A Heave-To Trick

When you're settled down into the heave-to position and everything is balanced, use a preventer line to "prevent" the boom slapping around wildly in sudden gusts, save wear on the rig, prevent an accidental gybe, or worse a bonk on the head.

Using Heave-To in a Man Overboard Situation

Heaving-to can be a very effective in a man-overboard situation. The moment the victim goes over the side you can crash tack the boat and move immediately into a heave-to position. Be sure the victim is able to swim and that they did not get hurt while falling. Heaving-to in a man-overboard situation isn't often taught and therefore isn't considered in the panic of the situation. It's your decision to heave-to or not in this situation, but it will keep you from getting too far away from your friend in the water, which is clearly the biggest danger.

Ultimately, in a man-overboard situation, we recommend turning on the engine and getting the sails down. The biggest danger from turning on the engines is not chopping your friend up—you're smart enough not to do that—but rather getting a line wrapped around the prop in all the panic and then not being able to maneuver. So just make that part of your "engines-on" routine in crew overboard practice. Next time you're out practice man (or woman) overboard.

But we digress. Back to heave-to: So there you have it, you're now a heave-to expert. NOT! You haven't practiced it enough yet! And while you're out there practicing it, have fun.

Exiting a Heave-To Position

There are two simple ways to exit a heave-to. Either of which depends on where you want to head next.

1. Release the jib sheet, straighten the wheel or tiller, and haul in on the main sheet OR
2. Gybe out of heave to by turning the rudder the other way (wheel to leeward or tiller to windward) and gybing the mainsail. Use normal gybe precautions. Don't do this in high winds conditions.

Key Instruments

Instrumentation can be very sophisticated and intelligent. Most electronic displays provide a wide range of menus of useful information.

Depth and Speed

One of the key instruments you will constantly use is your depth and speed meter. The following is a typical device.

It shows that the depth of the water is 9.8 feet and the speed of the boat through the water is 6.35 knots. Take care to understand from where the depth is measured. Is it the water surface or is it the depth below the keel? If your keel is 5 feet (1.7 m) deep, your boat will hit bottom when the meter is

Depth and Speed Meter

still reading 5 feet (1.7 m) if the meter was set up to read from the surface. Most devices have the ability to offset the keel depth. It is also wise to add in another 5 feet (2 m) of safety factor.

Devices can get quite sophisticated and can show a bottom contour much the same as at right. The arrow will show you if the depth is increasing or decreasing.

Depth Animation

The speed measurement typically comes from an impeller mounted under the hull that spins from the passing water. The speed indicated is the speed through the water, not relative to the land. If you are operating in high current flow, your water speed will be quite different from your speed relative to the land (speed over ground).

Your GPS device will also have a speed measurement. This is the speed over ground and can be very accurate. When there is no current, the speed from your depth and speed meter (via its impeller) and the speed from the GPS should match. If they do not match, clean your water impeller since it can become clogged with algae—which affects the measurement. Prudent sailors check and clean their impellers often.

Wind Instrument

Another key instrument used on larger sailboats is a wind meter that receives its information from a spinning anemometer at the top of the mast. It presents the wind direction and speed information to you in a display in the cockpit.

Wind Meter

The wind meter needle points to the direction of the wind and can be set to indicate apparent wind or true wind. It can also give other useful information controlled by the menu settings, such as wind speeds.

In the image here the apparent wind speed is 12 knots at an angle of 68 degrees from starboard.

Autopilot

An autopilot is an extremely useful device, especially when single-handing a boat. It gives you pertinent information but also allows you to make fine adjustments to your heading to port or starboard by touching the 1 or 10 degree buttons.

When the autopilot is connected to the GPS device, it can also steer automatically to waypoints that you set up in the GPS.

Some autopilots automatically steer the boat to maintain a constant wind angle.

Do not attempt to turn the wheel when an autopilot is engaged. You can damage the electric servo connections to the wheel.

GPS and navigation instruments will be covered later in the Chapter 9, Navigation.

Autopilot

Helpful Hints about Wind

Since the existence of wind is the primary reason we can sail, it is prudent to know all we can about it. Here are a few helpful tips:

Trimming the Sails

- 1/2 second glances ONLY at the wind vane at the top of the mast or the wind meter.
- Simpler signs of wind direction and velocity include flags, telltales, your hair, and birds. Birds, when given the opportunity, generally sit with their beak into the wind.
- Ripples on the water form 90 degrees to the wind.
- If you put your nose directly into the wind, you will hear the wind equally in both ears.

There are many ways to judge how the wind is hitting your vessel, and these tend to become intuitive with experience—you simply sense the wind. This is when you truly have the "feeling" of sailing.

Take Note When the Boat Heels Over or Stands Up

At a sailing group meeting, someone mentioned they were having trouble determining if the boat was pinching or not. My reply was that the boat stands up. After a moment of uncomfortable silence . . . I had to explain myself.

Pinching is a term to describe the boat heading too close to the wind. Someone is usually pinching if they are trying to sail to a destination that is too close to where the wind is coming from. When you do this your boat speed reduces dramatically and you're better off bearing away from your destination, picking up speed, and tacking one last time to your destination.

When you start pinching, the apparent wind will be less than 30 degrees off the bow of the boat. It means you're heading too close to the origin of the wind, so the wind cannot provide lift and pressure properly on the sails. With no pressure, the heeling force is reduced and so the boat literally "stands up" straight. If you're sailing along heeled over and you begin to feel the boat stand up straight, you're starting to pinch. Bear away.

Pinching Animation

Go through the animation here several times to view what is happening to the boat.

The concept of increased wind speed and changing course will potentially bamboozle you when starting out. From the NauticEd FREE Basic Sail Trim course, you gained a better understanding of true and apparent wind than most sailors on the planet. You know that if either the boat speed or true wind speed changes in magnitude this affects the direction and speed of the apparent wind. This creates the need to make course corrections.

Some Wind Shift Definitions

- Forward wind shift means the wind that you feel comes more from the front of the boat.
- Aft wind shift means the wind that you feel comes now more from the stern.
- Veering wind means the wind changes in a clockwise direction: If it was a northeaster then a veered wind might be an easterly.
- Backing wind means wind changes in a counterclockwise direction: If it was a northeaster then a backed wind might be a northerly.

You can almost instantly tell what the true wind is doing by the action of the boat. If the boat suddenly stands up taller (less heeling), the true wind has gotten lighter or has shifted forward—thus you should bear away. If the boat heels farther over, the true wind has gotten stronger or has shifted aft—thus you should head up.

Lifts—Knocks and Actions to Take Advantage

On close-haul headings, a wind lift is when you can change the boat direction in a more windward direction and keep power in the sails. You are "lifted" toward your destination. A wind knock is where you must change the boat direction to maintain power in the sails to a more downwind direction. You are "knocked" down off your course.

- True wind gets lighter—boat stands up—bear away—called a knock.
- True wind shifts forward—boat stands up—bear away—called a knock.
- True wind gets stronger—boat heels over—head up—called a lift.
- True wind shifts aft—boat heels over—head up—called a lift.

In other points of sail you simply trim the sails to take advantage of the wind shift.

Holding a Straight Course

Holding a straight course is an imperative skill to master as you learn to sail. As an experienced sailor, nothing is more distracting to a good day out sailing than a novice helmsperson swinging the boat in all directions. What I've found is that often a new sailor has been taught to "fly the telltales" too early in the learn-to-sail-process. Telltales are short pieces of ribbon mounted on the sails. When they fly backward along the sails it means that the airflow is flowing smoothly; in turn this means the sail is set correctly.

There's no question that all sailors are keen to introduce and teach others to sail. What a great community of passionate people. So whether you're a novice sailor learning to sail or an experienced sailor who loves to teach, this will be important.

As a sailing instructor and having owned my own practical sailing school, I have taught many people to sail. I've discovered that teaching to fly the telltales too early almost inherently invites the novice to be sailing all over the map. This is because the sailor is spending too much time watching the sails, watching the wind indicator and the wind meter, and not enough time looking out of the sailboat.

The issue really lies in that there is a delay between a course change and the telltales. So the new sailor tends to wait until the telltales are flying correctly before looking up and straightening the helm out. But by the time the sailboat is straightened out, the new correct point of sail has been overshot. The novice then tries to bring the sailboat back but overshoots again. And thus there is a constant "S" curve of trailing wakes out behind. A good thing to do is to point out the curvy wake to the novice so they can see what they have been doing.

The biggest mistake occurs when adjusting to go upwind to a close-haul position. If this is over turned, the boat can auto tack over to the other side. An auto tack occurs when the wind catches the headsail on the opposite side pushing it through the wind and causing an involuntary tack. It's an extremely common occurrence with new sailors and creates a lot of confusion as to why this happens. It also creates a lot of calamity and is a pretty embarrassing thing to do as the helmsperson. And you'll find that you're resorting to saving face by blaming the wind for a big change in direction. LOL. The term for a big change in wind direction is called "the wind clocked." But in reality the wind doesn't clock. You just over stood the wind and got auto tacked.

So let's fix that shall we?

Introducing Rule A thru Z, 1 through Infinity: **Keep your eyes out of the sailboat.**

When you drive a car and you want to speed up to 50 miles per hour (mph) (80 kph) you don't do the following: Set your car going straight then watch the speedometer intently until you reach 50 mph, then look up to make sure everything is okay. No! Instead, you keep your eyes out of the car, watch the road and traffic, and make small steering adjustments to stay between the lines. You flick your eyes to the speedometer for perhaps 0.5 seconds every 5 seconds or so. When you reach 45 mph, you lift your foot slowly and if you're a good driver you'll probably land right bang on 50 mph having stayed between the lines all the way.

Let's bring that concept over to sailing.

What you don't want to do is the following: hold your eyes on the telltales (speedometer) until they are flying right and then look up. No! What you want to do is keep your eyes out of the sailboat, watching your heading and traffic and flick check your eyes to the telltales and wind indicators for 0.5 seconds about every 5 seconds or so.

With this simple revelation, you'll never auto tack again and your wake will be straight.

Now, here's how to make adjustments for wind changes. You're sailing along toward a distant hilltop on a distant island and see that you need an adjustment to leeward. As you begin to become more experienced, you'll be able to determine from the telltales how much of an adjustment is needed. For now a 5 degree adjustment is a good starting point. First, make the adjustment with your eyes. Pick a 5 degree change on the hilltop and turn the sailboat toward that new point. Wait until the sailboat straightens out on that new point then check the telltales. If more adjustment is needed, repeat the process. Note that you're not watching the telltales. You're just checking them when the boat is heading straight. Using this method you'll reduce or stop any over standing on the points that you want to sail to.

When teaching this, I always get the question, "Um duh, what if I'm not head-ing toward an island?" Well, there is always something, and if there's not some-thing, there is a cloud. I doubt very much that you'll be learning this in the middle of the ocean without land in sight. Even if land is not directly ahead, there is land to the side. Make your adjustments according to the relative position of land on a shroud line or something on the boat. The point is that with your eyes out of the boat you can see your boat turning. Once you're an experienced sailor you won't have to worry about holding a straight course, it will all be inherent. But for now, get out and learn to hold a straight course with your eyes out of the boat.

Just like watching telltales or the wind meter, by watching a compass instead of land or a cloud is also not a good idea. Compasses lag like the telltales, as do wind meters. Get your eyes out of the sailboat.

So the secret to sailing a straight line is always be aiming at something in the distance or have a relative bearing on something in the distance against something on the boat so that your eyes are telling you if you are turning or not. When mak-ing adjustments to your heading, keep your eyes out of the sailboat so that they are telling you how much your boat is turning. Make small adjustments according to those distant objects and flick check your eyes for half a second to the telltales or wind meter (or compass if you're turning onto a new compass heading).

Keep your eyes out of the sailboat. And besides it's safer; you're keeping your eyes out for traffic at the same time.

And if you can't remember "Keep your eyes out of the sailboat" remember this one.

> You're a sailor if you can . . .
> hold a drink
> hold a conversation
> . . . and hold a course.

And if you can do that while telling a joke, then you're an advanced sailor.

Practical Suggestions

Remember each vessel, including sails, has a personality reflecting its construction and how it reacts to conditions in which it is sailing.

- The closer to the wind direction you are sailing, the closer you should set the sails toward the centerline of the boat.

- Let the sails out until each sail just begins to flutter, then pull them slightly back in. This will give you a perfectly trimmed sail.
- There is a saying regarding sail trim: "when in doubt—let it out." This works well because if the sail is luffing, there is no doubt you should pull it in. Thus, only doubt can exist if it is set too tight or just right (see the bullet above).
- When the wind is directly behind the vessel, sails should be out as far as possible. However, in this situation the mainsail will block all the wind from getting to the headsail. One way to counter this is to fly the headsail on the other side. This is called sailing wing and wing.
- Every point of sail has a distinct personality or feeling relative to the vessel.
- When the vessel is sailing dead downwind and the sails are set wing and wing, the specific tack defined for give way issues is determined by the side the main boom is set. For example, if the boom is set on the starboard side it means by definition that the wind is coming from over the port side and therefore the boat is determined to be on port and must therefore give-way to vessels "on starboard." Even if you are sailing by the lee, the give-way rule is determined by which side the mainsail is on. If the mainsail is not raised then the give-way rule is determined by which side the headsail is on. That is if the sail is on port, you are on starboard.

Sailing Regatta

Sail trimming provides physical and mental exercise for the crew, especially in regattas. As sailors gain experience, they add these to their personal bag of skills.

Motor Sailing

If the wind is light and your time is short you might want to consider motor-sailing—using your auxiliary engine for propulsion, sometimes in conjunction with your sail(s). When using sails and engine power, be careful to make sure the boat does not heel to the point the water intake comes out comes out of the water. You will burn out the water impeller and damage the engine.

If you are sailing directly into the wind in waves or swell, keeping the mainsail up and tightly sheeted will stabilize or at least reduce rocking. Certainly, douse the headsail otherwise it will flog, luff, flap, and make a lot of noise. Also, flogging fatigues the sails and the parts to which they are connected.

For purposes of give-way versus stand-on in the navigation rules of the road, you are now a power vessel, even if your sails are up. When your engine is used for propulsion, the sailing vessel under the rules becomes a power vessel.

Rule 25 (e) also applies: *A vessel proceeding under sail when also being propelled by machinery shall exhibit forward where it can best be seen a conical shape, apex downward.*

Conical shape with apex facing down = vessel under power

Below, the sailing vessel under power and sail is on a starboard tack, correctly displaying the under-power day shape. She must give-way to the port tack sailing vessel.

A sailor who refuses to learn is indeed a dangerous sailor. Knowledge of sailing techniques is infinite and continually evolving. It is the heart of sailing. Even if you are experienced, you will continually

Motor Sailing

be adding to your sailing lexicon each time you get on the water. Always keep an open mind, douse your ego, and raise your ears. We guarantee you'll be a better sailor for it.

Chapter 8
Communications

Non-Electronic Communications

Sailing has been around for thousands of years. Electronic communications has been around for less than 100.

The Slow Old Days

My Dad was a radio operator on a DC-3 during WWII. His stories of communicating using Morse Code were boundless and exciting, from gaining landing patterns to communicating emergencies—such as the times their landing gear would not come down or when another plane in the squadron was shot up on a mission. He was a pioneer in a new age of communication. Today we can't even imagine that slow of a data rate. Some of us once used 14.4 k dial up modems. Arh!

Before the harnessing of electrons and radio waves, humankind used many other forms of communication. Many are still used today.

Forms of non-electronic communication include:

- Verbal.
- Hand signals.
- Flags and pennants.
- Sound-making devices such as bells, horns, sirens, whistles, and cannons.

- Megaphones—just an improvement on verbal.
- Flares.

Each of these forms has unique uses depending on the situation. Yet most require users to understanding their meaning. Even with verbal communication, you have to be careful because of all the terminology.

Verbal Communication

Unfortunately, many a newbie sailor has been turned off sailing by a few crusty captains because of their harsh verbal communication style (AKA abuse). Don't be a crusty sailor. Below are a few people skills inserted into this course.

A loud clear voice is often preferred to gain the attention of someone not looking. The most common of these would be to announce "STARBOARD" in a potential sailboat-on-sailboat collision situation. By stating this, you are stating that there is a close-quarters situation, that collision is possible, and that you are stating you are the stand-on vessel—all in one word.

As captain it is your responsibility to state this: the other boat might not have seen you, they might be completely unaware of the rules, or they might believe they can squeak by. It is also your responsibility to understand such communications before you assume the role of skipper of a vessel.

Yelling is out and unacceptable. Loud, clear voice is in. We say this because the word yelling has a negative connotation. And creating negative situations only heightens emotions. We are all familiar with road rage and the truthful person would admit that they, at some time, have been guilty of it even to the slightest degree. If you've ever shot the bird at someone—the finger—then you have been suckered into your negative self.

We address yelling and road rage (on the water) here in more detail because it's important. Despite the wide expanse of the ocean, there is no room for negativity on the water.

Viktor Frankl, a WWII concentration camp prisoner and renowned psychiatrist, developed the notion of logotherapy, the theory that we try to attach a meaning to everything. We attach a meaning to someone cutting us off in traffic; we attach meaning to being on the receiving end of the bird; and we attach meaning to being yelled at. Steven Covey, in his popular book *The Seven Habits of Highly Effective People*, integrates Frankl's notion and adds that we as humans have the ability to see an action, make a decision on how to react, and then perform the reaction. Animals, on the other hand, only have action followed by instant reaction.

As an example, let's assume we get cut off in traffic. As humans have the ability to think about that, to make a decision about the meaning of that (if we want), and the ability to decide what to do about it. The key word is "ability." It does not necessarily mean that we act upon what we think or decide. Just that we have the ability. What is it about someone cutting us off in traffic? What meaning do we attach to that? Did they do it on purpose? Maybe, maybe not. In most cases, probably not. Even in addressing the case that they did it on purpose, we still have the ability to decide "Should I let that person continue with their crappy day or should I teach him a lesson so he'll never do that again in his entire life?" In the decision process, we get to bring in our human selves and decide that we don't have to attach meaning to it; that it might have been a mistake, or that even if it was on purpose, who cares? Why let it ruin my perfect day?

The trick, Covey states, is to practice inserting ourselves into the decision before the instant animal reaction.

On the water, you'll find there are a lot of inexperienced people out there. Novices, newbies, old hats who have not bothered to learn the rules, whomever— are all out there. But there is only one reason you are on the water and that is to enjoy yourself. To recreate = re-create. Re-create your good experiences. Don't let others ruin your day. Make a decision to make a decision between the action and your reaction.

Instead of yelling *"Learn the #@$% rules ya &*&^%,"* which, as we all know, is only going to get you the finger in return, you might buy the guy a drink back at the yacht club and say something like, "Whew that was a close one out there. I thought I was the stand-on vessel but perhaps I was wrong. What were your thoughts?"

Another way of looking at this all is to put yourself in their shoes. Have you ever made a mistake in traffic? Well, maybe that was you in another body making a mistake. It was a wise man many years ago who said, "Let he who is without sin cast the first stone." We all make mistakes. Let it go.

The point is to act like Abraham Lincoln, who was known as a great leader because of his leadership skills, not because of his title. What are your leadership skills at the yacht club or on a boat? People will follow you on a boat because they think (even unknowingly) that you are a good leader. It's not because you are a self-proclaimed captain; it's not because of your experience. In the corporate world, people go back to work the next day under a bad leader because they have a job to try to keep. On a boat you will find out about the quality of your leadership skills pretty quickly by the number of your solo sailing days. In the corporate world, you can expound upon your experience, berate and belittle as much as you want; on a boat, it's back to solo sailing if you behave like this.

Leadership Article

We really encourage you to read this article on our blog site on how to be a good leader on a sailboat.

Take, for example, the yeller, the skipper who yells at his crew, his spouse, and his friends. This is just a bad leader. "But," the skipper says, "it was necessary, we were about to hit the dock." The best way to hit a dock is to freeze up your crew by yelling at them. If you use an authoritative clear loud voice with specific instructions you will get things done smoothly and perfectly and maintain or even increase the respect you get. For example, "*Mike. We are going to hit the dock. Please take this fender now and go up front. Put it between the boat and the dock so we don't crash into it. Thanks.*"

Back to using a loud clear voice, think about your audience. Can they understand what you are saying using the terminology? Can they even hear you? A classic case where communications are compromised is between the bow and the helmstation; it is near impossible in wind. Hand signals are preferred, although bigger and more sophisticated boats use microphones and earpieces.

Hand Signals

There are universal signals that work for most people, but it is a good idea to agree on a set of hand signals that work with your crew.

Important ones:

- A closed fist is *stop* or *put it in neutral.*
- Virtual hand with a horizontal hand creates a T shape for *time out—wait a second or so.*
- Crossed arms in an X with closed fists is to *make fast—lock it off—cleat it.*
- A flat open horizontal hand pumping slowly up and down is *slow down.*

Using Hand Signals

- A flat open vertical hand pushing aft is *stop the boat in the water*.
- When retrieving an anchor, the bow person points to the anchor so the helmsperson can steer that way.
- A hand with flicking open and closed fingers means *ease that line (let out slowly)*.
- A twirling upward finger means *bring in that line*.
- Patting yourself on top of the head means *OK* (taken from scuba diving).

Start using these on your boat with your crew and stay consistent with their use. Pretty soon you'll be easily communicating with your regular crew.

Watch this video from our friends at Yachting Education (.com):

Video Hand Signals

Flags and Pennants

Flags and pennants are not used extensively. The most important ones to know are diving flags. There are other flags are used for emergencies and these are covered in Chapter 11: Safety and Emergencies, under the Raising the Alarm section.

Diving

You need to be aware of two diver down flags that indicate the vessel has scuba divers below. You are required to stay 300 feet (100 meters) away from such a vessel.

In the USA, a red flag with a white strip is used, while in most of the rest of the world, the Code A flag is used.

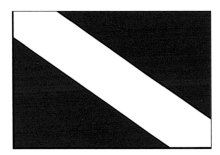

USA Dive Flag

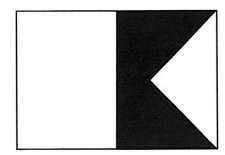

Rest of World Dive Flag / Code A

Sound-Making Devices

Sound-making devices are extensively used as warning devices and for maneuvering announcements on larger ships.

An important note is to always have a loud horn accessible within 1 to 3 seconds to the helmsperson. This simple self-imposed rule WILL prevent a collision at some point in your sailing life.

Flares

Flares are used in emergency situations. This topic is covered in Chapter 11: Safety and Emergencies, under the Raising the Alarm section.

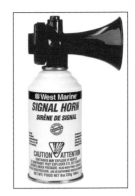

Sound Horn

Electronic Communications

A Thought

Imagine if humans had 16 fingers instead of 10. We'd all be able to grasp hexadecimal code a lot easier. Just sayin!

Morse code uses a long blip and a short blip. Combinations of these blips represent a letter. A fast human Morse coder could send ten letters in a few seconds but the accuracy depended also on the human receiver's ability to decode the message equally as quickly.

Nowadays gigabytes of data can be sent in a second as a digital signal. It is all a complete Wow! and we've seen this invention of technology, including all the working satellites, launched into orbit our lifetimes. Signals travel and are coded and decoded at the speed of light.

All these signals benefit our communicating with each other. AND the field of electronic communication continues to explode. Knowing the importance of knowledge and data, sailors have embraced technology. Even the laggards and Luddites carry an iPhone in their pocket to communicate with their grandchildren via video over 4G or to retrieve tidal information about a port.

Most larger sailboats these days make use of most of the systems in this diagram. Compare this to what

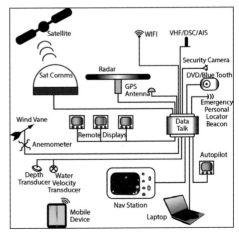

Data Communications

Captain James Cook would have carried on the *Endeavor* when he set out to measure and observe the transit of Venus across the sun in 1769 from the island of Tahiti.

Although telecommunications technology is improving quickly, people at sea need to know how to use many specific maritime communication methods including:

- Communicate with other ships and shore.
- Receive real-time weather information.
- Send or receive distress alerts in an emergency to or from rescue coordination centers ashore and nearby ships.
- Receive navigation information.
- Send and receive traffic information.

So given all the above, the following is a discussion of what you are expected to know when operating your vessel.

VHF Radios

VHF (Very High Frequency) radios are a primary source of radio communications between vessels and shore installations. More importantly, crucial in fact, VHF radios are a primary source of communication during an emergency. Most maritime safety organizations monitor VHF radio signals and specifically channel 16—the international distress, safety, and calling channel.

Operating VHF radios is easy, but there are protocols to follow. One thing to keep in mind is that the sender and the receiver cannot talk at the same time. This is often difficult to remember in an emergency. Transmissions should be kept short and cover only vital issues.

If you put out a distress signal on channel 16, the chances of it being heard by someone who can rescue you is almost 100 percent. The "almost" lies in the distance VHF signals can travel and land mass obstructions in the way.

VHF is essentially a line-of-sight system, since radio waves don't bend very much to follow the curvature of the Earth. Sometimes the signal can reflect and refract around land masses but mostly if there is a land mass in the way you cannot expect your signal to get through. For most reliable VHF communication, the VHF antenna must "see" the antenna of a distant station. Therefore, antenna height is more important in determining the range than radio wattage. The

VHF Signal

effective useful range of a VHF radio is 20 to 25 miles for ship to shore and 10 to 15 miles for ship to ship. The distance a VHF signal can reach between ship and shore installations is usually a bit further since the ground-based antenna is higher.

Fixed-Mount VHF Radios

Fixed-mount units are just that—they are permanently fixed into your boat and are usually high wattage, up to 25 watts. They gain their power from the house battery system.

VHF Radio

Handheld VHF Radios

VHF handhelds also offer many of the same features found on fixed-mount units. They offer portability in the same way a cordless phone allows more mobility at home. A handheld radio may be just what you need for use in a dinghy, small boat without electrical systems, or as an emergency backup for your boat's radio. Handhelds have a maximum output of six watts. Due to their short antennas, they have a limited range of five miles.

You can achieve a significant increase in range by connecting an external antenna or using a telescoping antenna mounted to the handheld radio. Battery life varies with the size of the battery pack. Many models have optional battery packs with longer operating times, greater transmitting power, or both. Some have battery-saver circuits that turn off the receiver to save power. The battery life of a handheld can

Handheld VHF

be increased by switching from full transmit power to one watt of transmit power.

If you have handheld VHF radios on board, make sure you also have a way to charge them.

Check out a handheld VHF/DSC radio product review video from West Marine.

Handheld VHF Video

Channel 16

Channel 16 is the most important VHF channel for sailors. It is essential for all emergencies. The United States Coast Guard and most other country's coast guard systems monitor channel 16, 24 hours a day, 7 days per week.

Channel 16 is designated as the single channel to be constantly used by all vessels at sea. This channel is a sailor's best link for communicating problems with other vessels or ground-based stations.

You can find the proper procedure for using your VHF—Channel 16—radio in an emergency in Chapter 11.

General Calls to Other Ships or to Shore

You can refer to the Wikipedia marine VHF Channels website for a table of VHF Channels for the UK, USA, Canada, Australia, New Zealand, and Finland.

VHF Channels
Wikipedia Article

Each channel has a specific use. Note carefully the channels you as a recreational non-commercial boater can use to communicate. Each channel operates on a different VHF frequency. Here is a summary for USA:

- **Channel 09**—Boater Calling. Commercial and Non-Commercial.
- **Channel 16** -International Distress, Safety and Calling. Any ships that are required to carry a VHF radio. Global Coast Guards, and most coast stations maintain a listening watch on this channel.
- **Channel 68**—Non-Commercial traffic
- **Channel 69**—Non-Commercial traffic
- **Channel 71**—Non-Commercial traffic
- **Channel 72** -Non-Commercial (Intership only)
- **Channel 78A**—Non-Commercial traffic

All others are for port operations, commercial traffic government and the like. They should not be used by recreational boaters. Note in particular that **Channel 70** is for DSC distress signals. No voice is allowed on Channel 70. Sometimes you'll see an A and B switch. A is typically used in the USA; B is used outside the USA (sometimes labeled as "international").

Procedure for Hailing a Ship by Radio

You may use channel 16 to hail a ship or shore station, but if you do so, you **must, must be brief!** We recommend this same procedure be used over channel 9, if channel 9 is used as a calling channel.

A hailing example:

Blue Duck: "Mary Jane, this is Blue Duck" *(the name of the vessel being called may be said 2 or 3 times if conditions warrant).*

Mary Jane: "Blue Duck, this is Mary Jane. Reply 68" *(or some other proper working channel).*
Blue Duck: "68" or "Roger".

Both switch to channel 68 (as an example). Have the conversation. End each turn with "over." End conversation with your station name and "out."

Operator's License

Some countries in the Mediterranean require that you have a VHF operator's license before entering their waters. If chartering a yacht, the charter company is required to ensure you have the same before heading out.

DSC—Digital Selective Calling

DSC Introductory Video

View a quick introductory video on DSC:

Digital Selective Calling, or DSC, is particularly excellent for distress signals. When the red distress button is activated, it automatically broadcasts an encoded digital distress call that will be picked up by all nearby vessels equipped with DSC. The designated VHF channel for DSC transmissions is channel 70. Therefore, you cannot use channel 70 for any reason other than DSC calls. The radio then automatically switches to channel 16 to allow voice communication. Since DSC uses VHF, it also is limited in range. The advantage is that it can send digital data that can be received much clearer than a garbled voice. The data sent in an emergency situation will include a distress signal, the GPS location, the vessel information, and much like pre-formatted texts, conditions like "sinking" can be included.

If the radio is interfaced with GPS, it will also automatically broadcast the distressed vessel's position. All DSC radios have an input connector protocol that allows GPS data input. If you have a GPS and a DSC radio, CONNECT THEM. Many DSC radios now include GPS as a built-in feature.

To use DSC, you must obtain a MMSI (Maritime Mobile Service Identity) number. You may do so free of charge at this web address: http://www.boatus.com/mmsi.

Note that DSC signals on VHF radios are still limited to VHF ranges. But through the network of DSC-listening vessels in the area, your distress is likely to be heard. For this reason, if your vessel is fitted with DSC you are required to have the device on when you are on board.

DSC Video

Here is another video that talks more in depth about DSC radios:

Telephones

Maritime Rescue centers do not recommend relying on cellular phones as a means of communication during an emergency.

Ordinary cell phones do work well so long as the unit is in approximately line of sight of a receiving tower.

In regards to using the phone for emergency; first, who are you going to call and do you have their phone number? You can't speak to the helicopter to coordinate the rescue via cell phone. The best you might manage is to call your mother in-law (why she is on speed dial we don't know) and tell her to call the authorities. Then you're expecting her to write down a latitude and longitude number? Is her daughter on board? Does she really like you? Is this her chance?

Bottom line: Make sure your vessel has an up-to-date VHF unit with DSC.

EPIRB

Pronounced "*e-purb*," an EPIRB is an acronym for Emergency Position Indicating Radio Beacon and is an emergency communication device that, when activated, continuously emits signals to be picked up by satellites that then can direct rescue efforts. They float and are practically indestructible. A Category I EPIRB that gets wet will automatically activate. A Category II EPIRB requires manual activation. If a vessel begins to sink, the now-submerged mounting device for the EPIRB will automatically release the EPIRB, allowing it to float.

EPIRB

As soon as an EPIRB is activated, its signal is received by satellites and is rebroadcast to ground stations or other ships equipped with receivers. Old EPIRBs relied on satellites triangulating the signal to obtain a location within a little more than a mile (2 kilometers). Newer EPIRBs broadcast GPS signals with a unique device number that is specifically registered to a vessel. In this manner, SAR (Search and Rescue authorities) have valuable information about the vessel and its accurate position immediately. The signal is picked up by satellites, airplanes, and ground stations, and triangulation of the signal is not necessary because the GPS location is contained within the signal itself.

You are well advised to ensure your vessel has a Category I EPIRB. It could save your life.

As with most electronic gear, the costs have dropped while their performance and reliability have improved. For sure, you are now no longer alone on the big oceans.

Personal Overboard Locator Beacon (POLB)

Personal overboard locator beacons are electronic tether devices worn by each crew member, dog, cat, or other items you care to save. When a POLB goes overboard, it starts transponding and sending alerts. The frequencies and alerts depend on the type of system. Some go via satellite, some via VHF/DSC.

POLB

AIS

The **Automatic Identification System (AIS)** is an automated tracking system used on ships and by Vessel Traffic Services (VTS) for identifying, locating, and tracking vessels. With an AIS unit on board, you can see if a ship is a threat to your current course and position. AIS information supplements marine radar, which continues to be the primary method of electronic collision-avoidance for water transport. Information provided by AIS equipment, such as identification, position, course, speed (or at anchor), closest point of approach (CPA—how close will the vessel get to my vessel?) and time to closest point of approach (TCPA—when will the CPA take place?) can be displayed on a screen for analysis by the watch person.

AIS operates at 161.975 MHz on the VHF band. Currently only ships over 300 gross tonnage or passenger ships of any size are required to broadcast AIS information about their vessel. However, some recreational vessels now have opted to broadcast AIS for safety reasons; but many don't. Thus, you're not going to get an accurate picture of all traffic with AIS. As a result, AIS should not be considered an automatic collision avoidance system but rather a way to gauge risk of collision. Keep in mind that if you're transmitting an AIS signal, then large ships have a better chance at seeing you, even if you are way out at sea, which creates some peace of mind.

In 2007, a new class B standard of AIS was introduced that enabled a new generation of low-cost AIS transducers and thus triggered recreational mariners to invest in the AIS technology for their vessels. A third class is a receive-only AIS, meaning you can see information about them, they can't see you.

The transmitting AIS units (A and B) require a GPS transponder unit to collect your GPS position in order to transmit.

The video in the QR code to the right is an excellent summary of the AIS technology.

AIS

Radar

Radar stands for **Ra**dio **D**irection **a**nd **R**anging. The acronym was coined by the U.S. Navy in the 1940s, just prior to the U.S. entering World War II.

Radar Animation

While the electronics of radar are pretty complicated the principle is quite simple. When you send out a signal and measure the time (t) for an echo to come back, the distance (D) to the object reflecting the signal is found by:

$$D = c \times t/2$$

Where c = the speed of the signal. And in the case of radio waves, c = the speed of light = 299,792,458 m/sec.

It's pretty amazing that we have electronics that can measure time differences at those kinds of speeds. For example, if an object is 1 nautical mile (1852 m) away, the time for the reflection to come back is:

$$t = 2 \times D/c$$
$$= 2 \times 1852 / 299,792,458$$
$$= 12 \text{ microseconds}$$
$$= 12 \text{ millionths of 1 second}$$
$$= \text{wow!}$$

But even better than that, the electronics can distinguish things that are 10 meters apart from the time differential. Double wow!

With radar, you can "see" weather systems approaching, land masses, and other vessels even if you cannot see them. Just a note however: the Rules for Prevention of Collision at Sea DO NOT allow for the replacement of a visual look out with radar (or AIS for that matter).

Even if your vessel does not have radar, you can utilize weather radar information broadcast on the Internet with your handheld phone or tablet. If you see dark clouds, you are well advised to pull out your device and view the local weather radar.

Global Positioning System (GPS)

GPS stands for global positioning system. It uses a network of satellites in orbit. Although the GPS is used as a navigation device, it is also a form of communication to the vessel. Thus we include it here. It's pretty interesting stuff.

Deep Thoughts

Imagine if in the 1700s John Harrison gave Captain James Cook a few satellites and an iPad loaded with a Navionics app instead of a chronometer. Oh man! Cook would have probably taken about 20 minutes to master the concepts. Us? It'll take a little study.

Global Navigation Satellite Systems (GNSS)—Global Positioning Systems (GPS)—give navigators unique real-time tools, but there are a few things to learn before jumping in. Don't just assume that a GNSS will do the job for you once you're out there. Now's the place and time to understand the power of knowledge and the depth of information such a device can give to you.

A GPS receiver calculates its position by precisely measuring the time difference between specifically timed signals sent by GPS satellites high above the Earth.

Each satellite continuously transmits data messages that include:

- The time the message was transmitted, and
- Satellite position when the message was transmitted.

The receiving unit uses the time differences between the messages from each satellite. From this, it determines the transit time of each message and thus computes the distance to each satellite using the speed of light. These distances are used to compute the location of the receiver using spherical geometry equations.

Basic GPS measurements yield only a position, not speed or direction. However, most GPS units can automatically derive velocity and direction of movement from two or more position measurements over time.

Notice from the above that the device on your vessel does not communicate back to the satellite. The information received from the satellite: time of day and satellite location is sufficient.

A final wonder in regard to this whole concept is that we have instruments that can measure difference in distance using light traveling this fast. It's incredible and kudos go to all the engineers (and begrudgingly the politicians) who made all this possible—and as a free service to the world.

Satellites in Orbit

Practical Navigation with GPS

Today, it is probable that in addition to your main chart plotter, you will have multiple other GPS devices on your vessel, things like phone and tablet devices. So reliability and redundancy is high. Additionally, there are multiple satellites being used. The more satellites the device can see, the more confidence in the accuracy of the position. A GPS device will allow you to see how many satellites it is seeing and will thus give you its own confidence value. This value is called the Horizontal Dilution of Precision (HDOP).

It is unlikely that multiple satellites go offline at the same time. So given all the above, it is reasonably safe to say that relying on GPS navigation is a sane(*ish*) thing to do. HOWEVER, given that you can't breathe water, it is NOT prudent to rely solely on GPS for the following reasons:

- GPS units can fail.
- Your batteries and thus recharging ability is down.
- Your aerials fail.
- You roll in a storm and everything is shorted out.
- There is a solar flare interruption of the satellite signals.
- You are struck by lightning and everything is fried (it happens).

In addition, the information stored in a GPS digital chart is only as good as the information originally entered. Older paper charts are scanned and digitized into a chart plotter. The accuracy of your information presented by the GPS will depend on the age of the charts.

Prudence means regularly maintaining a logbook of your positions, double checking your position on a paper chart, and using visual aids of landmarks, buoys, depth soundings, and oil platforms, for example. At sea, a prudent captain will contact passing container ships for a double check of position.

Knowledge of both paper charts and how to use them combined with electronic chart information is the wise thing to do.

GPS and the Speed of Light

Galileo is often credited with being the first scientist to try to determine the speed of light, in 1638. His method was quite simple. He and an assistant each had lamps that could be covered and uncovered at will. Galileo would uncover his lamp, and as soon as his assistant saw the light he would uncover his. By measuring the elapsed time until Galileo saw his assistant's light and knowing how far apart the lamps were, Galileo reasoned he should be able to determine the speed of the light. His conclusion: "If not instantaneous, it is extraordinarily rapid." Galileo deduced that light travels at least ten times faster than sound.

(Source credit http://www.speed-light.info/measure/speed_of_light_history.htm)

The speed of light was further refined over the centuries. In 1862, Leon Foucault determined the speed of light was 299,796 km/s. Today the adopted speed of light is 299,792.458 km/s—only 4 km/s different from Foucault.

Simplified: How GPS Works

It's pretty simple really. Place three people around the edge of a duck pond at known angles from each other. Each holds one end of a piece of string with the other end tied to a rubber duck. By knowing the length of each piece of string you could very accurately determine the duck's exact and *unique* position inside that circle.

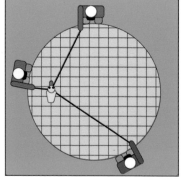

How a GPS Works

With GPS, the length of string is the time it takes for the signal to get from a satellite to you. By knowing the time traveled for at least three satellite signals, the software inside the device can accurately calculate your unique position on Earth at the particular moment in time. One second later the same calculation can be done and a new position established. Armed with this information, the device can report speed and direction findings.

Electronic Charts

Lesson Number One: Sailing instruments do not replace a sailor's natural senses; they help only to enhance and validate them.

GPS charts use the same data accuracy concept as computers, but keep in mind the concept of GIGO, which stands for Garbage In Garbage Out. Initially, when digital data first came on the scene, digital maps were created from paper charts and paper charts were created from the latest information available. Going back a few more years, charts had serpents and giant squid—these could equally have been digitized. Remember that your digital charts are only a representation of known information—not all information. In some cases, chart information still exists based on sextant celestial navigation information from way back. For example, we know where the Kingdom of Tonga is, but are the positions of rocks and reefs known around Tonga exactly within 6 feet?

Today, many coastal areas ARE accurately charted using high-tech hydrographic equipment. Airplanes beaming red and green lasers down into the waters can digitally document with ridiculous accuracy the landscape of the bottom. Red lasers bounce off the surface and green lasers bounce off the bottom. The time differential tells the depth. Using this method, a pass by an airplane at 250 knots can digitize a swath of coastline 250 meters wide. The data collected is hundreds of terabytes, detailing rocks the size of a basketball on the bottom. This data is then reduced to create a very accurate chart. The trouble is, we don't know if the digital chart we are using was created from a paper chart with serpents or from lasers.

A Plane from the Australian Hydrographic Office Gathers Depth Data

Hydrographic Office Airplane

Another example to keep in mind was an accident report of a yacht hitting a long pier at night. It wasn't on the digital chart. The pier was built after the yachtsman had updated his digital charts. And think of a recent sunken vessel that is not on the charts. It is thus prudent to keep watch as well as checking your charts.

Interesting Question

Here's a situation from a recent bareboat charter trip to St. Vincent and Bequia Island in the Caribbean: Pick which of the following statements is true.

1. We got up enough speed to ram right over the top of an island.
2. There is a giant tunnel through this island.
3. The island doesn't exist but is shown on the digital charts. See below.

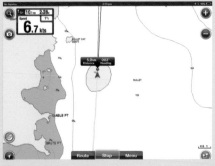

Electronic Navigation Error

The truth is the island does not exist and for purposes of this exercise and our electronic navigation discussions, I purposely steered the boat right through it. There was no change in depth as we went through it. It is not named nor does it have a height listed on the chart, but all the other islands do list a height.

Ultimately we must also be cognizant that electronically stored information is subject to failure because of lightning strikes, coffee spills, a knock down, battery failure, hard drive failures, aerial failures, solar flares, satellite failures, and much more. A lot can go wrong with disastrous consequences if you're not thinking. So always make sure that you back up your positions on paper in your logbook and on the chart.

Chapter 9
Navigation

Introduction

The history of navigation is fascinating and dates back to as many centuries as we can imagine.

Padrão dos Descobrimentos

Above is Padrão dos Descobrimentos (Monument to the Discoveries) in Lisbon, Portugal. The monument is dedicated to Henry the Navigator and the other discoverers of the 15th and 16th centuries who opened the trade routes to India and the Orient.

The Duke of Viseu, better known as Henry the Navigator, opened what is known today as the Age of Discoveries. Henry was son of the Portuguese King

John I and was responsible for the early development of Portuguese exploration and maritime trade with other continents through his planned and gradually expanding exploration of Western Africa and the islands of the Atlantic Ocean as he searched for new and faster route to the wonders of the Far East.

Today with Google maps in our pocket, we can't even conceive what these brave souls went through every day.

Years ago, the French mathematician and philosopher René Descartes cleverly invented a way of locating points on a flat surface. He simply drew two perpendicular lines, called them the x- and y-axis and then put a scale of numbers on each axis.

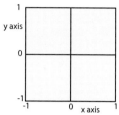

Cartesian Coordinates

Descartes showed how convenient and powerful it is to locate a point in a plane (flat surface) by using a set of two numbers—called the x and y coordinates. This arrangement became known as the Cartesian coordinate system and because it linked geometry and algebra, mathematics was forever changed.

If you wish to locate a point in space you need a third coordinate for depth. This is known as the z-axis.

Everyone is familiar with using a tourist street map in which a pair of coordinates—often a letter and a number—is given for any point you wish to locate. For example, you might see in a street map index that 100 Sir Edmund Hillary street is at coordinates A-6.

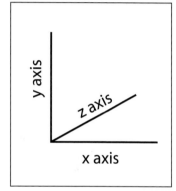

Three Dimensional Coordinates

Airplanes and submarines use three sets of numbers because they need to depth or altitude to identify their exact location in three dimensions.

A pair of coordinates also assists in surface navigation for sailors. However, there is a problem with Cartesian coordinates: the globe is round, not flat.

Early cartographers quickly realized that since the Earth is round, putting information from a sphere onto a flat piece of paper created distortions. They needed another system.

The major difference in locating points on a flat surface and a round surface like the globe is that on a flat surface, distance can go on indefinitely, while on a spherical surface you keep going around and around. Thus, there has to be a slightly new set of rules that allow unique coordinates to continue to work. These involve equators, meridian lines, hemispheres, and poles for example.

Maps commonly used for navigating are Mercator projections. Named after Gerardus Mercator, a Flemish geographer, who developed a system in 1569 that is still used by sailors today: latitude and longitude coordinates.

Navigation Units

Sailors are forever measuring stuff. This brings us to the subject of navigation units. As we all remember from the good ol' school days, measurement is the process of comparing something with an established standard. How these various standards were initially derived often makes for interesting reading.

Most measurement units have evolved over time as technology advanced. Many of the so-called English units of distance measurement are related to human body parts—for example, the foot. These units have associated seemingly random numbers for incremental measurements—12 inches per foot; 3 feet per yard; 5,280 feet per statutory mile (which is different from a nautical mile). Be tolerant of these colorful units of measure; they have a rich history representing the evolution of humans and sailing.

Metric units were developed based on the distance between the Earth's equator and the North Pole and the fact that the human hand has 10 fingers, which created the decimal system. Thus a major feature and advantage of the metric measurement units is that they are based on the decimal system; this makes for simple computations: 1000 millimeters (mm) in a meter (m); 100 centimeters (cm) in a meter; 1000 meters is a kilometer (km). A liter of water measures 10 cm by 10 cm by 10 cm and weighs 1 kilogram (kg) (on Earth); 1000 liters of water weighs 1000 kg which is 1 metric tonne. And just by universal coincidence, objects accelerate toward the Earth at 10 m/sec/sec (9.81 actually, but who's counting?).

Air (weather) and water (seas) share many physical measurement units, including pressure, velocity, currents, temperature, directions, density, and cloudiness. These units evolved as measurement requirements became more critical and better instruments were invented. Some are highly technical terms while others are more familiar. Never be afraid to ask for the definition of words or concepts you do not understand.

Since we will use these terms throughout the book, we begin with a few common definitions. Keep in mind that many of today's units of measure were in use long before the highly sophisticated scientific measurement tools that now exist. Also, keep in mind that measurements are always approximations.

- Statute mile—our common "road mile" is 5,280 feet. It is an arbitrary unit used only in the United States and Libya these days. It is about 1.6 km. You may know that the length of a foot was based on actual human feet—how accurate can that be?

- Nautical mile (nm)—6,076 feet, 1852 m (1.15 times the length of a statute mile). The cool thing about a nautical mile is that a nautical mile represents 1 minute of latitude. If you add up 60 minutes of latitude you make up 1 degree. Therefore, every degree of latitude represents 60 nautical miles going in true north/south direction. **The nautical mile is the standard unit of distance measurement for marine navigation today and is used on all marine charts**.
- Lines of latitude are imaginary horizontal parallel lines that circle the Earth. Each line is equidistant in a vertical direction from the others at all points around the globe. Thus each circle going north or south away from the equator is smaller in diameter until you get to the North or South pole where the circle becomes a dot.
- Note: Longitude lines are not equidistant. They start at the poles and fan at equal angles from each other then come together at the opposing pole. Longitude lines are farthest from each other at the equator. Thus longitude lines cannot be used for distance measurement in the same manner as latitude lines. 1 minute of longitude in a horizontal direction is most definitely not 1 nautical mile. You might suppose they might be at the equator due to the Earth being a ball, but the Earth is not perfectly spherical.
- Knot—a measurement of speed. 1 knot is equivalent to one nautical mile per hour. It is approximately 1.15 times faster than 1 statute (road) mile per hour. In early times, the speed of the boat was determined by letting out a rope with a board attached to the end. The board would stop in the water while the boat carried on moving. The navigator would count how many equidistant knots slipped through the hand before a 28 second sand timer emptied. Can you figure out the distance between the knots?

Original Knot Meter—on exhibit at Museu De Marinha, Lisbon

- 1 knot is about 2 km/hr (1.85 actually). This is good conversion to remember; it makes for an easy conversion when thinking about wind speeds. For example, 50 km/hr is close to 25 knots (might want to throw a reef in the sail).

- The metric meter is 39.37 inches, that is, it is close enough to a yard (actually 3.37 inches longer than a yard).
- The kilometer is a 1,000 meters or 3,280.8 feet or about 0.6 of a mile. 100 kilometers per hour is about 60 miles per hour. Did you know that it is about 10,000 kilometers from the equator to any one of the poles? That's convenient!
- A meter is 1000 millimeters.
- A fathom is 6 feet. Thus 1 fathom is close enough to 2 meters. Fathoms are very often used on charts to express the water's depth. We say often because many times it is not. Check the key on every chart before using it.
- Time: Universally measured in hours, minutes, and seconds. The time unit is now quite precisely measured using decaying radioactive materials. Chronometers (the common watch of today) were developed for marine navigation. One of the most famous chronometers, named H4, was developed by John Harrison in the 1700s. It is indeed a work of art. Harrison gave it to James Cook, who used in on his second and third circumnavigations in the 1770s. Cook praised it as being the future of navigation.

- Furlong—220 yards. You'll never use this so just forget it instantly, unless you're a horse racing fan.
- Fortnight—14 days. Just for fun,100,000 furlongs per fortnight is about 37 miles per hour.

Harrison's H4 on Display in the National Maritime Museum, Greenwich

Anyway, in summary for the American palate, and not to trivialize, but a nautical mile is a bit more than a statutory mile; a meter is a bit more than a yard; a kilometer is a bit over half a nautical mile.

Wikipedia discusses the history of the nautical mile and other interesting facts.

Nautical Mile History

Summary

Measurement is one of the most critical aspects of sailing (as well as flying and driving). Most of us are familiar with approximations, which generally serve us well, but to navigate precisely, when conditions call for it, it is imperative that we understand both measuring instruments and the units they use.

Latitude and Longitude

The latitude and longitude coordinate system is the key navigational concept for sailing. It is the mariner's coordinate system.

To express latitude and longitude, we use units of measurement called degrees and fractions of degrees. Recall from your math class that there are 360 degrees in a circle. Why? It comes from the original thought that the Earth took 360 days to rotate around the sun. Pity it did not take 100 days—this would have made school geometry much easier; but that may have created other evolutionary complications, so just go with 360 and be thankful.

Each degree is subdivided into 60 minutes of angle and each minute is subdivided into 60 seconds of angle. You will note similarities with the way we tell time.

1 circle = 360 degrees
1 degree = 60 minutes (of angle/distance, not time)
1 minute = 60 seconds (of angle/distance, not time)
How many seconds of angle are there in 1 circle?

Typically, instead of expressing degrees, minutes, and seconds, a coordinate is expressed in degrees and minutes with the minutes expressed as a decimal point. For example, 17 degrees 10 minutes 30 seconds is more often expressed as 17 degrees 10.5 minutes.

The North and South Pole

If you took a stick and jammed it down through the Earth about the axis where it spins, those points where it enters and exits are the poles. They are fixed in space on our planet. Have been and always will be. Thus, the cartographers were wise to choose these points as the basis for setting up the planetary coordinate system.

Latitude

Lines of latitude are man-made lines and can be thought of as circles going around the Earth that are parallel to the equator. Thus the circles get smaller in circumference as they near each pole. By their nature then, to jump directly north or south from one latitude circle anywhere on the planet to the next latitude circle is the same distance.

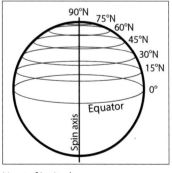

Lines of Latitude

The one non-man-made latitude line is the equator. This is universally ordained and defined from the axis of spin. Cartographers set the equator to be 0 degrees of latitude and since the poles are 90 degrees around the sphere, the poles became 90 degrees North of the equator and 90 degrees south of the equator.

A cool thing about latitude is that it defines the distance unit of a nautical mile on our planet. Ninety degrees of latitude on the surface of Earth is equivalent to the distance from the equator to the North or South Pole. One degree of latitude then is defined as 1/90th of the surface distance from the equator to the North or South Pole. Since degrees are divided into 60 minutes of angle as above, it was cleverly decided that 1 nautical mile should equal 1 minute of latitude. This is by definition not by coincidence. How many nautical miles are there from the equator to the North Pole then? 90 x 60 = 5400.

Remember this:

- 1 minute of latitude = 1 nautical mile
- 1 degree of latitude = 60 nautical miles

The easy way to remember which way latitude goes is that the "lat" in latitude rhymes with "flat," which is a horizontal line going around the Earth.

Longitude

Lines of longitude may be thought of as lines running around the surface of the Earth starting at the North Pole, going directly to the South Pole and back up the other side of the planet to the North Pole again. Thus, these lines are really circles.

The lines are obviously not parallel, but all have the same circumference. These imaginary lines are lines of longitude or meridians. Since they converge at the poles, their separation varies from the equator to the pole. Thus, it is imperative to understand that distance between lines of longitude cannot be used for any form of distance measuring.

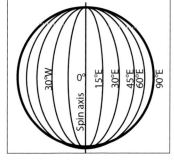

Lines of Longitude

Great Circles

A "great circle" is a circle on the Earth's surface whose plane passes through the center of the Earth. They are like longitude except they do not have to pass through the two poles. The shortest distance between two points on the Earth's surface is an arc that lies on a great circle. This is why when a plane flies from Chicago to Narita, Japan, or New York to New Delhi, it flies close to the North Pole instead of a straight line on a flat world map. The North Pole route lies on a great circle and represents the shortest distance for the plane to fly. All longitude lines are "great circles" since their plane passes through the center of the Earth. Latitude lines do not. You will use this information if you ever start sailing long distances.

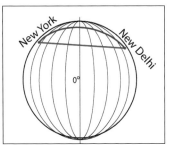

Traveling on a Great Circle Line

Since the Earth is round, we must decide which of the infinite number of lines of longitude should be the beginning line; the zero degree longitude line. Years ago, the British decided that the line of longitude running through Greenwich, England would be the beginning, and so they named it the prime meridian.

As we sail around the world, in either easterly or westerly direction, we can identify our location by the number of degrees and minutes that we are away from this prime meridian. For example, longitude 65° 35.8′ W means we are west of the prime meridian by 65 degrees and 35.8 minutes. Similarly, longitude 65° 35.8′ E means we are east of the prime meridian by 65 degrees 35.8 minutes.

Prime Meridian in Greenwich

So there you have it—given longitude (stated in degrees east or west) and latitude (stated in degrees north or south) you can locate any point on the surface of the Earth. That point is unique; no other point on the surface of the Earth has those coordinates.

Understanding this pair of numbers is the key to naval navigation.

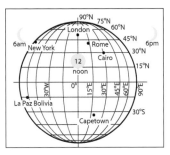

Latitude and Longitude on Earth

The following shows latitude and longitude laid out on a sphere (the Earth) with several key world cities placed. At this instance, it is noon in London, 7:00 a.m. in New York, and on the other side of the planet, say Auckland, New Zealand, (36 degrees 52 minutes south/174 degrees 45 minutes east), it is midnight.

What's cool about longitude is that it helps us with time. A day is defined by a full rotation through 360 degrees of our planet. This takes place in exactly 24 hours. Our time zones then (disregarding political intervention) follow every 360/24 = 15 degrees of longitude. Thus, if it is noon where you are and it is 6:00 a.m. where I am, then I must be 6 x 15 = 90 degrees of longitude to the west of you = 1/4 of the way around the planet.

As an example, say I knew it was 6:00 p.m. in London but the sun just apexed overhead where I am, then I know my longitude will be 90 degrees west.

An amazing, clear, and fun book to read on the subject is *Longitude*, by Dava Sobel. It describes how sailors came to accurately determine their longitude. It wasn't until the King of England offered a £10,000 reward for the first person to be able to accurately position a vessel within 1/2 degree in the early 1700s did the challenge really get taken up. The answer wasn't discovered until the 1760s.

After you have read this book, take a trip to Greenwich, England. It's a 20 minute train ride from London and there you can see the zero degree meridian (the prime meridian) line for yourself. While you are there visit the National Maritime Museum, and a quick sampling of the local pubs around Greenwich doesn't hurt either.

Longitude Book

Surface Geometry

Below is a brief summary of how locations are commonly expressed on different surfaces.

- Plane Surface (flat)—Two numerical coordinates (x and y) for locating objects in a plane
- Space (3 dimensions)—Three numerical coordinates (x, y, and z) for locating objects in space
- Earth's surface (curved surface)—Use latitude and longitude
  - Latitude (North or South of the equator)—expressed in degrees
  - Longitude (East or West of the prime meridian)—expressed in degrees
  - Additionally, airplanes use latitude and longitude and altitude

Aids to Navigation (ATONS)

Aids to Navigation include buoys, lights, lighthouses, and markers, among others.

Lateral Mark

A lateral buoy, also called a lateral post or lateral mark, is defined by the International Association of Lighthouse Authorities (IALA) as a sea mark used in maritime pilotage to indicate the edge of a channel. The red and green shapes are called either a Nun or a Can depending on their color and part of the world they are used.

Each mark indicates the edge of the safe water channel in terms of port (left-hand) or starboard (right-hand).

A vessel heading into a harbor and wishing to keep in the main channel should:

- keep port marks to its port (left) side, and
- keep starboard marks to its starboard (right) side.

And obviously a vessel heading out of a harbor should proceed opposite to the above.

For aid of memory, it is prudent to learn only what you should do when entering a harbor. Then you just apply the opposite when exiting. The last thing you want to do is to get flustered at night and try to remember which is which. Just learn one of the entering-harbor mnemonics presented below.

Sometimes lateral marks are not necessarily used solely in a harbor. They are also used in a river or coastal waterway. Logically for rivers, the upstream direction is treated the same as entering a harbor. For coastal waterways you need to check the chart as to determine which way is considered "returning."

International Association of Marine Aids to Navigation and Lighthouse Authorities (IALA) had adopted two systems, IALA-A and IALA-B, whereby the colors are swapped.

The USA and all the Americas, the Caribbean, North Korea, Philippines, and Japan use the IALA-B system. The rest of the world uses IALA-A. (Who could have guessed?)

The following is a guide to understanding the Aids to Navigation in the IALA-B system. If you are under IALA-A then just learn the opposite colors (colours).

Essentially, for IALA-A and IALA-B, the colors are swapped (but not the shapes) for entrances into harbors/

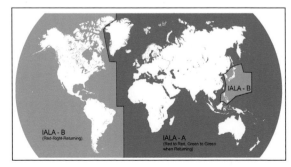

IALA Regions

harbours. The reason is said to be that the Americans during the War for Independence wanted to confuse the British ships and so swapped the colors.

You absolutely must learn the difference between IALA-A and IALA-B and where they are used—particularly if you are chartering in various parts of the world. But don't worry, they are easy. All you have to do is remember the mnemonic **"Red, Right, Returning"** under the IALA-B system. That's it! So, for example, under IALA-B, when you are returning from sea into the channel (or going upstream) keep the red markers on your right. In the case of the preferred channel, take notice of whatever color is on top. That is, if red is on top, keep the marker on your right for the preferred channel. Red Right Returning! Right?

If you live in under the IALA-A system then just remember **Red to Red and Green to Green** when returning. So when you are returning from sea into the channel (or going upstream), keep the green markers facing your green light and the red markers facing your red light. Our advice is to only learn one of these that suits you best. Then just apply the opposite logic/mnemonic when visiting a different IALA system.

Shapes of Lateral Marks

Lateral marks have shapes as shown below. A mnemonic to remember the shapes and colors for IALA-B that is commonly used is "even nuns blush red." Meaning nuns have even numbers and are the red lateral mark. Nuns have a cone shape or triangle shape pointing up. Consequently, under IALA-B the green lateral mark is called a can and are numbered with odd numbers. Cans have a square top.

Again, learn what you are used to in your local area and swap colors but not shapes when

IALA-B System
(for IALA - A system use opposite colors)

Keep These Aids on Your Port Side
Upon Returning
(Odd Numbered Aids)

Lighted Buoy   Day Marker   Can

Keep These Aids On Your Starboard Side
Upon Returning
(Even Numbered Aids)

Lighted Buoy   Day Marker   Nun

For Preferred Channel, Keep These Aids On Your
Starboard Side Upon Returning
(No Numbers - May be Lettered)

Lighted Buoy   Day Marker   Nun

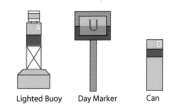

For Preferred Channel, Keep These Aids On Your
Port Side Upon Returning
(No Numbers - May be Lettered)

Lighted Buoy   Day Marker   Can

Lateral Marks

you travel to a different IALA region. Use the above to determine what color and shape is a return port lateral mark in IALA-A and IALA-B.

Safe Water Marks

One type of safe water mark is shown below, but there are other shapes as well—they are usually characterized by white and red vertical marks. They are not numbered but may be lettered. The letters have no significance other than individual identification.

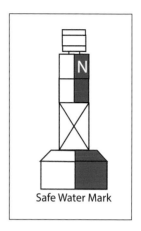

Safe Water Mark

Special Purpose Marks

Special purpose marks are yellow and are used to mark such areas as anchorages, dredging and survey operations, and fishnet areas. They vary in shape from cans to balls to day boards.

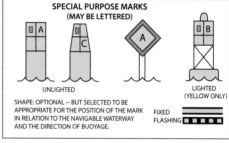

Mooring Buoys

Mooring buoys are white with a blue stripe. If they are lighted, they exhibit a fixed white light.

Isolated Danger

Isolated danger marks bear a black strip on top of a red strip. They may be lettered for individual identification. The chart marks show "BR" (for black red) followed by the letter designation if it exists.

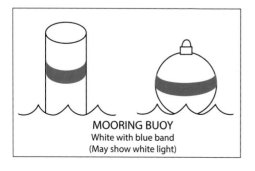

MOORING BUOY
White with blue band
(May show white light)

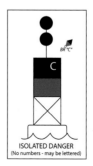

ISOLATED DANGER
(No numbers - may be lettered)

Bifurcated Lateral Mark

In the case where a channel may split, the preferred channel is has green and red horizontal bands. To follow the preferred channel, ignore the color of the lower band. For example, if red is the band on top, then pretend that the entire lateral mark is red. If returning from sea under IALA-B you would keep it to right. Right?

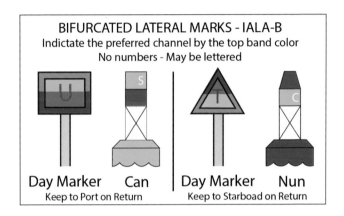

Putting It All Together

The diagram in the QR code is a simple example of how you might navigate a channel in an IALA-B area.

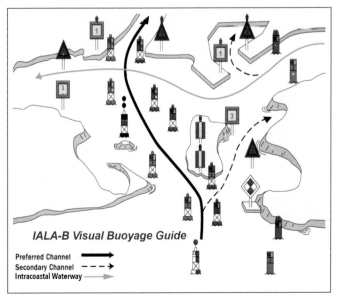

Daytime Channel

And again—if you live in or plan to visit an IALA-A area, then just swap these colors. Don't stress too much—there used to be 30 different systems worldwide until the formation of IALA and international acceptance.

Cardinal Marks

Various countries also use cardinal marks. While not prevalent in the USA, you will see them in other places, including the Caribbean.

Cardinal marks tell you on which side there is safe passage around a hazard. For example, a North Cardinal mark will tell you to pass to the north of the mark for safe passage.

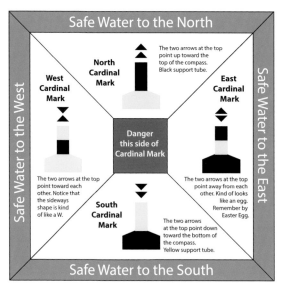

Cardinal Marks

Lights on ATONS

Lights are installed on *some* ATONS. The lights are usually alternating on and off on some consistent interval to distinguish one ATON from another. The series of "ons" and "offs" are listed on the charts. This helps identify exactly which ATON you are observing. The time between each series is called a "period."

Lighted ATONs are grouped into Flashing, Quick, Occulting, and Isophase.

- **Flashing:** A light in which the total duration of light in each period is clearly shorter than the total duration of darkness—and in which the flashes of light are all equal in duration.
- Example: a quick flash on then a longer period off.

- Example: the flashes might be grouped meaning that the ATON flashes quickly a number of times followed by a longer period of dark then repeating.
- **Quick Light:** A light turning on more than 60 (but less than 80 flashes) per minute.
- **Occulting:** Showing longer periods of light than darkness (opposite of flashing)
- **Isophase:** Showing equal periods of light and darkness—remember that «iso» means same.
- **A Long Flash:** (L Fl.) A light which exhibits a long flash of 2 seconds followed by a period of longer darkness.
- **Morse Code:** (Mo. (letter)) A Morse coded letter.

Colors of lights are listed with the ATON. They are red (R), green (G), yellow (Y), and white (W). Blue is reserved for law enforcement. If there is no color listed then it is white.

Examples of the various types are shown below

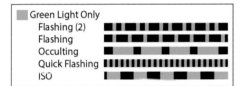

Green Flashing Lights

Red Flashing Lights

There can also be a composite group flashing light. This means that more than a group of flashes make up one signal. For example, in the example below the green light flashes twice then once—then repeats after some time.

Green Composite Group Flashing (2+1)

Composite Lights

You can identify the lights on the charts from the information next to the light. In the example below, the Bifurcated Lateral Maker "U" flashes composite green twice then once every 6 seconds—Fl G (2+1) 6s, while the Green Lateral Can number "9" flashes green twice every 6 seconds—Fl G (2) 6s.

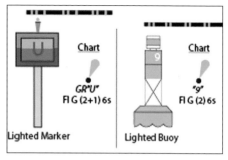

Lights Shown on Charts

At night, you'll be able to pick out the lights against their backdrop of city lights because of their alternating nature. In the example below you can see green and red lights. In a real situation, you have to concentrate on one at a time, so that the other does not distract you.

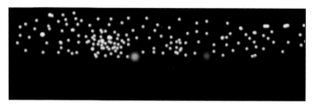

Example of Lights at Night

Caution Lights

In most countries, including the USA, the white quick flashing light is used to mark Cautionary ATONS.

Safe Water Marks

In many countries, including the USA, the Safe Water mark is used and is a white flashing Morse code "A". This is represented as one short followed by one long and then repeating at least 8 times per minute. Just remember A—ok.

A long 2-second flash over a 10-second period (L Fl. 10s) is specifically reserved for a safe water mark. But also, a safe water mark can be exhibited by other white lights as shown specifically on the chart.

Special Purpose Marks

If a Special Purpose buoy is lighted it displays a yellow light with fixed or slow flashing characteristics.

Isolated Danger Marks

If an Isolated Danger mark is lighted, a white light shall be used and the chart will announce the flashing sequence. The image below shows Fl (2) 5s, but this is just an example. Anytime you see a white flashing light you should be on guard. It is either safe or danger. Consult the chart immediately.

Sector Lights

Sector lights are sectors of color that are placed on lantern covers of certain lighthouses to indicate danger bearings. On a chart the sector bearings are true bearings according to the chart and must be converted from magnetic bearing if using a compass. A red sector indicates a vessel is potentially in danger of running aground. Note however, that red can be seen beyond the danger zone as well.

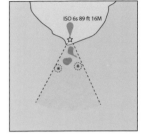

Sector Light

This is also seen here below in a real case of Nautical Chart #12354 Long Island Sound Eastern Port. Can you spot the Red Sector light?

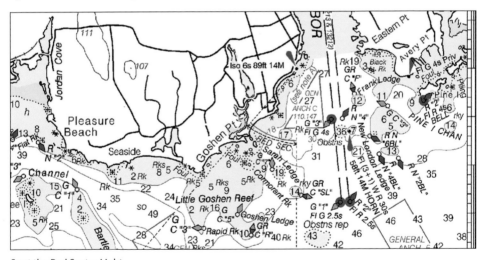

Spot the Red Sector Light

Cardinal Mark Lights

Cardinal Marks if lighted use white quick flash lights. They are easily remembered from thinking of a clock dial.

- North: Continuous quick flash
- East: 3 quick flashes (3 o'clock)

- South: 6 quick flashes followed by a long flash (6 o'clock)
- West: 9 quick flashes (9 o'clock)

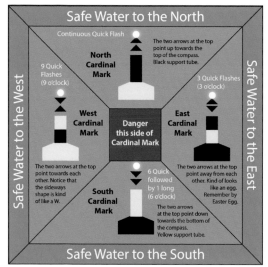

Cardinal Marks at Night

Light Lists

Publications that list all the lights usually exist for each country. In the United States the Coast Guard publishes the Light List, which can be found at http://www.navcen.uscg.gov/?pageName=lightlists

USA Light List

For your country, or the country you are visiting, just search on "coast guard light list (country)" or "navigation light list (country)."

Below is an excerpt. Each ATON is listed by number (from the index at the back of the light list), its name, and any distinguishing location, its latitude and longitude position, its characteristic, height (if it is a lighthouse), the range that the light can be seen from, the type of structure and any remarks about the light.

No.	Name and Location	Position	Characterisitc	Height	Range	Structure	Remarks
	Fox Island Thorofare						
3860	- Buoy 2A	44-07-54.801N 068-46-41.106W				Red nun.	
3865	- Buoy 2 South of shoal.	44-07-51.162N 068-48-05.977W				Red nun.	
3870	- Bell Buoy 4 Southeast from rock.	44-07-44.791N 068-48-28.719W				Red.	
3875	Channel Rock Daybeacon 4A	44-07-48.000N 068-48-30.000W				TR on iron spindle.	
3880	- Buoy 5 East of shoal.	44-07-52.901N 068-49-27.145W				Green can.	
3885	**Goose Rocks Light** On ledge.	44-08-07.500N 068-49-50.400W	Fl R 6s	51	11 W 12	White conical tower, black cylindrical foundation. 51	White sector from 301° to 304°. HORN: 1 blast ev 10s (1s bl).

USGC Light List Excerpt

Light List

Putting It All Together

The graphic below shows charted lights at a fictitious harbor entrance.

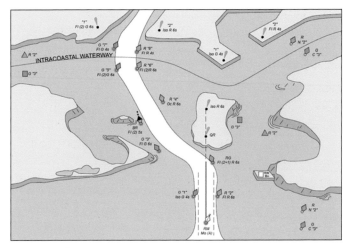

Lights on a Chart

Finally, here is a webpage which repeats the above information but with real animated flashing lights so that you can get the feel for what they really look like.

Animated Lights on Navigation Marks

The Nautical Chart

Safely maneuvering a vessel while using positions derived from various coastal and near coastal sources is called coastal navigation. These sources include buoys, markers, identifiable objects on shore, various points of land, radio beacons, and depth soundings as examples. The basis for all navigation is the nautical chart. These are categorized upon the amount of detail necessary—from very highly detailed harbor charts to those used offshore with very little detail.

Chart Briefing in Athens Greece

Charts for coastal navigation include:

1. Harbor charts that show conformations very clearly with great detail are the best source of information used to enter an unfamiliar harbor area.

2. Coastal charts, also called "large-scale charts," are useful for navigating along the shore and into the larger bays or harbors. They illustrate the local coastline features of a relatively small area in great detail, and enable movement between adjacent cities along the coast.

3. General charts, also called "small scale charts," illustrate a portion of the coastal area, with only larger objects on shore and lighted objects being identified. They are used by sailors navigating more extensive distances along the coast or when sailing to coastal islands.

4. Sailing charts used for offshore navigation are very small scale (1:3,500,000*). These show only ocean and land masses that border them. Water depths are available for regions of ocean and near coasts, but only major navigational lights (lighthouses, etc.) are available. They are designed to get us across oceans; we refer to larger scale charts as we approach the coasts.

*This would mean that 1 meter on the chart covers 3,500 km in distance. How much would 1 cm cover?

Positioning

All nautical charts display latitude, shown vertically on the left and right sides of the chart, and longitude, shown horizontally on the top and bottom of the chart. Latitude is also expressed with a North or South designation from the equator and longitude is always expressed with an East or West designation from the prime meridian. Remember that the prime meridian is a vertical line from the South Pole to the North Pole passing through Greenwich, England.

To help imagine this spatially, remember that any position in the northern hemisphere carries a north (N) latitude designation and in the southern hemisphere carries a south (S) latitude designation—that's easy!

Anything west of Greenwich and continuing in a westerly direction (<—that way) until about the middle of the Pacific Ocean to 180 degrees longitude, carries a west (W) longitude designation. This includes Ireland, Iceland, Greenland, the Americas, and Tahiti. Anything east of Greenwich and continuing in an easterly direction (—> that way) until about the middle of the Pacific to 180 degrees longitude, carries an East (E) longitude designation. This includes Europe, most of Africa, all of Asia, Australia, and New Zealand.

For example, on the following chart, if you were at 41 degrees 21.3 minutes North and 71 degrees 04.78 minutes West, the only place on the planet you could be is at the Groton Monument on the east side of New London harbor.

What is the latitude and longitude the New London harbor outer channel lateral mark G"1" Fl G 2.5s?

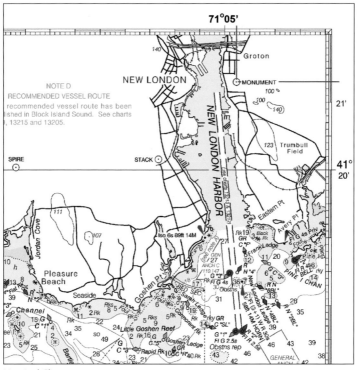

Nautical Chart

G"1" Fl G 2.5s is: Lat 41 deg 17.62 min N and Long 71 degrees 04.78 minutes W.

Updates

From the time that humankind first dipped toes in the water, charts have been made and updated. Today this is still an ongoing process. It is extremely important that you have the latest available chart. While rocks don't move very much, new wrecks are created, piers are built, channels are dredged or become in need of dredging, sandbanks shift, lights and buoys are moved, removed, and added, and positions on the charts are shifted from old celestial navigation positions to much more accurate GPS defined positions.

You would not want to be sailing at night thinking that all is clear because your GPS chart says all clear then suddenly crush into a new pier built last year.

Updates to charts are found on a Notices to Mariners—search under that chart number. The best advice is to check the publication date of your charts and compare to those available. The UK Hydrographic office and the USA NOAA Office of Coast Survey publish chart updates.

This paragraph is a repeat for emphasis. In this day and age, we almost expect that digital information is deadly accurate and is the latest and greatest. But if you've ever studied databases and programming, you're familiar with the term GIGO—"garbage in, garbage out." Many digital charts are created from scans of old paper charts. If that chart has old or inaccurate data then your beautiful chart plotter with incredible digital information can give you wrong, wrong, wrong information.

Check out me sailing through the middle of an island, that does not exist, east of Bequia Island in the Caribbean. This was a screenshot from a digital electronic chart plotter.

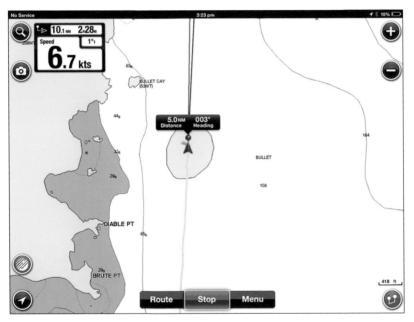

Nonexistent Island East of Bequia

Updates to electronic charts are often available. When you buy electronic charts, the company you buy from usually creates updates for download. Ensure you have the latest downloads of electronic charts.

True North versus Magnetic North

Chart directions are universally defined because of the spin axis of the Earth. That is, the directions are not made or defined by humans. A north direction is truly toward the point on Earth where the spin axis intersects the Earth's surface. Because of our celestial bodies it is highly convenient to define our north and south reference points this way.

Magnetic North is different from True North. The direction your compass points is independent (for the most part) from the spin axis of the Earth. Coincidently, it is close to the true North Pole. Like most planets, Earth has a magnetic field because of its iron core—as if a bar magnet at the Earth's core is sending out a magnetic field into space and circling back to the opposite pole. If it were not for this magnetic field, life as we know it would not be possible because the magnetic field protects us from the sun's radiation. The bar magnet is tilted permanently at about 10 degrees from the spin axis. But because of the motion of molten iron alloys in the outer core of the Earth, the surface pole of the magnetic field moves slowly over time. Currently, it is moving at about 60 kilometers per year and is relatively predictable from empirical data dating back hundreds of years. Thus, you will see listed on a chart the rate of change of the difference between True and Magnetic North.

When using a compass, it is important to realize that the north compass direction varies from the chart north direction and that this direction varies with your position on Earth. The difference between the chart True North and Magnetic North is known as the Variation.

For normal inhabitable places, the Variation ranges from 0 degrees to around 15 degrees. Of course as you approach the poles things go haywire. These Variations are well known and each chart will list the "Variation" between True North and Magnetic North. Thus, you simply apply this correction factor of Variation to your compass reading to find the chart direction or vice versa. The Variation will be listed as a certain degree amount and if the Variation is to be applied to the West or East.

The correction is simple and should not be intimidating. For example, suppose the chart tells you that the Variation is 7 degrees West. You simply ADD 7 degrees to your chart reading to get a magnetic compass reading. If the Variation is 7 degrees East, you simply SUBTRACT 7 degrees from your chart reading to get a magnetic compass reading.

Additionally, due to ferritic metal and electronics on a boat, the compass can be further distorted from True North. This factor is called Deviation and is also further discussed in Coastal Navigation courses.

These topics are more deeply explored in the NauticEd Coastal Navigation course.

Chart Symbols

Studying a harbor layout does very little good without understanding the symbols and what they signify. It pays to learn the symbols found on nautical charts.

These are widely available in an array of nautical books and on the reverse side of many charts. The most readily available and always up-to-date source is found from your maritime government; in the USA it is NOAA—Office of Coast Survey. This PDF downloadable book contains globally used symbols. The book is called **Chart No. 1: Symbols, Abbreviations and Terms.**

Download the Chart 1 on the Internet by going to: http://www.nauticalcharts.noaa.gov/mcd/chartno1.htm

Scan the QR code in the book image to get a spiral-bound hard copy on Amazon for $12 or so.

Chart 1 Symbols

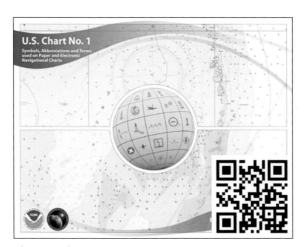

Chart 1 Book

Here is an iOS app for iPhone:

Chart1-iOSApp

Here is an Android app:

Chart1
AndroidApp

An example of the pages inside chart 1 is shown here. This is an excerpt from Section K.

K Rocks, Wrecks, and Obstructions

	General						
1		Danger line: A danger line draws attention to a danger which would not stand out clearly enough if represented solely by its symbol (e.g. isolated rock) or delimits an area containing numerous dangers, through which it is unsafe to navigate					
2	7₄	Swept by wire drag or diver	21 Rk	35 Rk	4₆ Obstn		‡ (15₇)
			4₆ Wk	4₆ Wk (1937)			
3	(20)	Depth unknown, but estimated to have a safe clearance to the depth shown	4₆ Wk	35 Rk	4₆ Obstn		
	Rocks						
	Plane of Reference for Heights → H			Plane of Reference for Depths → H			
10		Rock (islet) which does not cover, height above height datum	25	(21)			▲ (4 m)
11		Rock which covers and uncovers, height above chart datum	* (2)	(2)	4	+ Uncov 1m / Uncov 1m	⁘ ＊
12		Rock awash at the level of chart datum					⊛

Chart1 Section K Excerpt

View this animation, which takes you through some of the symbols and elements of a chart.

Chart 1

It is imperative that you not gloss over this section as you read, so we advise that you really gain access to Chart 1 now. Below we will take you through some of the more common symbols and give you a brief view into Chart 1.

Now look up the symbols on the following pages of Chart 1:

Chart Familiarization Animation

- C 13. Learn the heights of land.
- Not sure why Bridges are in Section D under Cultural Features—but they are. Check those out.

- F 14. Jetties and Piers.
- Peruse Sections H, I, and J to learn currents, depths, and bottom types.
- Pay particular attention to Section K—Rocks, Wrecks and Obstructions.
- View L 30.1 to see the submarine cable shown in the animation above.
- View M 10 through 18, then figure out the two examples of routing measures shown for paper and electronic charts.
- Study N 2 and N 12.
- Get a feel for Section P—Lights and Section Q—Buoys and Beacons. We'll go through these later. Study Q 130 in particular.
- Peruse R, S, and T.
- See that there is a list of abbreviations and an index at the end.
- Finish by viewing the Appendix.

Another Source of Information on Symbols

Admiralty Chart NP5011

Admiralty Chart NP5011 is the equivalent to the U.S. Chart 1 and is published by the UK Hydrographic office. Visit https://www.admiralty.co.uk

Know Your Chart

Always familiarize yourself with any chart before using it for navigation and plotting of positions; there are significant differences between charts that could lead to mistakes. Always check:

- Scale: Be certain you've selected the right chart for your purpose. There may be another sub-chart that shows more detail.
- The units in which depth soundings are measured—which also vary on different charts. Soundings can be in fathoms, meters, or feet. Be sure, for example, that when you're reading the number "5," it doesn't refer to 5 feet instead of 5 meters.
- Depth contours and colors: Color charts and electronic charts show shallow depth by color following a contour.
- The local Variation. This is the difference between Magnetic North and True North. Courses calculated need to take this into account. More on this later.

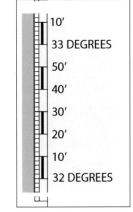

Latitude Scale Lines

- Increments of the latitude scale. The scale at the east and west edges is that of latitude, used to measure distance on a nautical chart. One minute of latitude = one nautical mile of distance. Be sure to understand what hash marks represent one minute on the latitude scale. The image on page 181 illustrates a latitude scale on which each small hash mark represents two minutes of latitude.

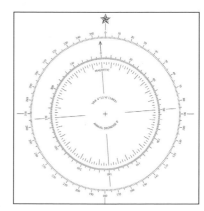

A Typical Compass Rose

- The **compass rose**, shown here, is an important feature of nautical charts. It is usually comprised of two concentric rings; the outer circle represents geographic True North, whereas the inner ring depicts magnetic directions that reflects local Variation and corresponds more closely with readings of the vessel's compasses. The Variation is usually given in the center of the rose.

Directions

Directions are given as zero through 359 degrees in clockwise direction. (360 = 0) relative to the North Pole.

- North (N) is 0 deg (= 360 deg)
- East (E) is 90 deg
- South (S) is 180 deg
- West (W) is 270 deg

There are various combinations of N, S, E, and W to divide the directions as shown. For example, NNE is 22.5 degrees. When someone is quoting a direction they will follow the number by T (True) or M (Magnetic) when in writing. When spoken use "True" and "Magnetic" sounded out—not "T" or "M". Details, but we're saving you from VHF embarrassment here.

See the compass rose below and also note how the designations of NSEW are listed. Note that it

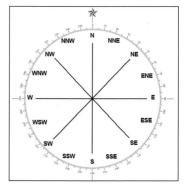

NSEW Direction Combinations

is, for example, NNE not NEN, and WSW, not WWS. The order of the letters is important and should be followed as such below.

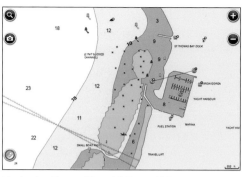

This chart below from Navionics of Spanish Town in the British Virgin Islands shows the shallow depths by colored contour lines. Green is usually represented by the Drying Depth, which means the area is above water

Navionics Chart of Spanish Town, BVI

at low tide. Blue often represents shallow. Light blue is less shallow. The depth of the contour line will be shown on the contour line; often in a different font than the font marking the actual depth.

Depths

Many charts will have a "Source Data" table listing areas of the chart and how the depth data was obtained. Surprisingly, you might still find charts where depth was obtained by lead lines and not by the far more accurate electronic depth sounders. The source and date of when the data was obtained is thus very important.

Navigation Tools

Tools commonly used for navigation include:

- Charts (of course). They are essential since they give you a visual orientation and features regarding the body of water you wish to sail. Charts are now available online, and are included as software in many navigation instruments.
- Dividers. This is a handy tool for measuring distances on a chart.
- Magnifying devices for reading small print, especially in subdued light.
- Compass. In spite of GPS the compass is still a major navigational tool.
- Parallel rulers used for moving lines on charts.
- Drawing triangles.
- Course protractor (Breton plotter is one example).

No matter the chart in use, the navigator's work largely involves determination of direction and distances. The most useful tools for actual chart work are:

Parallel Rulers

The parallel ruler is thought by many to be the most important tool of this trade. It is used to draw course lines, determine direction, and transfer course headings from the compass rose to the desired location on a chart. Scan the code to see a video of a parallel ruler in use.

Parallel Ruler Video

In the video, we want to establish the magnetic heading from one ATON to another. The parallel rules are set on the course and then that course is transferred to the compass rose. The rule is "walked" to the center of the compass rose and a line drawn to the inner rose. In this instance the course reveals 300 deg magnetic. Additionally the rose reveals that the variation between true and magnetic is 15 deg west in this part of the world, which translates to a true heading of 300 – 15 = 285 deg True, which is also shown on the outer dial of the compass rose. The compass rose is marked so that the inner dial shows magnetic while the outer dial shows true.

Parallel rulers are also used to place a known location on the chart. Given a lat/long position from a GPS, the rulers can transmit the latitude from the vertical edge the chart, and the longitude from the horizontal edge.

Scan the QR code here. The video illustrates the procedure for transferring a known latitude and longitude position to the chart. In this instance, a GPS reading gave us 41deg 15.2 minutes latitude and 70 deg 46.3 minutes longitude. The parallel ruler is placed on the closest chart drawn latitude line of 41 deg 20 minutes. The ruler is then walked down the side of the chart to the 15.2 minute mark. A line is then drawn across the chart to approximately the longitude position.

GPS Position Transfer to a Chart

Then the ruler is moved to the closest meridian of longitude that is marked on the chart. Once the ruler is lined up with this meridian, then the ruler is walked to the 46.3 minute mark. An intersecting line is drawn giving our position on the chart. As an additional note we notice that we are directly south of an ATON. We use the dividers to measure the distance, then transfer the distance between the points on the dividers to the latitude marks on the chart. In this case we were .5 minutes of latitude difference, which equates to 1/2 of a nautical mile.

The Protractor

Another useful and time-saving device is the course protractor—a protractor with an arm. You can simply determine angles by aligning the grid on the protractor with lines of latitude or meridians of longitude on the chart. You place the center of the protractor on the point from which you are measuring and then turn the arm to the second point. Note that the output angles are aligned with True North. Appropriate conversions to magnetic must be made if needed.

Scan the QR code for a video that shows the course between the same ATONS in the previous example. The course protractor is first set to ensure north is up. Then the protractor center is placed over the point on the chart by viewing through the hole in the center of the protractor. The grid on the protractor is then aligned with the chart lines and then the arm is turned to the second point. The reading is then taken off of the protractor. Note that this is a true heading, not a magnetic heading.

3Course
Protractor

The Breton Plotter

The Breton plotter tends to be more widely used than either a compass protractor or the parallel rulers. Here we have added an animation of using the Breton plotter to determine a course in Long Island Sound from a buoy we are passing close to— to the entrance buoy to New London Harbor. We want to know the true and magnetic course. Note this is not equivalent to your heading. Heading will take into account leeway and current.

Bretton Plotter

The Nautical Slide Rule

The nautical slide rule is one of the handiest and simplest devices to have around. If you have two of the three variables of speed, distance, and time, it will calculate the other.

- If you know speed and distance it will calculate time.
- If you know distance and time it will calculate speed.
- If you know speed and time it will calculate distance.
- Just spin the dials to align with the marks and read the remaining dial.

The QR code shows a video in which you can see how the slide rule calculates the distance traveled by a boat traveling at 7 knots for 3 hours.

Nautical Slide
Rule

Dividers

Dividers are used to measure distance by placing the two extensions across an unknown chart expanse, then transferring the tines to the latitude scale to determine the distance. I also use them instead of parallel rules to place the ship's latitude/longitude position once it is determined. This is done by first measuring the latitude from the chart's closest parallel, and then transferring that distance to the chart. Place a light line there with the pencil. Repeat the procedure for longitude; use the distance from the closest meridian of latitude, creating intersecting lines with the latitude reading. I find this much easier and far less frustrating than using parallel rules.

Scan the QR code, which shows a video where we use the same given GPS position example as previous: 41° 15.2 N minutes latitude and 70° 46.3 minutes W longitude. The 70° 50 minute median of longitude is transferred to our longitude position of 70° 46.3 minutes. Our latitude of 41° 15.2 minutes is then found on the side scale closest to the nearest line of latitude that is marked on the chart. The dividers are opened to this distance and then transferred to our penciled-in longitude line. Our position is exactly where the dividers touch the line.

Dividers

Pencil sharpener

Keep pencil leads very sharp for pinpointing positions. Sharpening with a sailing knife is not the way to go!

Other Tools

The **hand-bearing compass (HBC)** is fundamental and used in measuring bearings of charted objects from a ship's deck.

A **sounding**, the water depth, is another important element in coastal navigation. Soundings are usually determined by the ship's depth sounder. In case of instrument or electrical failure, it is wise to have a lead line on board to find the water's depth in those situations. A lead line is a length of line with a weight attached to one end. The weight is dropped into the water and allowed to reach the bottom. Depth is determined by reading a scale on the line, or by measuring the length of line that spanned the weight to the surface.

Binoculars are invaluable for sighting objects on shore or in the water to be used as navigational aids. They are of course essential in our efforts to monitor other traffic as well.

Whenever a vessel is maneuvered during limited visibility, a **spotlight** can become essential gear to locate navigation aids.

Electronic Navigation

We are well into the 21st century. Chances are that within 30 feet (10 meters) of you right now there are 2-3 GPS enabled potentially lifesaving devices: your iPhones and iPads, Android phones and tablets, and perhaps even your watch. Given that these are so accessible, it would be irresponsible for even a rudimentary introductory boating course to not include the basics of using these devices to get you home or navigate out of a bad situation.

With these mobile devices you can download navigation apps that will accurately show your position on a chart and give you lots of other data. Try it out now by following along.

It seems like we all end up in the British Virgin Islands sometime so we are going to work with the Navionics Caribbean and South America Electronic Chart.

Here are the iPhone and iPad links:

Navionics
Caribbean iPhone

Navionics
Caribbean iPad

Here are the Android links:

Navionics
Caribbean
Android Phone

Navionics
Caribbean
Android Tablet

Scan the QR Code for an animation of the lay of the land of the BVI. Tap on an island to zoom in then tap on the home button to zoom out.

BVI Lay of the
Land Animation

Next, here is an animation using the iPad.

Start by tapping the Play button then continue following the instructions or hit the CONT. button.

You will first measure the distance from the Road Town outer navigation markers to The Indians (one of the best places in the BVI to go snorkeling; it is often the first stop for charterers visiting the BVI).

Road Town
to the Indians
Animation

Then you will Start the navigation and you will see a data window pop up which shows Speed, Track, and Distance. The Skipper will exit from Road Town then turn onto the correct track to sail directly in a straight line to the Indians.

The great thing about this that it shows your track in a red line ahead of you. This is your real projected Course Over Ground (COG). It is not your heading because the mobile device has no way of knowing which way your boat is pointing, but it does know based on previous GPS positions where it has been and so projects a track out in front. So for wherever you need to go, you just turn the boat until the mobile device projected track lands on your destination then take a note of your heading and lock that in. This is your real direction of movement of the boat no matter what the current or leeway. Kinda feels like it is cheating. But it's not. Note however, the currents and leeway change and so you need to check often to make sure the red line is still landing over your destination. You also need to be very aware that your projected track is safe with no reefs, rocks, islands, or continents in the way.

There is a lot more to know about electronic navigation. This is just enough for now to get you home.

In fact, there is so much to learn and grasp that NauticEd has an entire course on electronic navigation.

Conclusion

Surely, navigation is the most challenging part of sailing for sailors. In the water, you cannot simply stop a passer-by and ask directions to the nearest café. Navigation requires a lot of mathematics and spatial understanding. It is a deep and seemingly endless complex topic.

But, like the early navigators, understanding is essential and required in order to be a responsible skipper. You should not rely upon line of sight sailing. There are other sinister factors at play like, fog, currents, tides, storms, hidden rocks, and electronic and mechanical breakdowns.

Remember, you are in command of a vessel and responsible for the lives of others. Your crew rightly or wrongly assume when they step on your boat, that you know what to do in any situation that may present itself. Take the following example: this is a picture of a gorgeous coastline. The second picture was taken 20 minutes later. This shows a kind of situation that is unavoidable as a sailor. One moment you are sailing along in clear air, the next you are enveloped in fog. How do you get home, avoid reefs, communicate with other vessels to avoid collision?

For this reason, we highly recommend that you take the NauticEd Coastal Navigation course. It will get you out there and home safely.

Twenty minutes later

Fog Rolling in

Chapter 10
Anchoring and Mooring

Introduction

Ensuring that your boat is in the same place you left it is a very important skill. When anchoring, there are many factors to consider: depth under keel and depth of the surrounding area, tidal currents, low-tide depth, other boats nearby, changing wind speed and direction, type of bottom, and length of stay. All factors play into your anchoring decisions.

"Yacht Heart" Taken in Corsica

Why Anchor?

There are many reasons for anchoring your boat:

- Emergencies.
- You are on an extended sailing trip.
- You love warm romantic evenings under the stars.
- Lunch in a gorgeous bay.
- The kids (yourself included) want to go swimming.
- Extreme hunger and your need to catch a snapper.

- You have butter, garlic and mango and it would go really nice with a barbequed snapper.
- Just because.

Sometimes the "just becauses" in life are the best reasons.

A Beneteau 41.1 Anchored

While we might be able to forgo lunch in the bay, as a responsible skipper you have to understand that emergencies do arise (often) and thus anchoring knowledge beyond "dropping the hook" is absolutely essential.

Those types of emergencies include:

- Medical needs.
- Gale force winds and waves that force you to hide it out behind shelter.
- Engine failure (in current flow it is even worse).
- Fog.
- Tired crew.
- Rigging failure.

Pure Skill

While sailing in a race in Auckland, New Zealand, we were in current so strong and winds so light that boats were being pushed sideways and backward rather than ahead. We drifted sideways through the finish gate with line honors while others who missed the gate had to set anchor to wait out the tide. Some call our win luck; we called it skill with local knowledge.

Given the "whys" above, a "wise" sailor will carry at least two sets of anchors.

Types of Anchors

Anchor design has been the focus of much research over thousands of years, and as a result, there are now many different kinds to choose from. Selecting which anchor to use is often a matter of good sailor's judgment combined with experience.

Weight is a big factor in selecting an anchor. The weight of the anchor must match your boat's size. Most chandleries will help you do this matching.

Below are a few common types and comments about them.

Danforth

- **Danforth:** A pre-WWII lightweight anchor used extensively by various landing craft. It has a very high holding power compared to its weight. Some are made from aluminum. It is easy to deploy and store. Holds best in sand, mud, and clay. Poor in grassy bottoms.

CQR

- **CQR:** An example of "plow" anchors. Invented in the 1930s, we can only recommend this anchor as lawn art.

Bruce

- **Bruce:** A British design that rights itself when it hits the bottom. Intended to reset itself should it be pulled loose. Relatively easy to break loose from its setting. Useful in sand, rocks, and mud.

Plough

- **Plough type anchors:** Seemingly one of the best all-around anchor type. They dig in and hold well. They may not be the best in really, really soft mud but great for regular mud, sand, and gravel.

Scoop

- **Scoop type anchors:** The newest type on innovation on the market. These anchors love eating sand, mud, and grass for breakfast. Some come with a roll bar to flip the scoop to the bottom, allowing it to quickly dig in. Here is a video about the designer of the Rocna brand scoop anchor and why he invented it.

Scoop Anchor
Video

Fisherman

- **Fisherman or kedge:** Invented over 1,000 years ago, probably. Reminds us of the classic movies about the 1800s like *Master and Commander*. It is mostly seen in gardens outside seafood restaurants.

Here is a blog article showing these anchors mounted on real sailboats.

Here is a short clip we took at the Annapolis Boat Show of some anchors in a tub.

Anchors on Sailboats

Rode and Scope

Anchoring Video

Rode

To hold a sailboat, the anchor must naturally be attached to the vessel. This is accomplished by using "rode," which is either all chain or a combination of rope or line and chain. Rode, then, is the stuff in the middle between the anchor itself and the boat. In this discussion, the words rope and line are interchanged. Some people say "anchor rope" and "anchor line" when they mean the rope part of the rode. Then there are the people who say there are no ropes on a boat. But from the rigging discussion earlier, we know is wrong.

Nylon line for the rope part is good because of its elasticity and light weight and low comparative cost. Chain is good because of its strength, weight, and ability to withstand abrasion. Chain weight is both good and bad. Good because it helps hold the anchor to the bottom, bad because it adds significant weight to the bow of the boat when stored in the anchor locker.

A typical combination chain and line anchor rode is made up of one boat length of chain and 250 to 300 feet (80m to 100m) of nylon line.

The "bitter end" is the opposite end of the rode from the anchor.

Scope

"Scope" is the ratio of the length of the rode compared to the depth of the water the anchor is set in.

Like gravity, scope is a universal law and it is vital you understand the concept. You cannot simply dangle your anchor on the bottom. For all chain, the length you let out should be at least 4 times the depth of the water. Take into account when looking at the depth on your depth meter that you have an offset from the keel. For example, if the depth is 15 feet on the meter, the real depth will be 20 feet if your keel is 5 feet long.

Scope then is the amount of rode you let out divided by the depth. For example, in 20 feet of water your scope will be 4 if you let out 80 feet of chain.

Just as an aside, you get a weird sense of lengths when anchoring. Consider this: if your boat is 40 feet long, 80 feet is only 2 boat lengths. To gain experience and confidence with this concept, consider snorkeling the anchor after you have laid it.

If your rode is made up of chain and rope, you should use at least 6 times the depth of the water. In higher wind conditions you might elect for a 7:1 (7 times the length of rode than the depth of water) ratio or in lighter winds, you might think a 5:1 ratio is appropriate. In the above example, a 7:1 scope ratio means you would deploy 140 feet, making your total swing diameter 280 feet. This is why it is desirable to anchor in shallower waters.

What is the maximum practical depth to anchor in if a 6:1 scope ratio is desired and you have 30 feet of chain and 250 feet of nylon roper? The depth is 280/6 = 46 feet (14 m). That's not very deep!

Some people have a hard and fast rule of 7:1, but you will always have some balancing decisions to make around scope. Some factors to consider in your decision include:

- The harbor is crowded.
- Some boats may be using all chain (and thus less swing).
- Your own swing.
- Predicted night wind shifts and strengths.
- Tidal change.
- The amount of chain before rope on your rode.
- The closeness to shore or underwater rocks.

Because of all these factors, it is best that you set a GPS anchor alarm and a depth-change alarm to warn you if you have moved and multiple time alarms just to get up multiple times in the night to check.

Why use a large scope? Because an anchor relies on the flukes digging horizontally in the bottom, not hooked under a rock. Thus, the rode must lie flat across the bottom while pulling on the anchor. The heavy chain acts to keep the rode on the bottom. The more rode you let out, the greater the chance the rode stays lying horizontal in wind gusts, which will pull your boat backward and lift the rode off the bottom. If you have sufficient length and weight of rode, the rode next to the anchor will remain lying flat across the bottom.

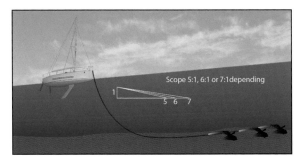

Proper Scope

At right is an example of too little rode being let out. You can fairly much guarantee that your boat will "drag its anchor" at this scope.

Play the animation to see how a proper amount of rode keeps the rode laying horizontal in a wind gust.

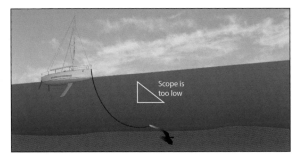

Scope Too Low

Letting out more rode gives better holding power, but this must be balanced with your diameter of swing if the wind changes direction. This is why most sailors elect for tried-and-true ratios that work: 4 to 1 for all chain, and 6 to 1 for chain/rope combination. Keep a watchful eye to ensure the anchor is not slipping across the bottom.

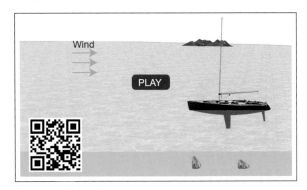

Anchoring Animation

The path (curve) of the anchor rode from the bow to the anchor is mathematically a "catenary," created by gravity pulling down on the rode. Since chain is much heavier than rope/line, the catenary shape is much different for chain than rope/line, as you can imagine. Chain tends to sit on the bottom for as much of its length as possible and because of this:

- The anchor is held flat, which gives it better holding ability.
- The curve is much greater; therefore, when the boat is hit by a wave the shock is taken up by the rising of the chain and not stretch in the rope/line.

- Abrasion on sharp rocks on the bottom is not an issue.
- It is heavy and also difficult to pull up without some sort of mechanical advantage such as a windlass.

Finally, you need a way to determine how much anchor line has been "paid out." A good suggestion is to mark the chain and/or nylon line at every 25 feet (7m). Chandleries carry a variety of markers for this purpose. Paint of different colors on the chain is good and also many people use nylon tie wraps: 1 at 25 feet, 2 at 50 feet, and 3 tie wraps at 75 feet.

Here's a fun video where we dive the anchor and check its set and a few other things we found on the bottom.

Dive the
Anchor Video

Notes

- If you plan on staying awake and aware, and anchoring for a short time, and the wind is light, you might be able to lessen your scope.
- Be aware that depending on the water depth a 6:1 ratio or more can create a large diameter circle for your boat to swing around, which is sometimes not desirable.
- In general, try to anchor shallower keeping in mind tide, swing, and obstacles.
- In general, the more rode you let out, the better holding power of the anchor.

Anchor and Rode Inspection

Since your boat and life depend on your anchor's ability to hold your boat off the rocks, it's a good idea to ensure that the rode will not let you down.

At least every six months:

- Inspect the rode length for rust and abrasion.
- Inspect the connections from rope to chain and chain to anchor.
- Ensure that the pin in the D-ring connecting the chain to the anchor is secured tightly with stainless steel wire so it cannot work free.
- Inspect the cleat that holds the rode to the boat to ensure it is solidly mounted.
- Ensure that the end of the anchor line, called the "bitter end," is firmly attached to the vessel, usually to a special cleat located in or near the anchor locker.
- Inspect the mounting of the windlass (if fitted).

Electric Windlass

An electric windlass is a powerful electric winch that greatly helps in the lowering and raising the anchor. Since they are powerful, they use a substantial amount of DC power that can rapidly drain your battery. You are therefore advised to run the engines when using the windlass.

Electric Windlass

The size and strength of electric windlass required depends upon vessel length, displacement, and type of rode. Most windlasses will accommodate both chain and line.

Usually there is an electric breaker/reset switch for the windlass. The breaker prevents too much current from overheating the wires to the windlass. If this "pops" you had either too much tension on the rode or you held the button on too long. You'll need to hit the reset switch, which is usually in an inconvenient location. For some unknown reason, manufacturers put the windlass reset switch in the most obscure locations. On some boats it's next to the battery switch. When skippering an unfamiliar boat, you should always ask the location of the windlass reset switch. Manufacturers, if you are reading this book, for goodness sake, please put the windlass reset switch in a logical location. Why do you hide it? Is it some sort of a sick joke amongst all of you?

Windlass Reset

In the image to the right, the yellow lever is in the tripped off position. It needs to be rotated up under the black bar to be reset to the on position.

The electric windlass is not designed to pull the boat toward the anchor. The way to pull in the anchor using a windlass is to use what is called the catenary effect. This is the weight of the chain rising in a curve off the bottom. When the chain is pulled in a little, the new curve formed by the chain weight pulls the boat forward. In this manner then, when pulling in the anchor, you should first hold the windlass "up" button down for only 5 seconds or so. Then let off and watch the boat move forward. Then use another 5-second burst and repeat. If you don't do this you could overload your windlass and certainly reduce its working life.

Watch out also for the chain stacking on top of itself in the anchor locker. It can quickly back itself up into the windlass and cause a nasty jam, which is difficult, at best, to get clear. Train your crew to watch for this.

When letting out, most windlasses allow you to loosen the winch spindle a little so that the rode can free wheel out. On some, you simply place the winch handle in the top of the center of the winch and turn counterclockwise to loosen.

Finally, you will find many windlass handheld controls on which the connecting cord has been repaired with black electrical tape. This happened because an amateur was not watching everything as the anchor rode came up and allowed the cord to be bound up with the chain and sucked into the winch. But you're better than that—right?

Anchoring

Anchoring is not simply throwing a "hook" and letting out line. Although, after watching some sailors, this seems to be their theory. Successful anchoring requires a plan considering all the factors.

Be Aware of These Things

The biggest failures to safely anchor and properly hold an anchor are lack of attention to wind and tides and poor "setting" of the anchor in the first place.

- Shelter from wind, swell, and waves.
- Out of the way of traffic.
- Out of the way of other anchored vessels.
- Sufficient depth of water around the entire 360-degree swing of the vessel if wind direction changes.
- No dangerous rocks in the 360-degree swing area.
- Rising and falling tide.
- Changing current caused by tidal flow.
- Bottom conditions (good or poor holding ability compared to type of anchor).
- Prohibited areas.
- Cables and lines across the bottom. These almost always exist in a marina. But also check the charts for subsurface electric and telephone lines to an island or peninsula.
- Scope.
- Makeup of your anchor line "rode." (All chain or chain/rope(line) combination?)

Anchoring in the Right Spot

Wind

Expect the wind direction and velocity to change. Use wind prediction apps to gain insight into what may happen to the wind during the night. In tight bays and bays with high cliffs, the wind swirls and constantly changes direction.

Tide

The tide goes up and the tide goes down. A rising tide will reduce your scope and will reduce the ability for the rode to lie horizontally across the bottom. View the animation.

Tide Animation

An ebbing tide will increase your swing and scope because the depth is reduced. This puts you closer to shore or can land you on the bottom or rocks, or all three.

As the tide ebbs and flows so will the tidal current direction. This can swing you closer to hazards.

Setting the Anchor

Once you select a spot and consider as many of the above factors as possible it is time to make crew assignments and discuss hand signals between the bow and the helm. Both the bow person and the helmsperson must know what is required and be able to communicate to anchor properly. The bow person must know how much rode to deploy based on the scope discussion above and be able to count the length of rode going out.

In the Communications chapter, hand signals were discussed. The skipper and the anchorperson are advised to learn these prior to anchoring and mooring operations. You can establish others as needed.

Here is how an anchoring maneuver is supposed to go in a perfect world:

- Motor the boat into the wind.
- Stop the boat in the water at the desired location.
- Deploy the anchor over the bow.
- Begin to motor the boat in reverse.
- As the anchor touches bottom the boat should moving slowly backward so the rode lies in a straight line across the bottom. It is important not to pile the rode on top of itself.
- When the appropriate amount of rode is released, it is made fast.

- The boat's momentum will tug on the anchor and set the anchor into the bottom.
- Additional pressure can be applied to the anchor by applying more reverse power.
- If possible, swim to the anchor to check it is set.

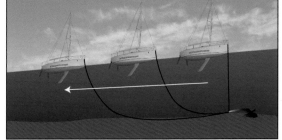

If you are lucky it will set the first time; otherwise you need to keep trying.

Using a Snubber

Setting the Anchor

Once anchored, for an all chain rode, it is recommended to relieve the direct connect of the chain to the boat by adding a length of stretchy rope called a snubber alongside the chain for 2 to 3 meters. The snubber provides the rode system with elasticity and is most commonly hooked (or tied) to the chain and then tied off to a cleat on the boat. The chain is then let farther out to relieve its tension. The snubber will absorb the impact of any wave action and removes the load off the windlass, which could possibly slip.

A Snubber Helps Absorb Wave Shock

To be effective, the snubber should be as long as possible—the longer the rope the greater the energy absorption.

Swing

Your boat position is always downwind from the anchor. When the wind changes direction your boat position changes. This change in position is called swing.

Swing should always be considered when anchoring, especially if anchoring overnight or leaving the boat alone. A change in wind can put your boat into a

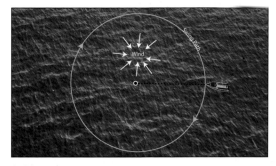

Swing

precarious situation by being too close to the shore or a rock or reef that was previously clear. As long as you don't anchor too close to other anchored boats, there is usually not a problem because those boats will also swing with the wind change.

Many times you'll find an area with mooring balls. These moorings are tied straight down to the sea floor and thus boats tied to moorings swing less than anchored boats. Therefore, it is generally a very bad idea to anchor in a mooring field. The golden rule is always "consider your swing."

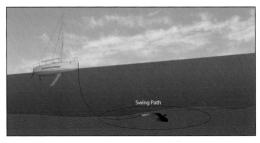

Swing

Swing

Consideration must be given to the tide. As the tide "ebbs" out, you not only get closer to the bottom but your swing circle grows and the shore becomes closer. The top diagram shows a boat's swing path with deep water and correct scope.

The bottom diagram shows that as the tide ebbed out, the scope increased as well as the swing path, bringing the boat dangerously close to the bottom, the shore, or both.

Monitoring

After the anchor has set and adequate rode has been paid out, take time to ensure you are not drifting. And considering changing winds and tide height and tidal current, it is important to periodically monitor how well your anchor is set.

Check your anchor set manually and electronically. Manually, sight bearings to objects on shore and determining that they are constant. Note that the boat will swing back and forth with the wind, making it a little difficult to check that you are remaining steadfastly connected to the bottom. But, over time, you will get a feeling that through each successive swing, bearings to objects on the shore are not changing.

Electronically you will have a more accurate determination. If you have a GPS device, turn it on and turn on "show track." Observe over time the history track of your boat. If the tracks overlay each other then you are holding steadfast. You can also use an anchor alarm on your depth meter. To do this, you set the maximum and minimum allowable depths. If the depth goes out of this range, the alarm sounds. There are also apps for your mobile device. Here are a few:

DragQueen for iOS

DQ-iOS

Drag Queen for Android

DQ-Android

Anchor Watch for iOS

AW-iOS

Anchor Watch for Android

AW-Android

NauticEd has its own anchor watch alarm built into its app for logbook tracking.

NauticEd
Logbook
App

Lighting

The International Rules of Prevention of Collision at Sea govern the lighting requirements for anchoring. These are described in Chapter 5. Not only must you know your own vessel's lighting requirements, but you must know others to be able to identify them. We recommend that you revisit the rules often. Visit our Sailing Apps page to download the free NauticEd app. You can then review all the NauticEd Courses off-line while you sit in the doctor's office or are stuck on an airplane.

Lighting

A sailboat at anchor must have one all-around (visible from 360 degrees) white light at the top of the mast. You may NOT leave on your green and red side lights or your white stern lights "for extra visibility." Those are running lights and indicate that you are NOT at anchor. A good idea, however is to leave on a cabin light; but consider your batteries.

A further life-saving idea is to always have a powerful flashlight available within quick reach in the dark.

Multiple Anchors

There are occasions when more than one anchor will add safety and comfort. One possibility is to use one or two anchors from the bow, one from the stern, or both. The conditions requiring this will usually relate to anchoring in heavy weather, tight quarters, or not wanting your vessel to swing onto the beach. The photo below was taken in Corsica, where a tight cove made it necessary to anchor off the front and then secure two lines off the stern to large rocks on shore.

Normally the bow anchor is set first; then the stern anchor is placed using a dinghy to take it out to the desired spot. Then the crew on the vessel will pull the rode until the anchor sets. When doing this you will want to ensure the anchor is indeed set. A bow/stern anchor combination has inherent danger if the wind changes to abeam. The area profile of the boat is much larger when viewed from its side, thus the wind loading is much larger when it comes

Multiple Anchors

from abeam. This can cause the anchors to drag. For this reason, stern and bow anchors are seldom advised.

In heavy weather, using two anchors off the bow may be prudent and desirable. The two anchors can be aligned extending out front or they can be positioned 45 to 90 degrees to the vessel's bow. Extreme care and thought are needed when using two anchors off the front. If the boat swings in the night the anchor rodes can become tangled.

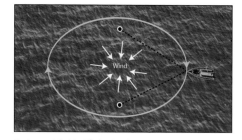

Swing with Multiple Anchors

In the following diagram, two anchors are set at 45 degrees. Notice the swing circle in the first diagram compared to the subsequent diagram whereby the anchors are set 90 degrees apart. Forty-five-degree set anchors are best in heavy wind conditions as each anchor takes half the load so long as the wind direction is constant.

Ninety-degree set anchors are best used in light winds in tight quarters where swing room is a concern. This style of anchoring is called the Bahamian anchoring technique.

In every case, if possible, you should dive down to your anchor with a mask and snorkel to ensure it is set properly. You'll sleep a lot better. Maybe not this time, but one time you will save your boat and possibly your life.

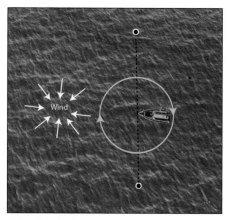

Bahamian Anchoring

Long Line Ashore

Convenient

Anchoring our catamaran in a bay off St. Vincent, we dropped the hook off the bow then backed up toward the beach until the rode was taut. Then we ran a bridle connected to both sides of the cat to a single long line that we ran ashore to the base of a palm tree. Many thanks to Morris, the local who helped us out with this maneuver.

The long line ashore is a good way to prevent swinging during the night and provides a convenient way to get close to the shore when desired. The long line runs from the stern to the shore while the bow anchor holds the boat out away from the shore. There is danger in this, however. A strong wind from abeam puts a large load on the anchor, which can cause the anchor to drag and thus pivot you onto the shore.

Innovative Anchoring

Anchoring Courtesy

After safely and securely anchoring your vessel, there are certain factors to contend with; most are common sense.

- Be courteous to those anchored around you; be quiet and mindful.
- If you run your engine, be aware of potential carbon monoxide fumes.
- Think about what you should and should not be dumping overboard.
- Anchor using the same method as the other boats around you so your swing will match theirs with changes in direction of wind.

Busy Harbors: Photo Taken in Hvar, Croatia

- Don't anchor in a mooring field; the swing on a mooring line is much less than that of an anchor rode.

Weighing Anchor

"Weighing the anchor" simply means raising it.

With an Engine

If raising the anchor is to be done by hand, make certain the assigned crew who will pull in the rode and raise the anchor are physically able. This can be a demanding chore.

When the time comes to leave an anchorage, there are recommended procedures.

Step One: Ensure all gear is properly stored and crew and passengers know what is going on. Ensure you have an agreed-upon set of hand signals between the crew member who is retrieving the anchor and the helmsperson.

Step Two: Start the engine and slowly motor toward the anchor, all the while pulling in the rode and placing it carefully in the anchor locker. Do not let the rode drift under the vessel as it could become entangled in the propeller, creating some real problems.

Step Three:

Plan A: As the vessel moves over the spot where the anchor rests, pull it up if you can. Stop the vessel's forward motion as you continue pulling in the anchor. If you use an electric windlass to raise the anchor, be vigilant to ensure it is running freely.

Plan B: If the anchor is set hard and you cannot pull it in, you may need to use the vessel's forward motion to break the anchor loose. This means maintaining slight forward motion and cleating the rode as you pass over the spot. The theory is that the vessel's momentum will break loose the anchor. Be very wary of the strength of the cleat on your boat.

Plan C: If the anchor fails to break loose, perhaps it's stuck on a rock. You can try to pull it out backward by motoring to windward. The flatter the angle you are pulling, the greater the chance of retrieval, so let out lots of rode when motoring to windward. Be conscious of the rode and propeller at all times.

Plan D: Try pulling the anchor out sideways. Let out lots of rode and alternate motoring across the wind on either side.

Weighing Anchor

Plan E: Persistence and various combinations of the above will normally work in your favor.

Tip: If you don't have a windlass and you're feeling a little tired, you can run the rode back to one of the winches atop the cabin.

Watch out that you're not stuck on a boat dock cable from a marina. In lakes, you might often be stuck on an old tree stump.

A variety of other techniques can be used when anchoring in rocky bottoms. One is attaching a line and a float to the backside of the anchor making it possible to pull the anchor out backward. However, this requires preplanning. If you're unsure of the bottom then this might be a safety precaution.

The Anchor Rescue Device: is an ingenious device that can save the day. You have to prepare for it however by purchasing the device and attaching to your anchor. Watch the video below.

Anchor Rescue

The very worst scenario is that you will have to leave the anchor and rode for later recovery with a dive professional. In this case, don't cut the rope rode, pay it all out and attached a floating bottle, such as a Clorox bottle, to the bitter end of the rode. If you do cut the rope, keep in mind that you will need to buy another complete rode, which is not cheap.

The best advice when weighing anchor is to remain calm and thoroughly think through your procedures before using them.

The possibility of losing an anchor to the bottom always exists. This helps underscore the need to carry an extra anchor and rode for just such an unfortunate occasion.

Without an Engine

At times, you may desire or need to retrieve the anchor without using the engine. In this case, use the forward momentum of the boat rather than fighting the tension in the anchor rode. Pull the rode enough to get the boat moving forward; once the boat is moving, it will tend to continue moving forward and the rode will slacken allowing you to pull in some more. Simple patience will save a lot of grunting and groaning.

Sea Anchor

Finally, there is something called a "sea anchor." These can be a variety of devices used to slow down a vessel caught in high winds and turbulent seas. There include commercially available chutes or small cones arranges on a long line or even a jury-rigged chain looped behind the boat. All are used to create drag to slow the vessel.

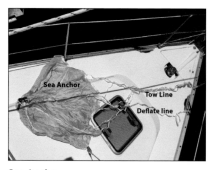

Sea Anchor

Mooring

Mooring a vessel means attaching it to a float that is firmly and permanently anchored to the sea bottom.

Some cities and communities provide mooring balls in lovely serene bays and coves; some free, some not. Many times, private individuals own the mooring balls. Some are available for rent and some are not. You will need to check the local cruising guide. Sometimes the mooring ball itself will have contact instructions.

To obtain a mooring ball, check the local guide to see the procedure. Sometimes you can call the harbormaster and make a reservation beforehand. It is no fun to arrive at a spot where you intended to moor and discover there aren't any balls available. Other times in popular chartering areas, you need to arrive early to be assured of a ball.

There are different types of mooring balls. Scan the QR code and tap the images to cycle through the various mooring buoys you will encounter. White mooring balls with a blue stripe are designated as overnight mooring balls for recreational vessels.

Various Mooring Balls

Mooring Procedures

The procedure for tying to a mooring is theoretically very easy. You simply motor up and using a boat hook, grab the float and attach to it to your boat. It sounds simple but you will see many dismal failures when watching others try it.

Success lies in establishing crew assignments: helmsperson, pointer, retriever, lines-person; and in making a proper plan.

Mooring

Crew assignments: Who is doing what? The pointer and the helmsperson must have a pre-established series of communications using hand signals. This is the most critical because the longer the helmsperson can keep the mooring ball exactly at the bow of the boat, the more time the retriever and lines-person have to properly secure the boat. Thus if possible, the pointer should have the job of only being a pointer— to continuously give hand signal instructions to the helmsperson: where the ball is, what direction to move, to slow down, to stop in the water, to disengage gear.

The retriever hooks the mooring pendant and brings it up out of the water onto the bow of the boat.

The lines-person prepares the bowlines ahead of time by cleating one end to a bow cleat and making sure the remaining line is untangled and clear to pull through the pendant eye. Then, once the pendant is brought on board he or she runs the bowlines through the pendant and back to a bow cleat. When shorthanded, the retriever and the lines-person can be the same person. It is best to have the pointer remain as the pointer only thorough out the entire maneuver. This is because the boat can quickly drift off and thus the helmsperson needs to know at all times how to maneuver the boat to keep the mooring ball at the bow.

The plan, once the crew assignments have been made goes like this:

- Select a mooring ball. Communicate that to the crew.
- Lines-person ready with clear lines? Ready.
- Retriever ready with boat hook? Ready.
- Pointer ready? Ready.
- As the boat approaches, the pointer essentially takes control of the boat via hand signals back to the helmsperson.
- The retriever and lines-person do their jobs to secure the boat as fast as possible. They do not try to get the lengths of everything correct initially. The primary objective is to secure the boat and then make adjustments to the bowlines after the boat is settled.

Notes

There are variances based on the type of mooring ball setup, boat type (monohull or catamaran), and the current flow versus wind strength.

Mooring Ball Setup

Most often the actual mooring line that you bring on board is a floating line attached to the mooring just below the ball. You simply hook the floating line and bring it aboard. When securing to a cleat, make sure it is a thick mooring line, not a thin messenger line.

With some mooring balls you can use the line on the mooring ball to cleat to your deck. With others you use your own bowlines to run through the pendant or through a ring on the mooring ball.

If you encounter a steel ring in the top of the ball, you loop your own bowline through the ring. The problem with this configuration is that you cannot lift the ball out of the water with the boat hook, nor can you reach down to it from your forward deck. There is another method to get to the mooring ball if it is configured this way. Simply back up the boat to the mooring ball with your aft facing the wind. The lines-person has a better chance of reaching the mooring ball in this manner because the aft of the boat is not as high as the bow and the helmsperson and the lines-person can work together easier. It is preferable to use a long line that is already attached at one end to a forward cleat and run around the outside of everything (stays, lifelines, and bimini). The lines-person then simply walks the free end back to the forward deck, pulling in the slack, and attaches it to the opposite cleat.

See our blog article on this.

Blog Article on Mooring

For Catamarans

With a catamaran, typically you will run a bowline from one hull to the pendant and back to the same hull. Then repeat for the other hull. This method stabilizes the catamaran from swaying with the wind.

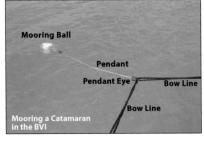

Mooring a Catamaran

Current vs. Wind Strength

Approach the mooring ball from downwind or down-current, whichever has the strongest effect on the vessel.

Safety Notes

- It is easier to go around and do it again than have your crew hurt themselves trying to hold the boat to the ball with the boat hook while the boat drifts away. Train your crew to unhook the boat hook and let the ball go if it becomes difficult to hold.
- The mooring configuration is always subject to weather, corrosion, currents, and rotting lines that erode the mooring integrity. Thus, you should be cognizant of potentially being released during the night and dangerously drifting away. For this reason, similar to anchoring, you should always check your position during the night. Use anchoring apps.

Summary

Flotilla Anchored

Anchoring is an essential skill needed by all sailors. In some emergencies, it is the only option. It is also a desired skill that allows you to simply enjoy and share moments at sea. Getting proficient in anchoring takes knowledge and some practice, but the results are safety enhancing and confidence building.

- Use plenty of scope.
- Check your swing.
- Select the appropriate anchor.
- Dive your anchor once it is set.
- Check your depth regarding tide changes.
- Ensure your scope will handle the tide change.
- Watch proximity to others who may not swing as much as you.
- Watch the anchor set for several minutes to ensure it is not dragging.
- Get up several times in the night to check your anchor.
- Assume the wind direction will change.
- Don't anchor in a mooring field.

Chapter 11
Safety and Emergencies

Introduction

Emergencies at sea extend from simple and almost funny episodes to major challenges that are extremely serious. When sailing goes well, life is good and we wish it would continue that way indefinitely. However, things can go wrong and when they do sailors must be prepared—including calling for help.

The best strategy is to try to prevent emergencies from happening. This translates into the following:

- Practice safety. Safe behavior is an insurance against an emergency.
- Learn the established rules. This is also a legal issue.
- Know your vessel and its capabilities thoroughly.
- Know your boat's equipment, how to use it and maintain it.
- Know yourself and your crew. This requires honesty, tact, and finesse.
- Prepare for possible problems. Have backup plans.
- Learn how to read weather forecasts. Get a forecast every time you go out.
- Use common sense, also known as good seamanship (you know what that is).
- Be patient and courteous and always prudent.

Safe practices and emergencies have much in common. Violate safety practices and the probability of emergencies increases dramatically. Rules for proper use of vessels and behaviors have been established and agreed upon; when followed, emergencies are less likely to happen.

The U.S. Coast Guard has established safety and emergency procedures that work globally. They have a variety of detailed publications and bulletins accessible at: http://www.uscgboating.org/recreational-boaters/index.php

USCG Boater
Safety Website

Safety Briefings

You can avoid many emergencies by conducting a proper safety briefing before leaving the dock. This also helps you to establish command and confidence in your crew.

Here is a PDF checklist for you to print out and leave on your vessel for the safety briefing.

Crew Briefing
PDF

Raising the Alarm

VHF

Procedure for VHF Channel 16 MAYDAY:

- Switch to Channel 16. All Distress signals via VHF are initiated on Channel 16. This is a worldwide protocol.
- Distress signal "MAYDAY," spoken three times.
- The words "THIS IS," spoken once.
- Name of vessel in distress (spoken three times) and call sign or boat registration number, spoken once.
- Repeat "MAYDAY" and name of the vessel, spoken once with call sign.
- Give the position of the vessel by latitude or longitude or by bearing (true or magnetic, state which) and distance to a well-known landmark such as a navigational aid or small island, or in any terms that will assist a responding station in locating the vessel in distress. Include any information on vessel movement such as course, speed, and destination.
- Nature of distress (sinking, fire, etc.).
- Kind of assistance desired.
- Number of persons on board.
- Any other information that might help with rescue, such as length or tonnage of the vessel, number of persons needing medical attention, color hull, cabin, masks, etc.
- The word "OVER."

Stay by the radio if possible. You'll probably need to repeat information and answer further questions, particularly concerning your location.

For example:

MAYDAY-MAYDAY-MAYDAY
THIS IS BLUE DUCK-BLUE DUCK-BLUE DUCK
Call sign WA1234 MMSI number 233006734
MAYDAY BLUE DUCK
Call sign WA1234 MMSI number 233006734

OUR POSITION IS CAPE HENRY LIGHT BEARS 185 DEGREES
MAGNETIC-DISTANCE 2 MILES
OUR CONDITION, WE HAVE STRUCK A SUBMERGED OBJECT

WE REQUIRE PUMPS-MEDICAL ASSISTANCE AND TOW
THERE ARE THREE ADULTS AND TWO CHILDREN ON BOARD
ONE PERSON HAS A COMPOUND FRACTURE OF ARM
ESTIMATE CAN REMAIN AFLOAT TWO HOURS
BLUE DUCK IS THIRTY TWO FOOT CABIN CRUISER-WHITE HULL-
BLUE DECK HOUSE
OVER

Repeat at intervals until an answer is received.

Keep in mind that you may know how to make a MAYDAY call but your crew may not: download this card, laminate it, and zip tie to your VHF mic cord.

Mayday Card PDF

Calls Other than Distress on VHF

Urgency: "PAN, PAN, PAN" (pronounced *PAHN PAHN PAHN*). This in the International Urgency Signal and is used when a vessel or person is in some jeopardy of a degree less than would be indicated by Mayday.

Safety: "SECURITY, SECURITY, SECURITY" (pronounced *SAY-CURE-IT-TAY*). This is the International Safety Signal and is a message about some aspect of navigational safety or a weather warning. You will most often hear this from the Coast Guard. Listen and take appropriate actions if necessary. For example, a navigational aid has drifted off station or a tornado watch has been issued.

The United States Coast Guard's website and recommendations on VHF distress signals is here:

USCG VHF
Distress Calls

Digital Select Calling (DSC)

Digital Select Calling (DSC) is a means by which a digital distress signal is broadcast via VHF Channel 70. Local Coast Guard stations monitor this in real time. DSC will report your GPS position, your vessel name and type, and the nature of your distress via a selectable text menu. However, there is a caveat; when you buy your DSC you must register it and hook it up to your GPS unit. Instructions for this will be with the unit manual.

It is important to send a DSC signal first when in an emergency situation, because pertinent information such as your vessel type, name, and position is broadcast digitally to all vessels in your VHF range vicinity, which gains more accurate and faster response times. After the DSC alert, you should send a voice alert. The Coast Guard monitors DSC 24/7. When they receive a DSC call they are instantly given extremely accurate and helpful information to speed and enhance the success of the rescue.

The DSC will likely have a selection of prescribed alerts from which you can select. If time is short, holding the red distress button will send a standard distress signal with your location. To initiate the DSC, open the distress cover and either (1) hold the distress red button for five seconds for the standard message or (2) press the red distress button and then select the best suited message from the menu.

USCG Video Interview

Watch the video interview with the Coast Guard.

Now watch how to send a DSC distress signal:

The United States Coast Guard's website with recommendations on DSC distress signals is here.

Sending a Distress
DSC Signal

EPIRB (Emergency Position Indicating Radio Beacon)

An EPIRB is an emergency device that will report a distress and your position to monitoring stations via satellite. It is automatically set off when immersed in water and is automatically released from its mount if the boat is sinking. While not required in most countries, it is a must for every vessel. This video from the USA-based chandlery West Marine describes the EPIRB best.

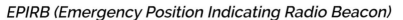

USCG DSC
Distress Calls

EPIRB

Mobile (Cell) Phones

Everyone carries a cell phone these days and people are more connected. Don't discount using your mobile phone for raising the alarm. It would even be prudent to input the phone number of your local Coast Guard station into your address book.

However, the downside to mobile phone alarm is that you are talking to only one person at a time. There is also a long list of reasons why a cell phone is not your best choice: the signal may drop, or be garbled, the range is limited to the closest tower, phones are typically not waterproof, you're relying on the battery being enough throughout the operation, you cannot transmit your position as well as a DSC, and the brave men and women that come to save you won't be holding their phone to their ears—they will be on VHF.

Learn to use your VHF and DSC.

Flares

This is a video created by Marine and Safety Tasmania. You should check your local country rules for the requirements of carrying flares that are mentioned in this video.

Flares Video

A bit of important basic information first:

Read the instructions on all flares and always store a set of protective flare gloves in the flare container to protect your hands when setting off flares. Keep all flares in a watertight container. Flares have a shelf life; remember to check their date stamps. Don't look directly at the flare when it is going off. Hold at arm's length. When possible, only knowledgeable and experienced persons should use the flares.

- **NEVER** activate marine flares in a non-emergency situation on or near regulated water. It is illegal.
- **NEVER** dispose of flares in household trash.
- **CONTACT** your local fire department or coast guard about disposal.

Types of Flares

Flares come in many different types for different alerting requirements:

- **Red Handheld Flares**
  A short-range distress signal used to pinpoint position during day or night. It burns with a light intensity of 15,000 candela for a duration of 60 seconds.

Hold over the side of the boat and downwind to stop red-hot sparks falling onto your vessel. Visibility is about 3 miles.

- **Orange Smoke Flares**
  This handheld signal produces a dense orange smoke for daylight distress signaling. Ideal to indicate wind direction to rescue helicopter in land or sea rescues. Burning time 60 seconds.
- **White Collision Flares**
  White handheld flares are for day and night use as a short-range collision warning signal and also for illuminating small areas.
- **Float Smoke Flares**
  This is a small and compact distress signal for daylight use only. There is a smoke signal that floats on the water for position marking during rescue operations. Indicates wind direction. Safe for use on oil- or fuel-covered water.
- **Red Rocket Flares**
  Longer range than a handheld, it ejects a red flare on a parachute at 1,000 feet (300 meters), burning for 40 seconds at 30,000 candela. This gives the flare around 30 miles of visibility, allowing vessels over the horizon and out of line of sight to potentially see your distress signal. Point the flare downwind. Fire a second flare a minute or so after your first. This gives the observer a chance to confirm the sighting and gain a bearing to your location.
- **LED Flare**
  A new innovation in the market is an extremely bright Red LED Stick. While it does not meet the legal requirements for coded and commercial vessels yet, that is only because it is under test and review. Major advantages are that it can "burn" for five hours and the unit can quick flash or send out a coded SOS signal.

SOS

What's in a Word

The origin of SOS is interesting. While people commonly think of it as Save Our Souls or Save Our Ship, in actual fact, SOS stands for nothing. It was created as such because the Morse code signal is distinct and difficult to confuse with other signals.

In Morse code, 3 shorts is "S" and 3 longs is "O."

SOS, then, is 3 short, 3 long, 3 short. You are not expected to know Morse code, so the easiest way to not get mixed up between shorts and longs for S and O is that the message is logically the shortest message for emergency purposes (that is, 3 longs—3 shorts—3 longs would be a longer message than the correct message of 3 shorts—3 longs—3 shorts).

A flashlight or sound device can be used to make this signal.

Other Distress Signals

The United States Coast Guard, in its navigation rules (rule 37), shows this diagram for other distress signals.

The Code V Flag, which is a large red X, is not a distress signal but it means "I require assistance."

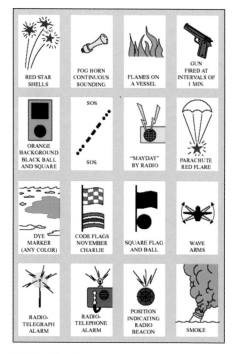

Distress Signals

Code V Flag

Safety Equipment

There is a plethora of equipment specially designed for a variety of emergencies at sea. Some are inexpensive, while others are very costly. Determine your specific requirements by the kind of sailing you will be doing and the location. But don't be cheap. If you can't afford to buy safety equipment for your boat you can't afford to go sailing. Any arguments?

Here is a PDF list of items you should keep on board. Print it out and keep with your boat documents on board. At least twice per season go through the list and write the date you last checked the items for completeness.

Safety Equipment List

Jack-lines

The possibility at any time of bad weather requires that jack-lines and harnesses be permanently carried on board. They must of course be strong and should be checked regularly for deterioration.

Jack-lines are typically webbing strips than run the length of the vessel on the deck and also mounted in the cockpit. They are attached to the vessel by points called jack-stays. Your harness then clips onto a jack-line during poor weather and will prevent you going overboard should a wave wash over the boat, a roll occur, or even if the vessel is hit by a jolting large wave throwing you down.

The jack-line then allows crew to move around the vessel performing necessary tasks at the foredeck, at the mast, or even in the cockpit.

One look at the guys in the Volvo ocean race will convince you that jack-lines are a good thing.

(Photo Courtesy of Wichard)

Radar Reflectors

Large shipping traffic relies heavily on radar to avoid collision. Since you and your boat are comparatively small and don't want to be squashed like a bug, it is a good idea to do what you can to be seen. Radar reflectors are usually smallish tubes with metal pieces packed inside arranged at many different angles that you attach high up on your shroud lines (side stays). They vastly increase the radar signal visibility of your vessel. These are especially important if your vessel is made of wood or GRP fiberglass, which tends to absorb rather than reflect radar signals.

Personal Flotation Devices

The terms "life jacket" and "PFD" are interchangeable, with the latter used in the USA and the former used in most of the rest of the world.

You might think this topic is pretty boring and that all we're going to say is wear one. Wrong. Actually, this is a pretty interesting topic. Research by a number of marine safety organizations found that many people did not wear PFDs because they were uncomfortable. As a result of the studies, manufacturers were prompted to design more comfortable PFDs and consequently the number of drownings has significantly declined.

Thus, what we are not going to say then is just "wear one." Rather, what we are going to say is "invest in a comfortable PFD and wear it." The biggest disservice that we do to children is to not have comfortable PFDs for them to wear. And you can imagine parents become so desperate for their child to enjoy boating that when the child starts whining because they are uncomfortable with an ill-fitting type I PFD, the parents take it off thinking, "All is okay—we'll just pay extra attention." And that is the death of little Johnny. Please invest in your children's comfort and think of your purchase of a comfortable PFD as an investment in them enjoying boating—so you can go out more.

Even if you don't have children, keep multiple, comfortable fitting child size PFDs on board. If children are coming out with you, ask the parents to ensure they have a properly sized comfortable PFD, one that the child can wear the entire time while on board.

Buoyancy Ratings

PFDs/life jackets are graded with a buoyancy rating that lists the amount of buoyancy force a PFD can hold expressed in units of newtons (N). Force is used rather than weight because force is a constant whether submerged in water or not, whereas our weight changes if we are submerged in water. On Earth (out of water) one newton force is about 1/10th of a kilogram.

Life jackets are rated in the following Buoyancy Rating Categories:

$$\textbf{275 N—150 N—100 N—50 N}$$

For example, a 150 N life Jacket provides 150 N of floating force. If a rock on the bottom of the ocean weighed 14 kg on a submerged weight measurement scale, then a 150 N rated life jacket would hold it afloat—barely. A 15 kg rock with a 150 N life jacket would have neutral buoyancy.

A 200-pound (91-kilogram) man requires about 10 pounds (4 kilograms) of buoyancy. The math here uses the person's body makeup of 80 percent water (neutral buoyancy) and 15 percent fat (positive buoyancy). 4 kg converts to 40 newtons. Thus, the 150 newtons is plenty for the average person and considered the minimum for an adult in offshore conditions.

Regulations and Recommendations

- International (and all local) regulations require that there be at least one PFD for every person on board. They all must be:
  - a type I, II, III or V PFD appropriately sized or a PFD of the proper buoyancy under the new system.
  - Properly fitting for each person.
  - In serviceable condition.
- Some local government regulations require all persons to wear a PFD under certain circumstances such as: on smaller boats, at times of

heightened risk, off the beach sailing yachts, sailboards, kayaks, canoes, and pedal boats.

- Children:
    - ○ Local regulations go even further and dictate age requirements for children to wear a PFD at all times. We recommend that right now you do an Internet search for your local government regulations for PFD requirements. In the United States and Australia, these regulations are statewide. In other countries, they are countrywide.
    - ○ Your children grow. At the start of each season, or more often, make sure your children fit their PFD and the buoyancy listed is correct.
    - ○ When fitting a child's PFD, test the fit by lifting the child by the PFD at the shoulders to make sure they don't slip out.
    - ○ Make sure you always buckle the strap that passes between their legs.
- Infants:
    - ○ Prior to boating with an infant, test out the fit of the selected PFD in a swimming pool. Since infants grow so fast, you should test the fit of the PFD often.
    - ○ The design should be such that the infant naturally rolls and floats face up without assistance.
- Don't forget to test each PFD at the start of each season. Remember, the law says your PFDs must be in good shape before you use your boat. Ones that are not in good shape should be cut up and thrown away.

Inflatable PFDs

Chances are that you will be switching over to an inflatable PFD pretty soon; especially now that we have convinced you to wear a comfortable PFD.

Inflatable PFDs are life-critical, semi-complicated devices that need proper maintenance and attention. They inflate when immersed in water either by detecting hydrostatic pressure or by a pill that dissolves when it comes in contact with water. The pressure bottle that holds the compressed air can be used only once and the mechanism that fires the pin to pierce the seal on the compressed air bottle must also be reset and replaced. Additionally, they need to be inspected annually. Beyond all that, however, once you realize how comfortable (and sometimes stylish) they are, you'll be happy you've made the transition. We have posted additional information about care and use of inflatable PFDs if you care to learn more on our blog site here:

Inflatable PFDs

Personnel Emergencies

As the skipper of a vessel, you are expected to be able to handle situations thrust upon you at a moment's notice. Many of these situations are boat-related issues, but there are also crew injury issues for which you should be prepared to assess and handle at least enough until professional assistance arrives.

Consider if you are knowledgeable enough right now to handle:

- a broken limb
- excessive bleeding
- a severe burn
- hypothermia
- dehydration
- head injury
- a diabetic with extreme low blood sugar level
- a heart attack or identify its symptoms
- extreme allergic reaction to shellfish
- severe seasickness
- alcohol, medication, or drug reaction or overdose

If you are in the slightest intimidated by any situation above, we highly recommend you take a Red Cross medical emergency class. The class is usually conducted over two evenings and deals with everything from cuts and burns to CPR. There is no substitute for professional instruction. There is a significant discussion of medical emergencies that are likely to occur at sea in the NauticEd Safety at Sea Course.

A Final Note: Human life is certainly the most precious entity on any sailing vessel. Preparation and knowledge of how to handle medical emergencies can make you a living hero with living friends and relatives.

Seasickness

Seasickness can quickly lead to dehydration. If you're a hardy old captain, don't look upon your sick crew as wusses. You're setting yourself up for a serious situation.

Here is some education about seasickness that can help you and your crew overcome it. You might even email it out to your crew beforehand. This was taken from Kona Hawaii Fishing with Captain Jeff Rogers (http://fishinkona.com/seasick.htm)

Thanks, Jeff!

Avoiding Seasickness

A fun day out on the water just might turn into one of the worst days of your life. While seasickness is somewhat rare in Kona because of the (mostly) calm seas, seasickness hits some people even on the calmest of days. If you or someone in your party is prone to car sickness in any way, they NEED to prepare. Seasickness is 99 percent preventable but not very curable. There are many remedies for seasickness and the most popular of these is the worst. I'm referring to Dramamine—DON'T TAKE IT! Not only is it a poor seasickness medication but the side effect of "sleepiness" can ruin your fun also.

Here's a list of remedies in order of effectiveness:

Scopolamine:

For the hardcore "I always get seasick" and "I get carsick easy" types. This remedy is also referred to as "the patch" and can be obtained by prescription from your doctor. It looks like a little round Band-Aid and is worn behind your ear. There are a certain percentage of people who have adverse side effects to this medication. I highly suggest that if you're using this remedy for the first time, try using one at home first. You don't want to find out that you have an adverse reaction to this stuff when you're several miles out at sea.

Bonine:

This is the best pill form, over-the-counter remedy. Highly recommended. Don't let a doctor or pharmacist talk you into any other kind of pill form. There are no others that are "just like Bonine." You will need to get this stuff working in your system well in advance of your trip. There's little to no side effect. The biggest mistake people make with pill form remedies is that they take their first dose either right before or right after stepping on the boat. That's too late! Seasick-prone people usually spew these pills out before they can take full effect. I highly recommend taking one dose of Bonine the night before your trip and another dose in the morning when you wake up. For long trips, don't forget to keep up with the recommended dosage.

Sea Band:

These are pressure point therapy wrist bands. Most people discount this remedy because it "sounds" like a gimmick. They work! There is also an electronic shock version but the non-electric ones work just fine. The nice thing about this remedy is that they can be added along with any of the other remedies without conflicting with them. I try to keep at least one pair around for those who didn't prepare, but too often people walk off the boat forgetting that they have them on. Many drugstores carry these bands as a cure for morning sickness. (Go onto www.west-marine.com and type in "seasick band" as a keyword.)

Ginger:

That's right. Plain old gingerroot. You can get this stuff in pill form, candied, raw, powdered, as a paste, dehydrated, in cookies . . . well, you get the idea. Ginger settles your stomach quickly and, just like with Sea Band, ginger can be added along with any of the other remedies without conflicting with them. I try to keep ginger candy on the boat and I can cure a good number of people with a combination of ginger candy and Sea Bands. Don't rely on me having either of them though.

Just one more note: Some people have a tendency to over do a good thing when they're on vacation. Go easy on the dinner the night before and breakfast in the morning before you go out. Don't stuff yourself. Don't get drunk the night before (hangovers are even worse out at sea) and get a good night's sleep.

Aloha, have a great day on the water!

Jeff also recommends a new product called MotionEaze. Here is a link to it on Amazon.

MotionEaze

We also recommend that as soon as someone begins to feel queasy that they take the helm and steer the boat. This is almost a guaranteed and instant cure. It completely takes their mind off the sickness.

Also try acupressure. Apply light thumb pressure to the inside of the wrist inside of the artery—just down from the hand and where your thumb can dig in.

Dehydration

Dehydration is the result of failure to drink plenty of water. Heat and wind are contributing factors. As skipper you need to be watching out for your crew and making sure your crew (and yourself) drink plenty of water (more than normal). This means never forgetting to bring an adequate supply with you. Usually there is a water tank on board but many people tend to shy away from drinking old tank water. As a precaution, you might consider storing water treatment tablets on board to treat tank water and convince a non-hardened crew member to drink, should bottled supplies run out.

One of the biggest contributors to dehydration on a boat is a crew member puking his or her guts out. Anytime you have a sick crew member you should be on high alert that they will begin to suffer from dehydration quickly.

A second major contributor is drinking too much alcohol combined with not enough water.

Symptoms:

- **Mild:** thirst, dry lips, dark urine color. Remedy: Rehydrate with water and electrolyte solutions.
- **Moderate:** partial heatstroke; very dry mouth, sunken eyes, skin loses elasticity. Remedy: Rehydrate with water and electrolyte solutions. Keep a constant watch on the victim and seek medical attention and guidance.
- **Severe:** heatstroke; all of above symptoms plus rapid, weak pulse, rapid breathing, confusion, and lethargy. Remedy: Rehydrate and get medical attention quickly; an IV for fluids will be needed.

Hypothermia

Hypothermia ensues when the body temperature falls below 95°F (35°C). It can occur without freezing temperatures, because a combination of cold, wind, and water can work synergistically to reduce body temperatures. Decreased core temperatures cause a gradual cessation of all body functions. An initial drop of only one or two degrees triggers the shivering response, followed by clumsiness, stumbling, slow reactions, confusion, and difficulty in speaking. The patient may be unaware that this is happening.

When the body temperature reaches 90°F (32.2°C), shivering ceases, and the muscles become rigid in an attempt to produce heat. Breathing and pulse rate decrease, and mental abilities diminish further, leading to coma, ventricular fibrillation, and death when the temperature approaches 80°F (26.7°C).

Hypothermia occurs most often to mariners who become wet from rain or spray with cold, windy conditions for extended periods of time. These are usually acute cases, and relatively easy to treat. **Submersion hypothermia** in near-drowning victims is far more serious because the person is not only hypoxic from lack of oxygen, but is subjected to the complications of lowered body temperature as well.

Symptoms of hypothermia		
Class	**Body temp°F (°C)**	**Symptoms**
Mild	<96 (35.6) 96-91 (35.6—32.8)	Intense shivering with impaired ability to perform complex tasks. Violent shivering, difficulty speaking, mental dullness, amnesia.
Moderate	86-90 (30—32.2)	Shivering ceases, muscles become rigid. Exposed skin is blue and puffy. Movements are jerky. Patient can maintain posture, and is aware of surroundings.
Severe	81-85 (27.2—29.4) <78 (25.5)	Coma, lack of reflexes, atrial fibrillation. Respiratory and cardiac failure, pulmonary edema, ventricular fibrillation, and death.

Definitive Assessment of Hypothermia

Assessing the degree of hypothermia guides treatment, so knowing the core body temperature is important. This is best taken by rectal thermometer, because an oral temperature will likely be lower than the rectal and is not accurate of the core body temperature. Be very attentive to breathing and pulse, both of which will likely be slowed and more difficult to detect. Do not initiate CPR until you're certain it's necessary by lack of breathing and carotid pulse.

Primary Care of a Hypothermic Patient

Emergency care has three primary goals:

1. Prevent further heat loss.
2. Rewarm the patient safely.
3. Avoid causing ventricular fibrillation.

Mild Hypothermia is defined as a core body temperature of 90°F (32.2°C) and above. A healthy individual who is shivering can be warmed relatively quickly with little risk. Remove wet clothing and dry the person; wrap the person in multiple warm blankets and cover the head, or use a hot shower to raise the victim's temperature. Administer hot, sweet liquids to the victim to elevate temperature and alleviate hypoglycemia.

Moderate Hypothermia presents in victims with a core body temperature below 90°F (32.2°C). The victim will lack shivering and begin to have muscular rigidity. To treat moderate hypothermia, take the same steps as noted above for mild hypothermia, but warm the victim gradually. Offer no fluids to the victim until swallowing is assured, and monitor vital signs and temperature continually while observing the level of consciousness. Seek medical advice.

Profound (Severe) Hypothermia or body temperature below 85 °F (29.4 °C) causes metabolic acidosis, and metabolic and electrolyte abnormalities with the risk of ventricular fibrillation. These result in a high mortality rate, especially in the absence of immediate medical attention in an intensive care unit. These consequences occur in spite of warming efforts, and in some cases are caused partly by the patient getting warmer. Our efforts to the victim must be to extricate from the cold, wet environment, prevent further heat loss, and allow warming to occur *slowly*. The best method of re-warming in these cases is wrapping the victim in a sleeping bag and covering the head. Seek medical advice immediately.

Breathing and heart rates are often difficult to detect in hypothermic patients. CPR should only be attempted after observing and assessing for several minutes, without signs of life, because CPR done when the heart is beating can cause ventricular fibrillation.

The exception to this rule is with a victim of **submersion hypothermia** who is not breathing. *Since drowning may be involved, CPR is indicated immediately.*

Sunburn

Direct, indirect, and reflective light can all cause sunburn. You can be severely sunburned even on a cloudy day. Ensure children are adequately protected; reapply sunscreen often. Wear-wide brim hats or hats with neck and side protection. Use sunglasses. Keep spare sunscreen, sunglasses, and hats on your boat. Protect your feet, nose, and ears. The risk of sunburn peaks during the day usually between 11:00 am and 3:00 pm.

Helicopter Rescue

Helicopter rescue is something you should be aware of; you will want such a rescue if you have a crew member who cannot safely wait until you reach the shore. While it may seem unlikely to you now, a little knowledge on this topic can save a life. Don't be timid about asking for this type of rescue if needed. The Coast Guard rescue teams live for and actually enjoy these types of rescues.

- The helicopter crew will give you instructions via VHF or phone before they arrive. Listen carefully and take notes; you will not be able to hear once they arrive.
- Start the engine and if directed by the pilot, follow the heading given.
- Dowse sails and secure tightly.
- Clear the deck of all loose and potentially loose gear.
- Ensure all your crew are wearing PFDs.

Helicopter Rescue

- A weighted line will be sent down first. Note that the rotor blades can cause massive amounts of static electricity. The helicopter crew will ground the line into the water to discharge this electricity.
- Once grounded you can take the line and gather in slack in a bucket (wear gloves). Don't attach it to the boat.
- One of the crew from the helicopter will be lowered to the boat. Follow this person's instructions once they are on the vessel.

An orange handheld smoke or buoyant orange smoke flare should be used to attract the helicopter. A RED PARACHUTE ROCKET SHOULD NOT BE USED. On a dull day a handheld or pinpoint flare may be used, but take note of the safety concerns and burn risk around a handheld flare.

Man/Crew Overboard

Man/Crew Overboard (MOB) is fortunately relatively rare, but chances are that in your sailing career it will happen. MOB means that someone has fallen off the vessel and (hopefully) is bobbing in the water as the vessel sails away. It can be life-threatening. MOB is a high-stress event, especially for the person in the water, and often the crew will panic. Even at five knots the distance between the MOB and the vessel increases rapidly. And given waves, it is very easy to lose sight of the person. Distance plus coldness of the water increases the chance that you might not be able to recover the person alive. **MOB is serious.**

Every skipper must have a plan and practice for this eventuality. And on every outing, the skipper should brief the crew on following the skipper's command and to remain calm in that eventuality. Next time you're out, simply throw a PFD overboard and try to recover it. You'll find that recovery is not that easy. Skippers should train spouses or regular boat buddies on the procedure to recover them-selves should the skipper fall overboard.

While MOB can occur in many scenarios, it is commonly the result of some-one slipping on a wet deck, equipment failure, or just not paying attention as the vessel lurches. Fast and rehearsed action is essential and can avert a real tragedy.

MOB Is Aptly Named

Sailing 10 miles out off Corsica, the crew sitting on the foredeck heard a small splash sound. They turned around to see that David, the helmsman, was not at the helm anymore. Fortunately for David, they decided to investigate. They discovered him floating and waving his arms frantically 100 meters behind the boat. David had made a near fatal mistake of setting autopilot and taking a whiz off the back of the boat without telling anyone and without the aid of a jack-line. MOB is called Man Over Board because of this exact reason. Men taking whizzes off the back.

The key to increasing the chances of recovering your friend/family member alive is practice-practice-practice. Why would you not? There is a reason emer-gency services conduct safety drills. And besides, practicing is actually fun.

The first order is to appoint a crew member to keep a watch on the MOB at all times. You must say these words to the appointed watch crew member:

"No matter what happens on the boat, no matter what else is happening, no matter what anyone says, DO NOT take your eyes off the MOB even for an instant. If you do, we could lose him."

Next, you must deploy to the MOB some temporary flotation as well as a flag marker if available. Next, get a position fix. (Most GPS systems have an MOB but-ton. Activate it immediately.) Now you must initiate a plan for recovery.

It is also vital that you gain control and the attention of remaining crew. Use names of people when issuing orders and make the orders specific. For example, instead of "Someone get a throw line," say "John, in the port aft lazarette, there is a long white throw line. Get it out now, please."

If a child is involved and you determine it is prudent for someone to jump in, be certain that individual (often a parent) has adequate flotation to prevent a sec-ond major problem. However, concentrate on getting the boat back to the MOB position first as fast as possible.

There are many suggested strategies for recovering an MOB. Every helmsperson, vessel owner, and/or person in charge should have practiced various procedures that they can become confident with.

The biggest thing to remember as the captain and leader of the crew is to keep your crew calm. Give complete and non-confusing orders and remain calm yourself. Your crew will pick up on your confidence and follow you if they see you're in control.

Methods of Recovery

It is your call as the skipper of the vessel as to which recovery method you feel is the safest based on the conditions and your experience.

The Heave-To Method

Heave-to is a very effective MOB recovery method and should be considered as a first option, especially if the victim can easily swim back to the boat. Review the heave-to discussion Chapter 7: Sailing. When you heave-to, the boat almost instantly stops dead in the water. The faster it is done, the less distance the boat gets away from the victim and often the victim is able to swim back to the boat. It requires little or no effort by the crew because the jib is left alone and only the main is let out after the boat is tacked.

MOB Recovery with Power

MOB recovery can be safely done using engine power. Many circumstances—cold water or high waves or your lack of confidence in your sailing skills—may make it more prudent to use your engine to get back to your MOB as fast as possible. Even with small waves, a person can be lost in only a few boat lengths.

When the decision is to motor to the MOB, several precautions should be taken.

- Ensure no lines are over the side before starting the engine.
- Be especially careful of speed in approaching the MOB. Maintain steerage.
- Be aware of propeller when close to the MOB.

MOB Recovery Under Sail

The following is a diagram showing an MOB recovery starting from a close-haul point of sail where the MOB situation occurs.

1. MOB happens: Immediately announce "Man Overboard." Appoint a dedicated watch person. Get life ring and anything else that floats overboard. Hit the MOB button on your GPS. Gain control of crew.

2. Ensure no lines are overboard. Start the engine. Head into wind and begin a crash tack.

3. Tighten up the main sheet. Maintain control of the crew. Act decisively with your crew. It is imperative that you lead the crew.

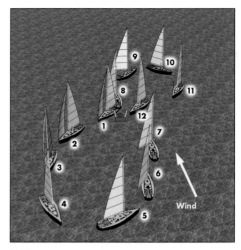

MOB

4. Furl or drop the headsail.

5. Head back downwind toward your MOB.

6. Get throw lines ready and cleated to the boat.

7. Communicate to the remaining crew the plan.

8. Drive the boat to a downwind position.

9. Bring the boat around.

10. Ensure the boat and your crew are ready for pickup.

11. Head toward your MOB from downwind.

12. Bring the boat alongside the MOB. If you don't have a rear transom on your boat you'll need a block and tackle, a spare halyard, or the boom topping lift to get your MOB on board. Be aware that pulling a person out of the water is virtually impossible. Your boat is equipped with all types of winches, blocks, and halyards—use them. Next time you're on your boat, plan what you would do to get a heavy person back into your boat. Buy equipment if necessary.

The Deep-Beam-Reach Method

The deep beam reach shown in the QR code is also useful for an MOB recovery when the course had been anywhere from upwind to a broad reach. It involves sailing a broad reach to a position slightly away the MOB, then tacking, then bearing downwind a little so as to make the approach on a close reach. The issue with the deep beam method is that it requires more space to make the maneuver, taking you further away from the MOB. In waves, this is not desirable as the crew may lose sight of the MOB.

A close reach is a good point of sail to approach an MOB under sail because you can easily depower or repower the mainsail to control the final approach and stop.

MOB Deep Beam Reach

1. MOB announcement, flotation deployment, crew assignments.
2. Bear away to a broad reach.
3. Trim the mainsail, furl or drop jib if sufficient crew.
4. Tack around.
5. Sail back toward the MOB such that the final approach will be on a close reach.
6. Prior to reaching the victim, depower the mainsail by letting it out and then turn upwind on to a close reach angle. Allow the boat's momentum to carry the boat to a point slightly to windward of the victim and stopping next to the victim. Be aware that the boat's momentum does not carry you past the victim. If you stop short, that's okay; you can power the mainsail slightly by bringing it in.

Positioning the boat windward of the MOB is generally the best because the windage will push the boat toward the MOB. In high waves there are complications of the boat being lifted on top of the MOB. In this situation you may consider leeward. However, you may find the boat being pushed away too fast. This is why you will find it easier to use the engine to gain closer control of boat and MOB positions in most circumstances.

The Quick-Stop Method

This is the fastest means for returning to a victim, always keeping the boat relatively close by. It is basically a tack followed by a big circle back to the MOB. View this video:

Quick-Stop Method

1. MOB announcement, flotation deployment, crew assignments.
2. Immediately tack the boat.
3. Begin the turn downwind; ignore jib if the crew is not available to tend.
4. Continue turning to directly downwind. Ease out mainsheet.
5. Sail downwind for only a boat length or two, trimming sails if possible, but not necessarily. Drop the jib if possible.
6. Control the mainsheet to prepare for gybing.

7. Gybe the boat.
8. Sail upwind to windward of the victim. Try to angle the boat to be on a close reach at the stopping point. Luff or drop all sails.

More MOB Thoughts

- Ensure no lines are over the side before starting the engine.
- Be especially careful of the boat's momentum in approaching the MOB. Maintain steerage. Be aware of propeller when close to MOB.
- Always during sailing have lines and throwable flotation available within quick reach.
- Consider specialized MOB hoisting gear when your boat does not have an easy entry transom.
- Stow a change of clothes and a blanket on your boat.

Final note comparing power versus sail recovery: It is your decision on how to get back to the crew member as fast as possible depending on conditions and your ability. Some instructors teach only the sail back method because they are concerned with lines in the water getting caught in the prop. Some teach to start the engine and motor back while dousing the sails because it does not rely on your expert sailing ability to get back to your crew member in the exact precise position. Some say the heave-to method is the way to go. It is a contentious point among instructors. We leave it up to you as the skipper who knows your own abilities the best. If you are not confident about sailing back then don't (check for lines in the water before you start your engine). If you can do a heave-to or a crash tack or some other method and sail back with confidence then do that. The key is to practice in all conditions. Train hard—fight easy!

The next time you're heading out, take this book and practice the methods discussed. You're the skipper. Become an expert at being able to save a life when called upon on an MOB situation. Note that you will be called upon at some time in the future.

Boat and Equipment Emergencies

The character MacGyver in the TV show of the same name would have made a great sailor. Why? Because he could fix anything and a boat is a concoction of a kajillion gadgets busting to rot, rust, short out, unscrew, break, tear, and generally just fall apart. And, Murphy is the guy who makes them do all that as simultaneously as possible, at the most inopportune time so that a seemingly benign failure can turn into an emergency.

The trick then is to prepare and plan for failure by doing lots of preventative maintenance and inspections.

Here is a handy Excel spreadsheet you can use. Customize for your own boat.

Recommended
Maintenance

Electrical Emergencies

Problems come in two forms: Your DC power supply has been drained or you have a circuit failure.

Loss of Power Supply

It wasn't too many years ago when sailboats operated perfectly without electricity. And since the laws of the universe have not changed since then, electrical supply failure amounts mostly to the loss of creature comforts. That is, EXCEPT for collision avoidance at night, highlighted by this example in which an acquaintance of ours was nearly run down by a high-speed ferry in the middle of the night in the cold waters of the Solent in the south of England. He had an electrical fire and had to shut down the breakers. ARHHHH!!!

For this reason, it is advisable to have readily available: one each of white, green, and red portable backup navigation lights as well as a flashlight you can reach easily. They are relatively inexpensive and a quick search on Google for portable navigation light will locate them, or just visit your local chandlery, which is are more than likely to have them in stock. Some have suction mounts, some have C-clamps and some mount on the pulpit railing. Obviously they should be stowed in an easily accessible place—AND the batteries should be checked often.

It is essential that you understand the "house battery circuit" and the "engine battery circuit" and that they are kept separate as described in Chapter 2. This reduces your chances of an emergency because you are not draining both batteries simultaneously and it is unlikely that you will have both house and engine batteries fail at exactly the same time. Thus, in a pinch, you can swap batteries around (or connect both house and engine circuits together) to get your engine started.

Preventative maintenance includes load testing your batteries every season and testing your alternator voltage output.

Circuit Failure

Circuit failure can be a result of corrosion of connections over time. Corrosion increases resistance at the connection point, which creates heat. The heat can create a failure in the form of fire. Loose connections also create heat or sparking, or they can just fall apart—disconnecting all together. Circuit breakers in the electric panel can also fail over time. Getting electrics or electronic devices wet especially with salt water is also a major cause of circuit failure. An acquaintance set his Apple TV on fire because salt water dripped from a leaking hatch onto it.

Preventative maintenance includes using an electric joint compound, a corrosion preventative conductive grease, on all circuit connections you make. A multimeter is also an essential part of the onboard tool kit for diagnosing problems.

Engine Emergencies

If your engine suddenly begins losing power and then stops altogether—you probably have a fuel flow problem. Chapter 3 highlighted the fuel flow system.

Possible causes are:

- Low fuel levels (duh).
- Clogged fuel filters.
- Bad fuel.
- Disconnected fuel lines.
- Air has leaked into the fuel line and the line needs priming.

The engine will also stop for a few other common reasons. A line wrapped around the propeller is a very common one. In this case, the engine will start fine in neutral, but as soon as you put it into gear, it stalls.

A worse scenario is that the water impeller inside the water pump has disintegrated and the engine's temperature alarm has sounded. This is bad—very bad! Usually, can fix this by replacing the water impeller, assuming you keep a spare on your boat. As soon as the temperature alarm sounds, you need to shut off the engine immediately or you could damage the engine and probably seize it.

Most mechanical emergencies are preventable by regular scheduled professional maintenance. But ensure you have an adequate tool kit on board, including a variety of screwdrivers, pliers, wrenches, hammers, and gloves for working around a hot engine for those times when you need.

Your anti-Murphy plan regarding engine failure, then, is to become adept at sailing the boat to the dock. When bringing the boat back to the marina, leave the sails in a position where they can be quickly re-hoisted if you have an engine failure.

Rigging Emergencies

Rigging emergencies seldom occur, and are usually caused by lack of regular inspection. At least quarterly, you should check all the cotter pins in the turnbuckles for your standing rigging stays. Cotter pins prevent turnbuckles from unwinding. Without them, a turnbuckle can unwind in a matter of a few hours of sailing causing a dismasting, which is certainly the very worst scenario beyond sinking for a sailboat. If a stay loses its turnbuckle connection, immediately turn the boat so that the wind load is taken off that stay. Then immediately rig a line to support the mast. A spare halyard can be used.

The points at which the side, fore, and back stays pass through the hull is a very important place to continually check. If they are not properly sealed, water leaks in and rots the chain plates. This will also cause a dismasting.

A dismasting is certainly an emergency. If this happens there will be a lot of lines and cables in the water. You have to clear all these away prior to starting the engine or you will have a bent propeller shaft and no means of propulsion.

Fire

Fast Action

Putting out fires quickly is essential. The sooner you find the source the quicker the fire can be extinguished. Crew knowledge of the location of fire extinguishers and fire blankets is paramount. Placement of these items with large clear signs should be carefully designed for ease and speed of access.

Fire Blanket

Immediately alert the entire crew. This is called sounding the alarm.

Many countries' laws require fire blankets to be installed on board. Law or not, fire blankets are a good idea. Fire blankets should be located near the stove and in each cabin that does not have a second way of getting out. A fire blanket should not be mounted above the stove. This would require you to reach through the fire to access the blanket. You can use a fire blanket to throw over a fire to smother it out or you can wrap yourself in the fire blanket to move quickly through a fire. Ensure your crew knows what a fire blanket is and where it is stowed.

Prevention

On the water, fire can be the death of you and your crew. Thus, it is overly important to take all preventative measures.

Electrical

- A leading cause of electrical fire is the AC plug to the boat. It is often not secured properly and thus leads to sparks and shorts. Each time you leave the boat, make sure the AC plug is securely fastened.
- Turn off nonessential electrical circuits when leaving the boat.
- Ensure your boat is properly fitted with an easy to reach and easy to find switch that disconnects the batteries from the DC system. When a DC electrical fire breaks out this switch is your first defense at extinguishing the source of the fire.

Stoves

- Turn off gas supply to cookers when not in use.
- Do not leave the cooker unattended when in use.
- Do not leave items close to the cooker.
- Take extra caution with cooking oils and fats. Especially because the boat may be rocking.
- Take extra care with children cooking.
- Train on the use of a fire blanket.

Smoking

We understand the addiction but we're talking about the lives of you and your crew. Smoking cigarettes in cabins below should never be done. Never! If you must smoke, do so outside. But even still, take note that when smoking off the aft end of the boat, the smoke circles back upwind through the cockpit. Be considerate.

Detectors

Smoke detectors should be fitted in the main cabins and each sleeping cabin for early detection.

Gas alarm systems are an easy install on a vessel and detect LPG spilled over from the stove. Since LPG is heavier than air, it can collect in the bilges over time. If the gas alarm sounds:

- Make the crew aware of dangerous gas.
- Vent the area by opening hatches.
- Turn off the LPG tank.
- Don't use any electrical devices.
- Don't activate the electric bilge pump. Any electric device can cause an electric spark.

Extinguisher Requirement

Remember, this is your life we're talking about. You spend thousands on insurance so please invest a few extra bucks in enough proper fire extinguishers to do the job. The job being—saving your life and your beautiful boat.

Here is a table of the required and recommended number, size and type of extinguishers you should have on your vessel:

	Boats 16 feet to less than 26 feet	Boats 26 feet to less than 40 feet	Boats 40 feet to no more than 65 feet
The Law	At least one Type B-I	At least two Type B-I Or At least one type B-II	At least three Type B-I Or At least one type B-I plus one Type B-II
Recommended	At least two type ABC-I and an ABC-II if you can fit it	At least three type ABC-I and a couple of ABC-II if they can fit	At least four type ABC-I and a couple of ABC-II if they can fit

The letters ABC refer to the type of fire that the device is able to fight.
- A = combustible materials
- B = combustible fuels
- C = electrical

An ABC fire extinguisher is an all-in-one chemical dispersion spray extinguisher and is the most commonly recommended for a boat since it can fight all types of fires that occur on a boat. The number refers to the volume of extinguishing material contained and thus the portability (weight). Type ABC-I is a lot more portable than Type ABC-II and can thus be more time-effective in the ability of the crew to get the extinguisher to the fire source. However Type ABC-I will run out of extinguishing material faster than Type ABC-II. So it's prudent to have enough of both types on board.

Ever been to a clean bathroom in a restaurant? You can bet that they are the ones with a signed inspection routine posted on the wall. Do that to your boat—post a signed inspection sheet regarding your extinguishers. It'll impress your crew and visitors. Add a note to the bottom to say, "If out of date, please inform the captain."

Set up the routine for extinguisher inspection:
- Check the gauge monthly.

- For chemical types, remove and shake upside down twice a year to keep the chemicals mixed. Have the bottle weighed and professionally inspected annually.

The ultimate key in firefighting is to not hurt yourself or the crew. Be prepared to abandon ship if necessary and let your insurance take the loss.

Sinking

A boat sits down in the water until it has displaced the same weight of water as the weight of the boat. It is a universal arrangement between boat and water. "You stay out and I will stay on top." When there is a breakdown in that agreement, a potential emergency arises.

Getting a hole in the hull (being "holed") can be minor or catastrophic. Often finding where the hole is can be a major problem. A first place to look is seacocks and sink drain pipes. The wood plugs stored in your emergency kit are used for driving into a burst seacock.

Tough Diagnosis

Once under sail, I stepped down to the cabin to grab a drink and into 6 inches of water covering the cabin floor. After serious diagnosis, I found that a drain pipe had slipped off the bottom of the forward bathroom sink. Water was coming in through the drain seacock, but only when we were heeling to port. You can't even imagine how difficult it was to determine the source of that breakdown.

If the issue is not a seacock, continue your search and look for flowing water. Stuff anything flexible like clothing or foam mattresses in the hole to reduce the flow. Chances are that you can stuff enough in the hole to slow down the water entry so the bilge pumps can keep up. However, should the hole be inaccessible or too large to patch, you may have to consider using a variety of pumps, buckets, and potential abandonment.

For whatever reason, should your vessel begin taking on copious amounts of water and sinking is a possibility, you must do something fast. If you have a dinghy or life raft, make it ready for use should it become necessary.

Because of the many air pockets in a modern vessel, it is unlikely it will truly sink. Abandon the vessel only if conditions become impossible. Stay with the vessel even if it maintains minimal floating. You are more likely to be seen by rescue aircraft if you stay with the vessel. If you are in a dinghy or life raft, tie it to the floating vessel but make sure the knot is easily undone and you have a knife available to cut the dinghy painter (line) in case the vessel sinks.

A life raft will usually have a sea drogue on board. This is a water anchor which slows the life raft from drifting away from the sinking area. It will also stop the life raft from capsizing and give the life raft stability in large wave conditions. It also keeps the tent opening facing downwind.

Luckily, sinking is rare. But this does not absolve the skipper for having a plan for serious events. A ditch-bag or grab-bag is an essential part of a ship's permanent inventory.

Prior to abandoning ship

Things to take:
- Ditch-bag.
- Water and food.
- Communication devices (should be in the ditch-bag).
- Other useful items such as warm clothing.

Things to do:
- Get life jackets on everyone.
- Send a mayday.
- Fire flares.
- Check the painter is tied to the vessel.

Scan the QR code for a list of recommended items in your ditch bag.

Ditch Bag
Contents

Running Aground

In the information age, running aground is usually caused by an amateur mistake, and besides the potential damage it is also highly embarrassing. A common error in thinking (or not thinking) is using an electronic chart with the zoom level too far out for the screen to display a low-water area.

Should the grounding cause you to be stuck, such as into a mud bottom, you may have difficulty getting off. If there is a rising tide, you may decide to wait it out. However, if the tide is going out you need to work fast to get loose.

To get out of your predicament use any combination of the following:

1. Luff the sails to stop the driving force.
2. Use the engine to try to back off.
3. If you cannot back off, put the wheel or tiller hard over and use power to turn the boat around. It should screw around fairly easily with the keel as the pivot point.
4. Heel the boat over by putting all the crew to one side. Leaving the sails up can also aid in heeling the boat. Heeling will effectively lift the keel up enough to get you unstuck.
5. Kedging: Once turned around, walk the anchor out into deeper water in the direction you came from. Haul in on the anchor with a winch. You may need to use flotation to swim the anchor out farther.

When chartering a boat it is prudent and ethical to report any grounding. If you've caused damage you may be endangering the next charter group's lives.

Propeller Entanglement

If there is a sudden slowing or stopping of the propeller, while motor sailing it is possible that you have picked up some floating line, hopefully not from your vessel. Should this occur, it is imperative to shut off the engine immediately to prevent overheating and/or damage to the transmission.

Depending on many factors, especially where this is happening, you need to get control of the vessel by sailing or anchoring. In a busy harbor, this can be a major problem. Immediately post lookouts to warn other vessels. Call for help on VHF Channel 16 if needed.

If a crew member is capable of diving down to investigate and remove the entangled line with a sharp knife, try it. For precaution, take the keys out of the ignition so there is no possibility of the engine being started should some distraction occur. For this reason, a dive mask and snorkel should be a part of your on-board inventory.

The line entanglement problem is too often a reality, especially where anglers, ski boarders, or some commercial fishermen regularly abandon lines.

Towing

The following diagram shows how you can tow another vessel. Form a "bridle" from the rear cleats on the rescue boat. On the boat being towed you need to make sure that the towline is attached to a place that is very strong. One suggestion is to wrap the towline around the windlass and then aft in a bridle to the headsail winches. This acts to spread the load. In heavy seas, ensure that there is plenty of distance between the boats so the rear boat does not slide down a wave and hit the front boat. Try to match the length of the towline to the wave pitch (distance between the waves).

Embarrassing

We once stopped in the middle of the lake to help a stranded powerboat that needed a tow. We ran a towline from his bow cleat to a bridle we made up to each aft winch on our boat. Then we raised the sails and towed the powerboat back in under sail. We could have motored but nah, I wanted the story to tell here. Hee hee, that must have been pretty embarrassing for the powerboater.

Dinghy Safety

When it comes to dinghy operations, the following is a dangerous attitude: "It's only a short distance ashore—jump in, she'll be right!"

Towing

Operating a dinghy safely is often overlooked, yet this is when you are in the most danger. Here are some issues to think about. Mostly the issues come from thinking that the trip is short and safety concerns can be partially relaxed.

Some considerations:

Dinghy Operations

- **Difficult to see:**
  In a dinghy you are low to the water and it is difficult to observe you. Often you've left the boat during daylight hours and returning at night. You forgot to prepare by taking a flashlight on board and so you are running dark.
- **Falling over:**
  There are no lifelines. The error margin for gaining your own balance is low. A dangerous spinning propeller is close.

- **Inexperienced operators:**
  Everyone is keen to drive the dinghy. What if someone fell out and the operator turned the engine the wrong way? In less than a second the prop could cause severe lacerations or even death. Balancing speed with total load and conditions requires experience.
- **Operating close to breakers and shallows:**
  Waves near the shore are a sure danger for capsize. And especially if the bottom is reef or coral cuts are going to occur. Never go side-on to a wave, especially approaching the beach. You cannot hold a dinghy against the force of even a small wave.
- **Tide and weather:**
  An incoming tide will sweep away your dinghy left on the beach. If you're ashore for longer periods of time, ensure the weather will be conducive for your return.
- **Often overloaded:**
  Heading ashore often seems like a hassle to run more than one trip for the crew. Thus the dinghy tends to get overloaded with gear and crew. Wrong balance or an inopportune wave can cause disaster. Water rushing in over the front due to forward overload can also create havoc.
- **Engine reliability:**
  Outboards suffer from many issues. An engine failure at the wrong time can be dangerous. Ensure you have oars on board and plenty of fuel.
- **Kill cord:**
  This is a lanyard attached to the engine cutoff switch and the driver whenever the engine is running. If the driver is thrown overboard the engine will automatically cut off, enabling the driver to swim back to the dinghy AND preventing the propeller from chomping body parts.

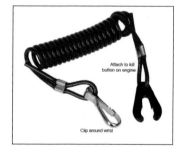

Kill Cord

- **Life jackets and pump:**
  Often, the crew and parents tend to negate the need for life jackets due to a short trip or just not thinking this has obvious potential consequences. A deflating dinghy is not a fun feeling while in operation. Carry the pump.
- **Boarding and getting out:**
  Our rule for these operations is always have three points touching something at any one time: for example two feet and one hand or two hands

and one foot. An entry and exit like this tends not to look so graceful but is much more graceful than wet clothes, salt water in your drink, and a bonk on the head.

- **No communications:**
  Often the dinghy crew will neglect to carry on board any form of communication to rescue. A dinghy with a failed engine caught in a rip current is a disaster. Consider taking a VHF and perhaps flares.

- **Returning from the bar:**
  Drink driving laws are often overlooked when operating a dinghy—and besides, the chances of being caught are minimal, right? Yet the law is there for safety, not to randomly write tickets. Operating a dinghy drunk, while perhaps funny at first, can have serious consequences on the water at night.

- **Secure the dinghy:**
  "Excuse me—is this your dinghy?" This was the question we heard once from a fellow boater towing our dinghy. It's pretty embarrassing! Don't rely on inexperienced crew to tie a proper knot.

In general, you've been applying good seamanship to your entire cruise. Don't slacken your guard around the dinghy.

Watch this dinghy training video:

Dinghy Training
Video

Summary

Sailing emergencies are real. However, their chances of occurring are greatly diminished by obeying rules, maintaining safe practices, making contingency plans, providing good maintenance, and having a comprehensive knowledge base.

Be prepared by studying and listening to those who have had emergencies. Avoid panicky behavior at all times. Practice emergency situations when you are under normal conditions, especially Crew Overboard. One day it may save your friend's or family member's life.

Afterword

Congratulations on working your way through this book. We really hope you enjoyed it and were able to enable the QR codes throughout to gain a more interactive and visual appreciation of the information presented.

What Now?

Well, get on the water, silly

That's an easy thing to say but in practice, many people don't own a boat. There are a few things you can do about that when getting started.

Join a Yacht Club

In virtually every city with a sailing waterway there is a yacht club

- Joining a yacht club is pretty simple and relatively inexpensive for the return you'll get. Costs range from $40 to $80 per month. And if you own a boat, many times the marina fees are less expensive than a regular marina.
- Some clubs are very racing focused; some are not. Even if you're not a racing type person, racing experience will improve your cruising sailing skills vastly. Racing is like learning a language by immersion.
- Yacht clubs are highly social and so you're going to meet a lot of very cool and interesting people who will become your friends. Throw away the

preconceived notions of the stereotype snooty stuffy yacht club and just join one and find out for yourself.

- Yacht clubs many times have a nice pool for the kids to hang out in and they will get to hang out with other yachting type kids. A vast improvement from learning life skills at the mall.
- Yacht clubs organize weekend sailing trips away. These are usually very fun flotilla events. Here you can learn a lot of overnighting and anchoring skills.
- Occasionally yacht clubs will also organize a bareboat charter sailing holiday to places like the Caribbean, Mediterranean, or the Pacific islands. This is a great opportunity to join in on the safety of a flotilla.

Yacht Club Notice Board

Some people think that if you don't own a boat, then what's the point of joining a yacht club? However, if you don't own a boat, then you should definitely join a yacht club. **Here's a big fact. Virtually all boat owners are desperate for crew for either racing or cruising events.** This is proven by the dozens of Post-it notes on the yacht club notice board from skippers looking for crew.

Join a Sailing Club

A sailing club is usually a for-profit company who have lots of sailboats that, as a member, you can rent quite inexpensively. They maintain the boat, pay for the slip fees and insurance, and all you do is walk on, sail, and walk off. Pretty convenient! And many times you will find this cost is less than owning one yourself.

Make Friends with a Boatowner

This is easier than you think. Surprisingly, virtually everyone who has a boat does not have enough friends to go sailing with. Why? People are just too busy these days. If this was not true, then boats would not sit in their slips for months on end without going out. Call a friend today and tell them you will help them make use of their boat. Heck, throw caution to the wind and put a note on Facebook or put an ad on Craigslist.

Share a Boat

Lots of boat owners are considering selling their boat because they don't use it enough to justify the costs. Having someone share in those costs can be very attractive to a boat owner. Again, post an ad on Craigslist.

Round Up a Syndicate of Owners

Lots of people you know want to buy a boat but the costs of full ownership are prohibitive. Start talking to friends about getting together and sharing a boat.

The point is that with a little bit of diligence, you can start sailing without owning a boat. And using the knowledge you have gained here, you'll be thoroughly and safely enjoying your experiences.

Thank you for reading *Successfully Skipper a Sailboat*. I'll leave you with a line used by Marlin to his son Nemo in the movie *Finding Nemo*.

NOW, GO HAVE AN ADVENTURE!